Advance Praise for *Brand Aid*

"John La Forgia's *Brand Aid* is an extraordinary account of a decades-long journey leading the marketing and branding transformation of the Mayo Clinic—one of the most highly respected and revered organizations in the world. Written in a highly personal and engaging style, La Forgia brings a human face to a brand that, at is very core, is about humanity itself. Many 'how to' books have been written about the technical side of building and managing brands, but this is one of the very few books that also brings people into the equation in a rich and vivid way. It is compelling reading that even the most casual student of marketing and branding will find rewarding. It is an absolute must read for anyone seriously interested in health care marketing or, more broadly, the marketing of professional services. Its lessons in how to infuse marketing and branding into organizations not accustomed to or even comfortable with those notions are relevant and invaluable to marketers everywhere facing that very difficult challenge."

—Professor Kevin Keller, Author of
Marketing Management and *Strategic Brand Management*

BRAND AID

THE REVOLUTIONARY TRANSFORMATION
OF THE MAYO CLINIC BRAND

— BY —

JOHN LA FORGIA

PRESS

A SAVIO REPUBLIC BOOK
An Imprint of Post Hill Press
ISBN: 978-1-64293-247-8
ISBN (eBook): 978-1-64293-248-5

Brand Aid:
The Revolutionary Transformation of the Mayo Clinic Brand
© 2019 by John La Forgia
All Rights Reserved

Cover Design by Tricia Principe, principedesign.com

This is a work of nonfiction. All people, locations, events, and situations are portrayed to the best of the author's memory.

posthillpress.com
New York • Nashville
Published in the United States of America

For Pamela

CONTENTS

FOREWORD

THE IMPORTANCE OF health care today is indisputable. It has become one of the most important issues in national elections and dominates the news and daily conversations. At the heart of the health care ecosystem are the health care providers and the doctors, nurses, and others at hospitals and medical centers all over the country.

Like many institutions that have a "higher calling"—e.g., education and other nonprofits—marketing is something that can make health care providers uncomfortable and uncertain. Yet there is growing recognition that health-care marketing is critical to the growth and success of health-care organizations and their ability to achieve their missions, and therefore needs to be understood, embraced, and practiced well.

The Mayo Clinic has been a medical pioneer for decades, and its three-shields logo succinctly displays why—patient care, research, and education all matter and blend together seamlessly. Recognizing the importance of health-care marketing, it is no surprise that Mayo has similarly pursued leadership and excellence in marketing too, with great success. Thankfully, this book tells you how.

I first met John La Forgia, along with his colleagues Kent Seltman and Scott Swanson, at a branding conference in Florida over twenty years ago. They were there to learn about the latest and greatest ideas in the field as they embarked on establishing the Office of Brand Management at Mayo. They asked for my input and advice, and I eagerly said yes, leading to a long-term working relationship I have always cherished.

Throughout that time, John was my key contact, and I got to know him well, greatly admiring his wisdom, judgment, and friendly working style. When he mentioned that he was writing a book to share his marketing and communication experiences managing the Mayo Clinic brand, I was thrilled. I knew John's keen eye and expressive storytelling abilities would be ideal for revealing Mayo's secrets of success and what makes this incredible organization tick.

I was correct in my forecast. *Brand Aid* is an extraordinary account of a decades-long journey leading the marketing and branding transformation of the Mayo Clinic—one of the most highly respected and revered organizations in the world. Written in a highly personal and engaging style, John brings a human face to a brand that at its very core is about humanity itself.

Many "how to" books have been written about the technical side of building and managing brands, but this is one of the very few books that also brings people into the equation in a rich and vivid way. It is the perfect companion piece to Len Berry and Kent Seltman's *Management Lessons from Mayo Clinic,* which astutely took a service quality, culture, and systems perspective to deconstruct Mayo's success. *Brand Aid* expands on those factors to also go deep inside the organization for a compelling account of the decisions involved and the roles of the many different people who contributed to its marketing success.

Like Scott Bedbury's up-close anatomy of Nike and Starbucks in *A New Brand World,* John blends his personal experiences running marketing at the Mayo Clinic with the many lessons and rules he learned along the way. It is compelling reading that even the most casual student of marketing and branding will find rewarding. It is an absolute must-read for anyone seriously interested in health care marketing or, more broadly, the marketing of professional services. Its lessons in how to infuse marketing and branding into organizations not accustomed to or even comfortable with those notions are invaluable to marketers everywhere facing that very difficult, but all too common challenge.

The Mayo Clinic is an amazing organization in so many different ways. At a most basic level, like any strong brand, the success of the Mayo Clinic as a brand rests on its ability to deliver on a compelling brand promise as the result of some key brand pillars, such as:

- ◯ Relentless collaboration and service
- ◯ Unrivaled expertise and innovation
- ◯ Compassionate commitment to health and healing
- ◯ Unimpeachable trust and integrity

As these pillars suggest, like the world's best brands, the Mayo brand is a powerful combination of coveted and distinctive intrinsic and extrinsic benefits. Fundamentally, the Mayo Clinic creates an unparalleled patient experience because of its utterly unique service delivery and its passionate belief in its mission. Rock-solid in character and driven to make the world a healthier place, the Mayo Clinic is the standard bearer of what a modern health care provider should aspire to be.

Yet, at the same time, the Mayo Clinic is so extraordinary in what it does and its reputation so impeccable, it may seem to be almost "too good" for the "average" person. Through the years, a long list of famous people have come to the Mayo Clinic to solve their serious and life-threatening health problems—from Yankee legend Lou Gehrig to Jordan's King Hussein, from golfer Arnold Palmer to Senator John McCain, from singer Glenn Campbell to television newscaster Tom Brokaw, among the many.

Their often well-publicized visits and treatments could easily make Mayo seem out of reach to someone without similar wealth and celebrity. Another marketing challenge for John and his team through the years was thus to ensure that the Mayo Clinic was seen as accessible and relevant to a broader target market who could—and should—benefit from all that Mayo has to offer.

All of this and much, much more is revealed in John's firsthand account. From strategy formulation at the top leadership circles to day-to-day decision making with clinic operations, John covers it all. Fun to read and easy to learn from, these confessions capture the marketing transformation of a preeminent organization and the development of a talented leader at the same time. Its lessons can be applied to drive similar transformations and nurture similar developments for thoughtful marketers in all walks of life.

Kevin Lane Keller
Dartmouth College
Hanover, NH
December 28, 2018

INTRODUCTION

WHEN I BEGAN my career in health-care marketing in 1980, the profession was in its infancy. My first hospital didn't even have a marketing department. Few hospitals did. Overt promotion of health-care services carried a stigma that lingers among some physicians and administrators even today.

Nonetheless, in 2017, according to The National Health Expenditure Account (NEHA), health-care spending in the United States amounted to $3.5 trillion, 17.9 percent of the GNP, with billions of dollars spent each year promoting hospitals, health-care systems, pharmaceutical companies, insurance companies, physicians, and every other health-care service imaginable through every medium available in the twenty-first century.

During my thirty-eight-year career, I have participated in this remarkable transformation. Starting with writing newsletters on an IBM Selectric typewriter, my career tracked progressively with changes in the health-care industry until my colleagues and I were implementing national and sometimes international marketing at a level of sophistication and effectiveness rivaling that of our more experienced and far better funded compatriots in other industries.

As a witness and coperpetrator of this massive change in the largest sector of the American economy, I experienced firsthand the evolution of health-care marketing, from folksy, photocopied employee newsletters that would embarrass a high school media class to targeting potential customers with predictive analytics, search engine optimization, and customer relationship management.

At times, the organizations I was part of embraced these innovations. More often, they resisted, sometimes with all the force of tradition and professional authority they could muster.

Regardless, they couldn't stop the forces that had been unleashed and, today, marketing, advertising, social media, and the rest are fundamental aspects of the American health-care system. As a result, the question for today's health-care organization is far more complex than "To market, or not to market." Persistently difficult problems plague every marketer, particularly in health care. To whom should we market? What is the message? How do we know if we are having any effect? What should we spend? How do we get the hospital and medical leadership to support our efforts?

Let's be clear—the Mayo Clinic brand was iconic long before I went to work there in 1991. The development of that iconic position happened organically and, to a large extent, unwittingly. I've always thought that the Mayo brothers had an intuitive sense of brand building, even though they almost certainly never used the term nor were purposely brand building. Just the same, their actions of perpetual learning, traveling, sharing, and participating in the larger worlds of medicine and society had the effect of growing the Clinic and building its brand.

To this day, physicians and other staff at Mayo Clinic emulate these behaviors to the same positive effect. For all intents and purposes, the activities of the Mayo Clinic areas of public affairs, marketing, and communications work in strategic partnership with the staff to enable, amplify, and strategically apply those same behaviors. The difference, of course, is that now we have a lexicon, a body of research, and a history of best practices to guide our efforts.

I would also like to be clear that this is not a textbook in the conventional sense. A vast trove of research, how-tos, journals, and textbooks is available to anyone seeking the factual aspects of health-care marketing. Rather, this book is a hybrid of stories, obser-vations, and learnings gleaned and synthesized from a professional lifetime attempting to answer the questions posited above, usually with some success, but also with some notable failures, which, as many have said, are almost always the most instructive experiences.

I confess to equal amounts of pride and trepidation regarding the writing of this book. My sense of its value derives from my work with many younger practitioners who lack the historical perspective that I have acquired, and while mentoring such professionals, I have found that stories and lessons from the hard knocks of decades in the marketing trenches resonate most and bring to life the abstract principles they've studied in college.

Finally, may I express the hope that the contents of this book can be a part of the shared knowledge upon which future genera-tions of marketers can develop better tools, become more effective, and do more good for the patients and families who are, ultimately, the people we are here to serve.

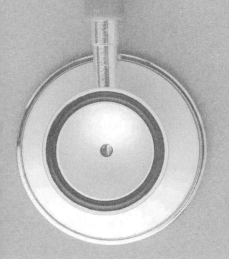

CHAPTER 1

THE PROBLEM WITH HEALTH-CARE MARKETING

WHAT IS MARKETING?

For thirty-five years, I have searched for a practical solution to this question and have found many answers that sound good in theory or in textbooks but are unhelpful in the day-to-day world of health care. To begin, textbooks will define marketing in academic business terms such as:

> *Marketing is the activity, set of institutions, and processes for creating, communicating, delivering, and exchanging offerings that have value for customers, clients, partners, and society at large.*
>
> *American Marketing Association*

Try using this on your leadership team. Even if they also went to business school and even if they studied marketing there, these definitions will leave the typical operations-oriented administrator or physician nonplussed. I can assure you the responses will be something like:

"Yes, we know all that, but what are you going to do?"

"I thought marketing was advertising."

"Marketing is puffery and manipulation. That's not appropriate for health care."

This last reaction was ubiquitous in the early years of my career. Even now, I might have a conversation with a physician that would go something like this:

Me: "Dr. Jones, I'd like to talk with you about our proposal for brand management."

Dr. Jones: "Brand management? We've been around for a hundred years. We've managed our brand just fine. What the hell do we need that shit for?"

Or:

Me: "Dr. Smith, I'd like to present to your committee about our brand management program."

Dr. Smith: "What? We're a brand now? What are we, Ivory Soap?"

Nowadays, brand management and marketing are all but omnipresent in health-care institutions. Yet anyone who works in the field knows that many physicians and executives remain skeptical of marketing's purpose and effectiveness in health care. After all, medicine is primarily a science, with well-researched practices and predictable outcomes—at least, most of the time. Few physicians are aware of the rigor of truly research-based marketing, and sadly, their experience of marketing over the years has borne out their prejudice that hospital marketing departments are often in-house job shops, producing materials at the whim of a physician or administrator with little thought given to the strategic purpose or standards of practice for effective marketing.

Recently, I had a conversation with the president of a substantial health-care network. As we talked, he warmed to the subject and shared his opinions about health-care marketing:

"I don't know. I suppose we need to advertise but I don't know why. I don't believe anyone ever chose a hospital because of an ad they saw on TV. No one believes that stuff. And we have all these people and spend millions on ads and pens and health fairs and all I know is it costs too much, and I don't know what we're getting for all that money."

He finished with a perplexed expression and looked at me as if I might have an answer. Instead, I asked him a question: "George, if you feel that way, why do you even have a marketing department?"

The question turned him thoughtful and, after a few moments, he said, "Image? Community relations? Keep our name alive in the community? Provide information about our services so people know what we can do for them?"

His delivery had been as much in the form of a question as it was a statement. Unwittingly, he had articulated the skeleton of premises that have become the bedrock of my approach to marketing health care.

- Provide mechanisms for an *exchange of information* that will help patients find the right service at the right time in the right place.

- Anything produced by the marketing department, whether words, images, interviews, or websites, must be based on substance and must provide *value as it is perceived by the patient.*

- *Marketing is a strategic partner* with the medical and business leaders and, as such, must ensure that all marketing contributes to the mission and strategic plan of the institution.

- Marketing must be based on *research, data, and measurement.*

- Marketing is the focal point for the *coordination and implementation of an integrated public presence.*

Although these five principles are easily stated, health care remains stubbornly resistant to their full adoption. I have found that health-care leaders will accept the truth of these axioms intellectually but, in practice, rarely follow their full implications in a manner that could contribute markedly to innovation and customer satisfaction in health care, as they have in other industries. For the rest of this chapter, we will explore why this is so. Subsequent chapters will address in some depth what is to be done.

THE EXCHANGE OF INFORMATION

Any simple definition of health-care marketing should include the fundamental principle of providing people with useful information that they can use to make good decisions about a product or service they want or wish to access, usually at a critical point in their lives.

That's not as easily accomplished as it may appear. Over and over again, I would review copy for a hospital website or ad that would essentially say:

"We have all the best stuff and the best people. And we love you and your family. So please come to our hospital."

In terms of effectiveness, this is the equivalent of an airline saying, "Please fly with us. Our planes won't crash."

Research has shown that most Americans assume their planes won't crash and, likewise, that their doctor and hospital are very good at what they do. Therefore, the trick, if you will, of communicating to patients is to give them real information that is relevant to them in terms they can understand.

Health care is a complicated subject. Most people don't really understand how our system—if one can even call it a system—really works. It is marketing's job to help the patient, family, or customer have a better understanding if not of the whole system, then at least of the components of the system they are attempting to access.

At Mayo Clinic in the early 1990s, we produced a multivolume physician directory with a bio of every staff physician. We mailed these to referring physicians all across the country. The result was a deafening silence. Considering the expense and effort that had gone into the project, this was a major disappointment. In an attempt to clarify what had gone wrong, we called some of the offices that had received the directories. They told us the books were very nice but, basically, were useless because no one had the time to riffle through hundreds of pages to find a specialist for a patient. (Remember, this was before the Internet became a common household utility.) We had printed a one-page summary of essential phone numbers and contact names in the back of one of the volumes. Tellingly, in most cases, the physician's office manager had simply torn this page out of the book and posted it on the message board at his or her desk. The tomes were placed on a shelf next to their collection of outdated *Physician's Desk References* and *Quality Circles* manuals.

This experience prompted us to do something rather new in health care at the time. The physician directory idea had sprung full-blown from the mind of one of the executives at the time, more or less as Athena had sprung from the head of Zeus. This purely internal perspective had not served us well. We had the revolutionary idea to ask the customer.

Focus groups were nothing new and I am not trying to imply that it was rocket science to suggest we do them. Health care, though, then and now, is an extremely internally focused environment. For most of medicine's history, physicians have had complete autonomy to consider the options and make decisions based upon their own perspective, or perhaps with consultation from others in their field. The idea of asking the patient her opinion was slow in taking hold. Likewise, hospitals and specialty centers are largely self-directed entities without perceiving much need for, or maintaining much interest in, a comanagement proposition with patients or physicians let alone insurance companies. To this day, the key factions of health care retain this fiefdom mentality, despite the many forces, and now laws, pushing these groups to break down the barriers and cooperate.

So, with some effort, we persuaded a group of referring physicians who were attending Mayo's renowned Internal Medicine Board Review course to participate in a few focus groups regarding referring physician communications. Physicians rarely hold back and so the conversations hit hard and hit home. One physician summarized the findings in a way none of us ever forgot.

"When I get those fat brochures from you or any other hospital I just throw them away. I don't have time to read that kind of thing. I know you have good services. I know who you are. Don't try to sell me on something. Help me. Help me help my patient."

Don't sell to me. Help me. This should be the motto of every person in health-care marketing. Are you helping patients find what they need at this stressful time in their lives? Or are you simply producing the formulaic materials packed with corporate health-care speak that are almost always mandated by hospital administrators, legal departments, and physicians everywhere?

The other pearl borne of these sessions was equally simple and trenchant. "I want something from you I can read in five minutes," one physician said. "Service, contact person, phone number. That's it. That's all I need."

Accordingly, we developed a one-page newsletter with the promise clearly stated in the masthead: *"Reading time—5 minutes."* We tracked much success in terms of response to the service features in the newsletter. Naturally, in subsequent years, electronic versions supplanted the printed piece, but the principle remained: "Stop selling and start helping."

VALUE AS PERCEIVED BY THE PATIENT

Often in my career, I was asked to reengineer a poorly functioning hospital marketing or communications department. After the fourth or fifth experience solving such a problem, I learned that the causes of a "broken" department's dysfunction fell into a predictable pattern. Later, we will go through these in detail, along with remedies. At this point, though, I want to address the issue of providing substance and value as perceived by the patient. You see, these broken departments were always perceived as "failing to hit the mark" and were held in low esteem for their unwillingness or inability to produce results. Executives often asked me if it was time to "clean house" or hire "experts" from an outside agency. They felt the symptoms, if you will, but could not diagnose the cause.

Because of the highly internalized perspective of medicine and health care discussed earlier, marketing and communications departments have been consigned to a low spot in the executive or professional hierarchy. Many health-care leaders don't consider marketing a profession at all. Traditionally, staff creating newsletters, brochures, and now digital media have been seen as no more than media production staff. As stated earlier, the marketing department was a job shop. For decades, these staff have been at the beck and call of their superiors to produce a commercial or a giveaway pen-and-pencil set simply because the person who requested the item outranked them. If the head of orthopedics wanted to distribute a brochure about, say, problems of the left wrist, because he wanted to start a left wrist clinic, he would not ask the marketing department to help determine the need for such a clinic or if a brochure was the best method for communicating about such a place. The leader's expectation was, and often still is, that the marketer would respond with a courteous "Or course, Dr. Tarsal. How many brochures will you need? When would you like to distribute them?" The inside joke among us in those situations was that we should then ask, "Would you like fries with that?"

Many of you reading this may demure and suggest that the situation has improved. I would be the first to agree. Today, many hospital organizations have MBA-trained chief marketing officers (CMO) who sit alongside their fellow executives at the leadership table. Having been one of those CMOs and knowing many others, I contend that the situation is still SNAFU. We have a long way to go before health care embraces true marketing as an essential part of the operations of a health system—not for our benefit, but for the benefit of the patient.

To be fair, the present condition is understandable. Medicine and health care are intensely empirical, operational, task-oriented, process-driven institutions and professions. These traits are hammered home through years of training, practice, credentialing, and regulation. They have to be. A person's life depends on that level of rigor and discipline. Can we say the same about marketing? I have seen marketing professionals stand in front of a room full of physicians and suggest a slogan or a campaign, and when asked by a physician why such and such a slogan was chosen, the answer will be some version of "We all liked it," or "It's what the agency recommended." Imagine the surgeon who walks into the operating room one morning and says, "I have an idea. Let's do the valve repair a different way," and, when asked why, replies, "I just want to try something new." Thankfully, this is crazy talk. Regrettably, marketers often engage in crazy talk or are perceived to be a bit crazy by their more practical colleagues, because health-care marketers often lack a firm grasp of the underlying strategy, data, and proven best practices that should support their recommendations.

Both sides share responsibility for the current state of affairs. Leaders ask for random projects, and marketers acquiesce, to the detriment of all.

Once, a prominent cardiologist brought me a logo he had designed himself for a conference series of which he was the primary director. An internal graphic designer had rendered the logo to his specifications. It was a human arm floating in air, cut off from the body at the elbow, the hand holding in its palm an anatomically correct human heart, as if said heart had just been torn from a subject's body and was being displayed as a trophy to the gods. The visual lacked only blood to complete the scene, which one's imagination could easily provide.

My initial reaction was instantaneous revulsion. Since Dr. Kaye expressed such happiness at this creation, and held a prominent position at the hospital, I told him I liked the concept but was not too happy about the execution. I said it was too graphic and would turn people off.

Dr. Kaye: "It's not for people; it's for cardiologists. They know what the heart looks like. I don't see a problem here."

Me: "Of course, they do, and I'm not a cardiologist. Dr. Kaye, this logo will be on the covers of brochures, on PowerPoint slides, on video screens around the country. We'll use the graphic in our internal publications. This image will be seen by thousands, maybe hundreds of thousands of people, and not just physicians. I think many people would see this as kind of scary, or gross, and I don't think it's the kind of image we want to present to the public."

This was by no means the end of the negotiations. Eventually, we presented his mock-up to people around the hospital (even cardiologists) and after this bit of "research" demonstrated general discomfort with the "heart-in-the-palm" graphic, Dr. Kaye conceded that the image could be improved. The designer stylized the image to make it less grisly, so Dr. Kaye had his logo and my concerns were alleviated. How much simpler and efficient for all involved if Dr. Kaye had consulted with marketing at the beginning—in other words, worked with the logo and public presence experts at the start?

This example is mild, and the story had a happy ending. Many other times, the tendency of leaders has been to insist that they know better than the staff that they have hired to do the work they are requesting.

Over the decades, hospitals have become far more attuned to understanding the needs of the patient in the nonmedical sense. Birthing suites, valet parking, luxury accommodations (for a price) are just a few of the many "innovations" that have put a glossy sheen on the health-care experience. As has already been established as a theme of this book, these niceties are not always implemented because of a strong sense of patient need determined through research. Often a leader learns that a neighboring hospital has put one of these hospitality services into place and feels the need to do the same—that is, to compete. Many administrators see the nonmedical aspects of their industry as being similar to the hotel industry. Disney has classes on how to provide excellent service, and it has even built a hospital in Celebration, Florida, as a model of their service excellence.

Marketers and marketing are, at times, involved in these projects. Other times, the entire service program is not seen as marketing at all by hospital leaders. This curious sense of perspective has arisen, in my view, because the valet parking and birthing centers and gourmet meals are typically incorporated into the hospital's operations departments, whereas marketing is usually seen as a peripheral, "extracurricular" activity. If health-care industry leaders seriously want to please their patients through an understanding of patient needs, they would do well to realize that companies such as Apple and Disney and The Four Seasons relentlessly review customer feedback and incorporate that feedback into their operations. They understand that marketing is not a peripheral activity but is a core operational necessity, as we shall explore further later. If we marketers are to be taken seriously, and if we are to have any effect on the success of the mission and business of our institutions, then the application of our skills must be based on more than an opinion. Focus groups, surveys, studies, and benchmarking all exist in abundance. Health-care marketers need to be able to demonstrate the correct course of action with something approaching the same rigor that supports the actions of an accountant or attorney or a hospitalist. Otherwise, marketing conversations devolve into an argument between two people over different shades of blue.

This tendency to see marketing as a peripheral matter of taste or one's gut instincts has its most significant negative impact when it comes to the value of what marketing provides to the patient. Often, materials for patients are written in an incomprehensible insider's jargon, or describe services such as gourmet meals or other amenities as if that were the only important criteria when considering one hospital over another. Many times, the "voice" of the materials, whether visible or implied, is a smiling, bland, corporate figurine telling the patient that everything will be fine, because she cares so much about you and only you.

Much hospital marketing imagery likewise presents photographs of operating rooms, Da Vinci surgical machines, and picture after picture of smiling healthy families posing in front of buildings, buildings, and more buildings. From the insider's perspective, this may make a certain amount of sense. After all, this stuff costs millions of dollars and leaders are proud of their buildings and their technology. They, or their marketers, seem to believe that the patient sees these pictures and associates the hospital with state-of-the-art capabilities. What they actually see is nothing, or rather nothing to distinguish one facility from the next. I have often held up an ad from a hospital and removed the identifying marks and asked a leadership team to name the facility. Nine times out of ten, they couldn't do it, even if the hospital promoted was their own. Most hospital marketing is as generic as the pills the pharmacy dispenses.

We know from serious research, not just my name-the-ad game, that all patients see in those ads is one more hospital and—let's face it—if you've seen one hospital, you've seen them all. Generally, hospitals look alike, have the same technology, and employ the same smiling, happy, caring staff. Patients have come to take all this for granted. Research shows it has no impact. So why is this still the prevalent mode for hospital marketing? In my experience, it is largely vanity. Physicians want to show that they are just as good as the famous doctor down the street and have the same high-tech toys. Administrators tout their facilities to each other at conferences and cocktail parties. Nothing says success like a twenty-story bed tower designed by a famed architect.

What I'm describing is, as Peter Senge wrote in *The Fifth Discipline*, a system that is perfectly designed to produce the outcomes it is producing. If you distill the last few pages, the feedback loop looks something like this: For deep, perhaps unconscious motivations, a leader asks the marketing department to produce a certain widget. The widget's purpose for existence is unclear to the marketer, but she builds it anyway. The widget is produced at great effort and expense, usually to the leader's precise specifications, and is then foisted on a large group of innocent bystanders at this point called the "target market." Since the target market has no use for this widget and can't understand what it is saying or why they are receiving it, they ignore it. Upon learning the fate of the widget project, the leader tells everyone that marketing blew it, and we should use experts who really know how to do marketing. Meanwhile, another leader has come to marketing asking for a doohickey, with the same, predictable results, and on it goes, with the reputation of the marketing department sinking by the day, the administrator lamenting the sorry state of affairs "with that group," and the bewildered patient finding her view of health care growing ever more alienating and frustrating.

STRATEGIC PARTNERSHIP

To an alarming degree, health-care marketers are ignorant of the mission, operations, and industry trends of the institutions they ostensibly serve. In one group I led, I found that 80 percent of them had never seen a surgery or spent any time at all in a hospital, save for the waiting room. They had no knowledge of the Affordable Care Act (ACA) or Accountable Care Organizations (ACOs) and knew nothing about how Medicare worked. When I asked them how our medical center made money, they were unable to answer the question except by saying we took care of sick people and got paid for it.

Once, I was asked to reengineer a health-care marketing group that had found itself in a particularly bad place—literally and figuratively. This institution had endured a number of years of negative margins. Eventually, a new leadership team was tasked with turning the tide. I was recruited to improve the marketing and communications.

The previous CEO held the marketing group in such low esteem that he had kicked them off campus and exiled them to a cinderblock office space in the middle of an industrial park ten miles from the hospital. The group felt distant, disrespected, and now, with the changes in leadership, scared for their jobs.

Our first meeting, though fraught with underlying tension, proceeded amiably enough. Once I assured them I was not carrying a pocketful of pink slips, I asked them to give me a rundown on their current projects. Sam was the first to speak up.

Sam: "I'm finishing up a brochure for primary care. It'll be at the printer tomorrow, and when it comes back, Mary and Lois will stuff the envelopes and take them to the post office."

Me: "Primary care. That's interesting, Sam. You know, I was just at a meeting of the leadership team where I learned that we have no capacity in primary care and definitely do not want to promote it. How did this come about?"

Sam: Well, Sally, the administrator for primary care, called and said Dr. Octavio wanted to promote his department and she asked us to put a brochure together. They had already written most of the copy themselves."

Me: "Sam, is there a marketing plan for this service? Do we have a budget or a target or goal for what we are trying to accomplish with this brochure?"

Sam: "No, Sally called last week and said she needed the mailing to go out this week, and so we had no time for any of that and we just put it on a fast track."

Me: "Is this pretty much how things work for you here?"

At this point, the group grew quiet, with many suddenly finding irresistibly interesting materials on their notepads. Betty, though, the administrative assistant for the area, whom I soon learned was the bravest of the bunch, said what we were all thinking.

Betty: "Yes, John, that's the way it happens all the time. We never know what we're supposed to do first and sometimes we might think a project doesn't make sense, but your predecessor would just say do it and if we questioned her, we'd be the ones to get into trouble."

To cap it all off, I asked the group about the marketing department's budget as a whole, and they looked at me and shrugged. "None of us have ever seen it," one said.

"How about a marketing plan for the hospital, or any particular service line?"

"We don't do those," another replied.

This group, banished to a distant industrial mall, didn't receive any information about anything important to the operations of the medical center, yet they were expected to produce meaningful results in support of the mission and strategies.

Or, perversely, perhaps no one expected this group to produce meaningful results at all. They were just a necessary evil, a master's-trained group available to make posters and lick envelopes and, once in a while, take a picture. Who else would photograph all those hospital grip-and-grins?

These examples are by no means unique. In my experience, they are all too typical. As to how this could be, equal fault can be found with leadership and the marketing staff themselves. I have yet to work in a medical center that orients its nonmedical or nonoperational staff on such matters as those listed above. As stated repeatedly, many leaders believe marketers are just there to do what they're told, and it doesn't matter if they understand the business. As for marketers, they concentrate on the core skills of their discipline: writing, graphics, photography, advertising, media buying, websites, and social media. The linkages between how these media affect medical center operations and sustainability are poorly understood by both parties.

In my view, the consequences for health care of this internal, siloed, and elitist approach to the public will be significant and, in fact, are already becoming apparent as physicians and executives see their autonomy slipping away, their income threatened, their revenues being squeezed, even their not-for-profit status being challenged by state legislatures and the US Congress. When you consider the lack of understanding that afflicts most people, the extreme guardedness of hospitals and physicians, the enormous costs involved, is it any wonder that "outsiders" view the whole enterprise with suspicion?

In many ways, I have seen the marketing staff as a bellwether of how the health-care industry interacts with the public since, for all intents and purposes, executives treat the marketing groups as if they were simply an extension of that public. Health-care leaders continuously bemoan the public's lack of understanding and support. Yet when the opportunity arises to alter that state of affairs, the leaders fall back into their comfort zone of banal statements and privately dismissive attitudes.

A strategic partnership among caregivers, administrators, and marketing, although by no means a panacea, could contribute to broader understanding and support for the health-care industry. More importantly, since innovation often derives from ideas and perceptions generated outside an industry's habitual frame of mind, marketing in its best sense could bring the outside in and help foster the transformation American health care so desperately needs.

RESEARCH, DATA, AND MEASUREMENT

In the previous paragraph, I used the phrase "marketing in its best sense." This doesn't refer to creating Clio-winning advertising or having copy praised by the International Association of Business Communicators or the Public Relations Society of America. Marketing is far more than simply marketing communications. Talk with any brand manager at Procter & Gamble or General Mills. The brand manager for Tide or Cheerios possesses intimate, immediate knowledge of his product's brand image, target markets, market share, and, most importantly, his customers' conscious and unconscious feelings, hopes, and dreams for Tide or Cheerios. Those insights are brought back into the company and applied to research and development for product improvements, better messaging, and, ultimately, higher customer satisfaction (and, by the way, greater profits). Recall the physician who was angry about being considered soap. Early in our brand management program at Mayo Clinic, we invited a marketing leader from General Mills to talk with a group of executives about how General Mills executes brand management for their products. Some of the physicians could not get past the bizarre phenomenon of sitting in a conference room at Mayo Clinic talking about a box of Cheerios. The notion that medical services were similar to products, or brands, in that patients develop strong emotional ties to their health-care providers just as they do to their breakfast cereal, and that those associations could actually not only improve patient satisfaction but improve the health-care experience, was a bridge too far. As brand management took hold at Mayo, these attitudes changed, and many physician leaders walked across that bridge, so to speak, although some are still wondering where it leads.

Data, qualitative and quantitative, collected over the course of years, then analyzed, synthesized, and applied strategically, are critical to the success of any enterprise, whether it be P&G, Apple, or General Mills. Why not in health care?

Certainly, the essential health-care service—medical care—does not lack for data. Physicians are drowning in it yet seek more and better data continuously. They know that innovation without data is Russian roulette when it comes to the life of a patient. Margins for error in health care must be—and are—miniscule, and every hospital works hard to make that margin as close to zero as humanly possible.

Evidence-based medicine is the bedrock and the glory of our health-care providers. As a marketer, I read the *Journal of the American Medical Association* (*JAMA*), the *New England Journal of Medicine* (*NEJM*) and *Lancet* so I could have a better understanding of the world of medical research and, indirectly, the mind-set of physicians. Over time at Mayo Clinic, I became friends and colleagues with some of the world's leading medical researchers. The Mayo brothers themselves based much of their reputation not just on their mechanical skills as surgeons but as men willing to examine scrupulously their own practices, learn from their mistakes, publish their results, and remain open to the teaching of others. We may now take such behavior for granted, but it was only in the late nineteenth and early twentieth centuries that such practices were slowly becoming the norm. Now they are established worldwide, no place more so than at Mayo Clinic.

Therefore, it should come as no surprise that at Mayo, every discipline, including "soft" areas such as human resources or marketing, is expected to base their decisions and activities on data, evidence, and outcomes.

When presenting to a group at Mayo Clinic about a particular tactic, I learned I would be asked questions like,"How do you know that [tactic] will be effective? Is there a body of evidence to support that?" I learned that any report purporting to present a conclusion based on data had better be statistically sound, for Mayo Clinic physicians are inherently skeptical, as every scientist should be, and will dismiss any study with too small an n (sample size) or too large a margin of error, that possesses any inherent biases, or any other statistical flaw. And, by the way, one study doesn't constitute a trend, so how do we know that this matters at all? You may think this seems elementary, but I have had interactions with other hospitals in my career that did not approach marketing with anything like this kind of rigor.

I relay these anecdotes with admiration and respect for my former Mayo Clinic colleagues. Marketers in other industries have been held to these high standards for years. Yet the health-care industry's reliance on data and evidence in marketing is inconsistent and often semicompetent and, as stated more than once, CEOs and other leaders are far too willing to "do marketing" without any data more persuasive than a gut feeling or a brief competitive fire in the belly or a "media opportunity" thrown across their desk by a golfing partner.

Marketers cannot evolve without data. Conversely, no financial officer, medical staff president, or hospital administrator will just take marketing's word for it about spending a few million dollars in hopes that spaghetti will stick to the wall, nor will marketing be elevated in their mind's eye without concrete data demonstrating outcomes both tangible and intangible.

One medical center I worked with had been struggling for years with lower-than-expected demand. The situation was a puzzlement and the CEO, a brilliant physician who readily admitted he was perplexed, asked our marketing group to investigate. Despite the fact that this medical center had been in operation for decades, there were large gaps in knowledge of the community and the reasons for its lack of interest. Indeed, certain basic questions had never been asked, and so, comprehensive surveys were fielded with patients, nonpatients, referring physicians, and community leaders. Concomitantly, we conducted internal surveys and focus groups, as well as operational analyses of the more poorly performing service lines, as well as supporting groups such as the appointment desks.

The results were counterintuitive for most of the leaders. While no one in the community doubted the excellence of the staff or its physicians, three key barriers prevented patients from choosing them:

1. I don't think my insurance will cover me.

2. I won't be able to get an appointment.

3. I don't think you want my business anyway.

In marketing lingo, we would say, the hospital was not competing on points of parity. That is, because people had these attitudes, the hospital wasn't in the comparison set from which patients and physicians would choose a provider. They weren't even in the game.

Further, the staff physicians, unaware of these attitudes, only aggravated the situation through behaviors that, from the public's point of view, gave evidence of the truth of these biases. Some patients were turned away for not meeting certain criteria about the nature of their illness. Call centers used templates to filter out patients not fitting the criteria. This was done because a particular physician wanted to develop a specific type of practice, perhaps for research purposes, perhaps because it was a special expertise of said physician. Regardless, word spread in the community that this hospital "wasn't interested in me and I could not get an appointment, so why try?"

Once the situation revealed itself, the remedies were clear, although hardly simple. Templates were changed or removed, physicians were encouraged to "see the patient," and a marketing campaign ran for years, letting people know that their insurance was welcome, that the medical center most certainly did want their business, and that appointments were available.

In this case, marketing and operations worked in tandem, as strategic partners, to change the community perceptions with target messaging backed up by operational changes. Over time, demand grew, and the hospital maintains that success to this day. The physicians involved would never have changed any of their behaviors if there had not been comprehensive, reliable, properly managed research that educated them about the counterproductive consequences of their actions. Nor would anything have changed if the marketing leader, or the CEO, or anyone else simply said, "The problem is x, the solution is y. Now go fix it." Physicians, and indeed most of us, do not work that way. We prefer to understand the situation so we can come to our own decision about how to participate in a solution.

Marketers also bear responsibility for the surprising lack of data informing their actions. Many hospital marketing staff are not trained in the discipline. Often, they come to health care from advertising or public relations agencies and are more schooled in marketing communications than in strategic marketing. Rarely have hospitals sought the statistical analysts and strategists that should form a part of the hospital marketing team. Often, those professionals are housed in finance or planning departments. The evolution of the hospital planning department and its current confusion with hospital marketing is a topic for a later chapter. For now, suffice to say that hospital executives often turn to the finance department or planning department for reports on market share, growth potential, and referral patterns, data that in any other industry would be part and parcel of marketing's purview in order to create a system-wide picture of the relationship of operations, consumer attitudes, and the marketplace. Instead, this legacy organizational arrangement contributes to the isolation of marketing as merely concerning communications or promotions.

Even in such situations, marketing staff need to avail themselves of these resources. They need to become literate in statistics, strategic thinking, competitive analysis, and planning. All of the marketing departments that I have had the opportunity to make over were heavily weighted with former journalists, public relations specialists, agency marketing communications specialists, and, a few times, staff with no previous training in any of these disciplines who were simply asked to be the person who would compile the weekly newsletter or produce a flyer in Adobe for the company picnic. Leaders of marketing groups have a responsibility for ensuring their hires are competent and appropriately skilled in areas such as data analysis and brand management, as well as production areas such as writing, graphics, or digital communications. Given the aforementioned lack of respect often exhibited toward hospital marketing groups, we have only ourselves to blame if the department becomes the last refuge of corporate deadwood or institutional teachers' pets for whom the CEO or HR VP wants to find a place in the organization rather than face the harsh reality regarding that person's employment.

Many times in my career, I have heard a certain refrain from fellow marketing heads, sometimes in private conversations, or at conferences around the lunch table, or even as part of conference presentations all across the country: "Marketing should have a seat at the table." A seat at the executive table has been the Holy Grail of marketing and communications for as long as I can remember. I have heard this refrain expressed with rational dignity, I have heard it spoken often as a persistent whine, and I have even heard a boss demand of his boss to be given a seat at the grown-ups table in a loud, angry, expletive-laden voice that shocked all around them (that didn't work either).

Yes, this book argues that marketing should have a seat at the executive table. My view is that it can be—indeed, must be—earned, and the key to that happy circumstance is data and demonstrable outcomes. As long as we participate in hiring poorly trained staff or focus on knocking out schlock at the whim of an administrator, and so long as we fail to present strategically valid recommendations based on data and a deep understanding of our institution's goals, strategies, and marketplace, we will remain on the periphery and will have only ourselves to blame. Marketer, heal thyself.

INTEGRATION

Throughout this narrative, I have used the word "marketing" in a broad sense to encompass what are traditionally siloed activities, including data gathering and analysis; marketing communications, graphics, and video production; and digital communications such as website development and social media. In truth, my contention is that marketing should be a department that integrates all the nonmedical activities that protect and enhance the institution's brand Government relations, community relations, brand management, internal communications, development communications, public relations, and traditional marketing. All should be united with a common purpose, consistent messaging, and mutually synergistic strategies and tactics. Over the years I worked at Mayo Clinic, the benefits of this type of alignment slowly took hold. The path is not easy and, later on, we will review the possibilities and the pitfalls of achieving this type of full integration.

As a principle of marketing as it could be, indeed, as it should be, there are many precedents outside of health care. The marketing head of Coca-Cola is also responsible for product development. At Ford, likewise, the head of marketing is also responsible for product development. In these cases, the dualism regarding operations and marketing that is so prevalent in health care simply doesn't exist.

These industries understand the symbiotic relationship that exists between the company and its customers, manifested internally by a close relationship with operations and marketing.

Steve Jobs famously dismissed some aspects of marketing, particularly focus groups. (Let us also remember he was the progenitor of the "1984" Super Bowl television commercial, still usually cited as the single greatest TV ad of all time.) Jobs was fond of quoting Henry Ford, who said, "If I had asked people what they wanted, they would have said a faster horse." Nothing can replace the kind of intuitive genius driving a Steve Jobs or a Henry Ford or a Jeff Bezos of Amazon.com. Leaders like these, though, also possess an intuitive genius for assessing market needs and applying modern technologies in ways that others did not see. They were in tune with the marketplace as it was evolving, not as it had been. Often, as with Jobs, learning and experience in other disciplines, such as design, were applied to industries that would ordinarily have ignored such thinking. Jobs also was known for having a multidisciplinary team that included marketing at the initial stages of product and service development. Marketing was not brought in as an afterthought. In this way, his company transcended traditional organizational boundaries to build a cogent brand based on substance, not just imagery.

This may be the most important principle of the five enumerated at the beginning of this chapter, and also the most difficult to achieve. As Mayo Clinic moved closer to this ideal, difficult conversations, hurt feelings, and outright angry opposition occurred. Change always produces anxiety and resistance. No organizational structure is perfect, nor can a chart of lines and boxes in and of itself produce meaningful change. Since Mayo Clinic is a paragon of consensus culture, colleagues needed to understand the rationale driving organizational realignments, and needed to be persuaded that the changes would indeed benefit the institution more than the status quo. Over the years, our experience at Mayo Clinic demonstrated this benefit, as will be explored in later chapters.

That integration would drive activities at Mayo Clinic makes perfect sense once one understands it is in the culture's DNA as it is nowhere else. Although Mayo Clinic executives would also say, "We don't integrate just for the sake of integration," everyone at Mayo Clinic understands that the burden of proof was on those who did not support what most others saw as an opportunity for better teamwork, greater efficiencies, and better outcomes for patients, families, and indeed the institution itself that could be accomplished by a proposed mechanism of integration.

Integration need not always be mandated by a strict reporting hierarchy. Committees, consensus building, work groups, and temporary blitz teams all help further the cause. At some point, though, people need to know who is in charge of what, and, as we shall see, there is more to marketing than picking a logo or writing a catchphrase.

As is by now clear, Mayo Clinic is the inspiration and the model for my thinking about marketing (in the broad sense previously described), its relationship with other disciplines within the organization, institutional operations, and the patients we serve.

During the course of my career at Mayo Clinic, we conducted hundreds of surveys interviewing thousands of people all across the country. We learned many things from them that aided us in our care for them and our services for them. When we isolated some of the differentiating characteristics of Mayo Clinic from other health-care providers, we learned that many Americans harbor two profound frustrations about our health-care system: feelings of alienation and feelings of fragmentation. Many people will tell the same health-care story, with individual variations. Susan feels ill, goes to her primary physician, and learns that she needs X-rays and lab tests. She may need to go to different facilities for these services. Then she anxiously awaits the results, which may take days, then goes back to her physician, who refers her to a specialist, an appointment that can take days or even weeks to materialize. She may then learn she needs surgery, and that again requires a different visit to a different office. Then the hospital stay needs to be scheduled, then the recovery, and then some form of rehabilitation or recovery assistance is required. And then we throw in the various medications prescribed by the different physicians, the different billing forms, the insurance requirements, and you have a recipe for extreme frustration. No one understands the hospital bill; physicians often explain things poorly if at all; most people don't know the right questions to ask; and insurance companies have a perspective different from the others, namely, reducing costs by any means available. Not knowing where to turn for help, patients and families usually do as they are told, and though in the end, an outcome may be reached that is satisfactory from a medical point of view, the human aspects of the experience are alienating and disjointed.

Mayo Clinic is an entirely different kind of institution, one that has solved the problem of integration by providing all the necessary services in one location (actually three: Rochester, Jacksonville, and Phoenix/Scottsdale). Patients who came to Mayo Clinic often told the story referenced with a few important revisions. Their decision to come to Mayo Clinic was almost always their own doing, after consultation with friends and relatives and now very often digital communications. Their frustration with the fragmentation and lack of humanity in the process had driven them to a breaking point or, sometimes, local physicians could not determine the problem they were having and Mayo Clinic could. I personally brought my mother to Mayo Clinic twice in her life when a physician in her hometown had told her she needed surgery, only to find that she did not. She did not live in a village of twelve people, nor were her physicians badly trained. The difference was the application of collective wisdom from a team of physicians at Mayo Clinic who brought together the perspective of many disciplines. Other medical centers in the United States have adopted some of Mayo Clinic's practices. Nowhere, in my opinion, has the whole health-care process been so well constructed, improved, and humanized as at Mayo Clinic.

My hope is that hospital marketing departments can attain the same level of interdepartmental cooperation and respect that prevented my mother from enduring surgery she did not need. Obviously, the prevention of an unnecessary operation is on a different order of magnitude in importance from stopping useless marketing materials or writing incomprehensible or meaninglessly bland messages to patients or failing to understand the real needs of a population. That said, consider this example: For a time, Mayo Clinic had three separate websites for each of its clinics in Arizona, Florida, and Minnesota. These three websites in some places had three different explanations of how to access the clinics, three different methods for presenting the medical specialties, and, at times, differing write-ups about services provided. Confusing for the patient, for the staff, and not the kind of integrated brand Mayo Clinic represents. Once we adopted a more integrated approach to website production, these discrepancies were eliminated, and now a unified web team produces all such materials for a unified website.

On every level, whether the internal weekly newsletter or a major national ad campaign, we owe our patients useful information of substance and value to them. We owe it to them that we show clearly that our house is not divided against itself, that operations and the other disciplines are working consistently in harmony. We owe them statements and promises that are true and provable. Most importantly, we owe it to them to listen to them and understand their needs, not just their diseases or conditions. Just as this is important to good medical care, it is essential to the best practice of marketing.

CHAPTER 2

MARKETING HEALTH CARE STRATEGICALLY

MARKETING FOR HEALTH care is unlike marketing for any other product or service. Most obviously, few, if any, aspects of a person's life are more highly valued than one's health or the health of a loved one. When illness strikes a family, the situation engenders fear, anxiety, and often tension within the family. Few, if any, products or services one markets carry the consequences of dealing with a situation that is often a matter of life or death.

Not all illnesses or conditions are catastrophic or potentially life threatening, nevertheless even the simplest of procedures, such as a tonsillectomy, results in a small number of deaths each year. Something as small as a medication error caused by a misplaced decimal point can result in serious harm or death. As one physician said to me, "There is no such thing as minor surgery." Every encounter with the health-care system is a serious, expensive, potentially harmful event.

Of course, people go to the doctor and into hospital every day, largely because they have motivations that override these apprehensions. Research shows that Americans have faith in the quality of their health-care providers. They may think the system as a whole is broken, too expensive, and too confusing, but when it comes to their own providers, though, people generally express positive feelings toward their physicians and hospital. Health-care marketers know that it's very difficult to persuade a patient to switch doctors. Usually, patients will change physicians only under duress; that is, something has gone terribly wrong with the outcome of an episode of care, or the relationship with the doctor, that compels the patient to make a change. Research we conducted at Mayo Clinic confirmed that most Americans, including patients and even referring physicians, see one hospital as pretty much just like any other hospital. Likewise, regarding physicians, they don't see much difference in quality between the neurologist at the medical center down the street and the neurologist at a specialty center a thousand miles away, for example, at Johns Hopkins in Baltimore, or Massachusetts General in Boston. This faith in the quality of the personal provider is accompanied by a strong sense of hope, largely driven by the miraculous progress in medicine during the twentieth century. Nowadays, the media are rife with stories of medical procedures and technology approaching the wonderment of science fiction. Media report patient stories on amazing comebacks from dreadful illnesses, or limbs being reattached, faces transplanted, conjoined twins successfully separated. These help fuel the strong belief in America that just about any illness can be cured or, at least, ameliorated because of the impressive science informing the high-level skill of American health-care providers.

What does it mean to market strategically in such an environment? It is important to realize that health care is not simply a product or a service in the traditional sense. Many physicians, perhaps more so in the early part of my career, often expressed the notion that their job was to produce a positive outcome for the patient. More than once in my career, I have had a discussion with physicians about patient complaints. One physician, world-renowned in his field, said to me, "I saved that man's life. His valve had deteriorated, and, without that replacement, he would be dead today. I did exactly what I was trained to do. And now he is complaining because I didn't smile enough? Is that what medicine is about now?"

He is not alone with these concerns. For many caregivers, overburdened as they are with too many patients, too little time, scarce resources, more regulation than the US Tax Code, and now, a burgeoning concern for service excellence, the comfort zone for their workday can easily turn health care into a largely transactional exchange, kind of like getting your car fixed. The battery dies, you get towed, the guy in back changes out the battery, you pay the bill, and off you go. Are you thinking, "Hey, that guy didn't shake my hand or say thank you?" Even if you are, by the second stoplight, your mind is on to other things.

Yes, we live in an age when even many car dealerships have developed an extraordinary interest in customer service, and, indeed, so have health-care providers. From the point of view of the provider, though, I maintain that they see marketing's job as primarily promoting the product (i.e., process and outcomes). Many physicians would bring my departments their quality scores and expect us to produce an ad with charts and graphs comparing them to other physicians or hospitals, believing that this would drive patient choice. Disregarding the ethics of such an ad, the notion that numbers alone will drive patient preference has been proven wrong by numerous studies. One such study published by the Health Care Advisory Board demonstrated that patients in New York City over a certain period of time were more likely to choose the hospital with the most effective marketing campaign, even though said hospital did *not* have the highest-quality scores. Studies conducted at Mayo Clinic confirmed that 90 percent of Americans do not base a provider choice on Health Grades or LeapFrog or UHC's rankings or any other of the numerous such systems published every year. The annual

"Best Hospitals" issue of *US News and World Report* has an impact with a small number of consumers. The vast majority, though, rely on word of mouth, recommendations of friends and family, and, increasingly, information from websites and social media.

Regarding service, though, the twenty-first century is the era of Apple Genius Bars, Amazon same-day drone delivery, and instant customizable streaming and downloading of just about every song ever recorded. Compare these scenarios with health care. Even today, you are told that you have a certain condition and need an operation. You go to the surgeon who tells you when she can do your procedure. You go to the hospital when it works best for the surgeon, surrender your clothes and your wallet, and find comfort in the belief that the people who are sticking you and probing you and, eventually, cutting you know what they are doing. The next thing you know, you are awake, in pain, and you have no idea what happened "in there," or what it will cost, but everyone is smiling and saying, "You did great," and "Everything is going to be okay."

Throughout this episode of care arise many opportunities for caregivers to provide service excellence as well as product excellence. In most facilities today, service excellence has become an all-consuming passion among providers. They know that outstanding service can be an essential in a world where the population sees very little difference among providers in the "product." Patient satisfaction ratings and other service indicators, once the province of a nearly forgotten group in the hospital hierarchy (often marketing), now receive regular attention from the hospital leadership team, not only because of the importance to the patient, but because the federal government now requires it as part of the basis for hospital reimbursement. Many insurance companies have followed suit and base hospital and physician reimbursement on similar standards.

HEALTH CARE—A PRODUCT AND A SERVICE

As you can see, health care is not a product transaction like buying Tide detergent or a service experience like a vacation week at the Hilton Hawaiian Village in Waikiki. Just as light is simultaneously a beam and a wave, health care is simultaneously a product and a service and should be marketed accordingly. Light behaves as a beam in certain situations and as a wave in others, yet it is always both. Marketers need to keep both aspects of health care in mind and balance messaging carefully between the two.

What is increasingly understood among marketers in health care is the overriding importance to patients and families of the health-care experience. The total of outcomes, relationships, facilities, service, ease of access, follow-up, and loyalty programs all combine to create an experience for the customer that must be managed in its totality if the health-care provider wishes to have outstanding metrics for customer preference and willingness to recommend.

Since the health-care industry is rapidly becoming commoditized, it is more important than ever that marketing understand the experiential nature of modern health care and work in concert with other leadership to ensure it is managed with the patient and family at the forefront.

A key first step in this process of understanding is to assess a given provider's marketplace positioning. Most MBA-trained marketing professionals will be familiar with the concept of positioning, and probably have read Al Ries and Jack Trout's *Positioning: The Battle for Your Mind*, a classic in its field that brought the term positioning into the marketing lexicon. Here's a good summary of the positioning concept:

> *Positioning is something (perception) that happens in the minds of the target market. It is the aggregate perception the market has of a particular company, product or service*

in relation to their perceptions of the competitors in the same category. It will happen whether or not a company's management is proactive, reactive or passive about the on-going process of evolving a position. But a company can positively influence the perceptions through enlightened strategic actions.

In marketing, positioning has come to mean the process by which marketers try to create an image or identity in the minds of their target market for its product, brand, or organization. It is the 'relative competitive comparison' their product occupies in a given market as perceived by the target market.

—Derrick Daye, "Great Moments in Marketing: Ries, Trout & Positioning"

In my work in marketing, I have found this concept fundamental to the successful development of a strategic marketing plan; in fact, it is essential to understand positioning if you wish to develop any kind of strategic plan for the business. How can you plan where you want to go and how you want to get there if you don't know where you are? How can you know you can really get where you want to go if you don't know what resources or assets you possess to get you there? And finally, what if the place you want to go is no longer a place at all, but a ghost town of last decade's trends and attitudes, and the population has moved on to places you did not know existed until it was too late?

Despite the simplistic nature of these questions, you would be amazed at the number of times I have been the first to ask such questions of a physician leader or an administrator. Whether an entire medical center or a service line, I have been in the position of being asked to create a brochure, or a website, and when I delve into the content for this marketing medium, I have been told that that is all still under development. In the 1980s, my marketing department was asked to create a brochure for one of the first women's centers in the country, when that was a hot trend in the healthcare industry. As I asked the administrator, who had been newly hired for the job, about the content, it became clear that she did not know what the center would provide as services. The institution could not agree on how to take components of women's care, such as mammography and osteoporosis screening, out of the hospital and into a separate building. Nor was anyone sure if the center should include OB or GYN services, nor had anyone done studies of the appetite for services in a separate facility, nor did anyone know what the strategy was for reaching the target market, which, at the moment, was "women," except for the creation of a "beautiful" brochure that would appeal to "women." We worked on this brochure for about a year. Twelve months of back-and-forth with the center staff and my staff, adding services, removing services, and reviewing copy and graphics by committee. After a year, my group and I decided to do something extraordinary. The next time I met with the administrator of the women's center, I said, "Katie, we have tried and tried, but it seems we cannot please you or the group with our work. I don't think we can do this project for you. I think you should take it to an outside agency. I'll even help pay for it."

Katie looked at me, shocked, and said, "You mean you won't do this for us?" I nodded, and she started to cry.

This was a first for me, a manager in my mid-twenties, to have a woman twice my age with a PhD crying in my office over a brochure.

After she calmed a bit, she told me the saga of her year of trying to get this center off the ground. As described above, and as I have said so often already, the project grew out of a brief conversation at a leadership table, as in "We should have a women's center," since, you know, everybody's building one, and, it'll be a profit center, and so on. So Katie was hired and told to get it done, but no one knew what it was, and every time she attempted to put something together, she had resistance and things would grind and grind as they can in any corporation.

In marketing, we call this the "If you build it, they will come" syndrome. Traditionally, this was more or less true. The country wasn't overbedded, not every hospital had every new gizmo, there wasn't the proliferation of specialists we have now, and the government and the private payers would get a bill from the hospital and pay it, usually in full, and all was well with the world. Additionally, no one questioned that doctors and administrators knew—they just knew—what was best for the patient. No need for marketing studies. Patients don't really know what they need in health care, after all.

To be fair, it did happen in the 1960s and 1970s that Health Systems Agencies (HSAs) were created, and the Certificate of Need (CON) process initiated. This required hospitals to receive permission before they could build a new facility or purchase, say, a major appliance such as a CT scanner. Consequently, reports would be generated about population growth, cases per thousand of certain illnesses, profit that would be generated by x number of patients over y number of years. This created a lot of bureaucracy and, in some cases, certainly put projects on hold or slowed their timeline, but it didn't stem the explosion in health-care costs. Most states no longer have the CON process.

Katie probably had just such a *pro forma* for her women's center, but that is hardly a blueprint for creating a meaningful service line out of thin air. After my meeting with Katie, we all resolved to give it one more chance, and we did get a brochure created, and the center opened and ran for a few years. It never established its position in the marketplace; it had a name but no discernible brand or identity—it was just a collection of a few services that could have been anywhere, not necessarily in a new building with flowers and mauve upholstery. The women's center is no longer there, and I still have a copy of the brochure we created. It was one of the worst brochures

I've ever produced and has been resting quietly in a file box for thirty years and will never again see the light of day.

STRATEGIC DIFFERENTIATION

If a marketing plan is to succeed, it must be based on solid strategy that derives from the overall strategy of the organization. My experience has been that most hospitals today spend a great deal of time on strategic planning, although this is not universally true. If you work for a hospital that does not have a strategic plan, you will need to spend time with the leadership determining what their thinking is on their actions and why they are moving in certain directions. The strategies may not be written down, but they exist in the minds and actions of the leaders. Marketers in this situation have the unenviable task of trying to codify enough of the strategy so that marketing strategies can be measured against them.

When I try to get to the heart of a problem of strategy, especially if there is no written plan to guide me, I have three questions that often provoke the answers I need. Someone suggests a tag line, or that we should open a women's center, or buy a hospital. I ask:

○ Why?

○ So what?

○ How do you know that?

One has to be careful with these questions. If you express them in the wrong tones, at the wrong table, or at the wrong time, you will be pegged as arrogant, questioning, negative, perhaps obstructionist. It is important to establish that marketing has the job of deeply understanding actions and motivations, so they may do the best job on behalf of the organization.

Imagine Michael, a staff person in your group, comes to you and suggests the hospital change its current tagline from "We Care" to "We Care the Most."

I might say, "Interesting idea. Why should we do this?"

Michael: "Every hospital says they care. We need to say we care the most to differentiate ourselves."

Me: "Michael, when I hear the line, 'We Care the Most,' I ask myself, 'So what?' If I'm a prospective patient, and you say to me, 'We care the most,' what would you say if I said, 'So what? What does that mean, anyway?'"

Michael: "It would mean we're better than the other hospitals. We have the most caring staff. We have the best customer service."

Me: "Really? All that from the addition of those two words? How do you know that?"

And so on. This is not an idle exercise. Many times, once the explanations are given for what was, admittedly, a pretty poor attempt at a tagline, I would ask Michael to think about all that he had told me when he delved deeper into his intentions and motivations, and then come back with some better ideas based on what he had said. "Oh, and perhaps, Michael," I would say, "we should do some focus groups with patients and find out whether any of this is going to make any difference to anyone at all.

Now, in conversations with leadership, the situation is far more delicate. A decision has been made to build a sports medicine center. You have been asked to market said center. You ask, "Can you help me understand why we've chosen to build a center in this particular place with these particular services? Is there a study or a report I can read? Some data that I can study?"

Ideally, marketing would have been involved in the initial decision to build the center. For the sake of this exercise, let's assume it was a bit of the "If we build it, they will come" syndrome. Asking why and getting information is essential. The next question might be in the form of, "How do we know a center is needed there and will do well?" Maybe the answer is in the report, maybe it isn't. Perhaps it is a "We just know" kind of answer. In this scenario, the "So what?" question is in your mind, because it's possible you haven't heard any solid criteria for the rationale behind this center. In this kind of situation, I have recommended marketing studies that would help us understand the needs and preferences of the targeted population, so we can do a better job of marketing the project and so that we can develop our own answers to some of the "So what?" questions. Whereas, in an ideal world, marketing wouldn't be asked to market a project they hadn't already helped study so as to inform the best possible decision, it will inevitably happen that marketers will be asked to market that which has already been decided. In those cases, further studies are vital if the marketing is to have any credibility at all. Furthermore, the marketing department does not want to be in the position of allowing others to say, "Well, the plan was solid, but we didn't get any support from marketing (or their support was ineffectual), so, really, that was the problem."

POSITIONING

So, one way or another, the marketing leader must ascertain and understand the strategy of the organization. Once that is accomplished, the notion of positioning comes into play. Given the position that the organization currently holds in the market, are the strategies in keeping with that position, antithetical to that position, or do they aspire to move the position into a new space?

Hospital leaders have been accustomed to thinking of their facilities almost the way Safeway might think of a grocery store. We are here to serve shoppers (doctors) with the goods they need (beds and technology) so that they can feed their families (take care of their patients). Given the population of this suburb, we can build two stores five miles apart and meet the needs of x thousand people. (We can build a 150-bed hospital in this neighborhood and our catchment area will be x thousands of patients.) This mechanistic perspective on health care is woefully out of date. Patients have far more options than even ten or fifteen years ago. They can go to a clinic at Target or Walmart or CVS. They can go to a specialty heart hospital, they can choose Lasik surgery at the center down the street, they can go online and find any care center or provider in the world, or they can call a nurse line and treat themselves (to a point). No longer is the hospital the center of the medical world.

This competitive landscape is what has driven hospital leaders to seek marketing and branding as they never have before. The challenge has been to translate traditional marketing practices and terminology and apply them to the odd business that is health care. Positioning is a perfect example of this aspect of the marketer's dilemma. Often, when I have introduced the concept of positioning into a health-care organization, say, at a leadership meeting, the initial reaction is a groan or a puzzled grimace. Most administrators and physicians have not read Ries and Trout, nor have they ever heard of positioning or, worse, the dreaded positioning statement. Marketers tend to be fond of this tool and often fall in love with their tautly worded, rigorously debated positioning statements. In my experience, leaders generally don't get what the fuss is about.

Once the initial explanations are dealt with, in itself a painful experience, the reactions vary from indifference to confusion. Most commonly, leaders ask, "How is this different from our mission and vision statements? Isn't this just a reiteration of the same concepts?"

PROMISES, PROMISES

This brings us to the essential, vital, *sine qua non* of the purpose and potential of hospital marketing: testing internal assumptions against external reality. As previously stated, medicine and hospital administration are historically highly internally focused. When I started at Mayo Clinic, I suggested that we do a study to determine how people perceived the Clinic, hoping we could use the information to better target potential patients. One of my supervisors at the time was incredulous. "This is the Mayo Clinic," he said. "We know what people think of us. We don't need to waste time or money doing that kind of crap."

Admittedly, this was the early 1990s, long before brand management swept through the health-care industry. Over the years, I learned that Mayo Clinic was not alone among hospitals in believing they had a firm handle on how they were perceived by the public. As community organizations, hospitals had close connections with their "catchment areas" through volunteers, patients, and their families, fund-raising events, and interactions with government and business leaders. What was poorly understood at the time was that such groups present a self-selection bias. Benefactors, volunteers, and even patients and families are far more inclined to speak positively about the medical center they have chosen to support, not to mention often having "drunk the Kool-Aid"; that is, they are sometimes so familiar with the hospital's self-perceptions and internal assumptions that they share the same perspectives and are therefore blind to some of the harsher realities.

Most hospital leaders now acknowledge the need for consumer data. Usually, they don't dig deep enough or stay with the program long enough to get an actionable information set.

The process of understanding market position is, of course, closely related to and a fundamental part of brand management. Positioning statements put into clear language the competitive advantage or competitive aspirations of a product or service line or facility. Through such data, one may find that hospital X is perceived to be acceptable by the public for "ordinary" illnesses but is not the first choice for more serious situations. One may find wide information gaps among consumers who don't know the full scale of services available at a given hospital. In my experience with this kind of research, we inevitably uncover some facts that leaders do not want to hear: that their hospital is poorly perceived for quality or service, it is misunderstood as to the levels of technology and sophistication, or that they are at a competitive disadvantage vis-a-vis the medical center down the street, despite the fact that they know—in fact, are absolutely sure—that they run a better hospital than those guys.

Based on research, positioning statements should embody the reality of a hospital's market position, whereas mission and vision statements are internally generated promises or aspirations that may or may not be in agreement with external perceptions. When serious conflicts are found between a leadership team's perception of itself and its activities versus those of the "outside world," the consequences are potentially dire. Just as General Motors fell into the abyss by dismissing consumer trends and producing cars nobody wanted to buy, so, too, can hospitals fall into a fog of believing they are creating just the right environment or set of service lines just as they have always done, while another hospital, far more in tune with consumer trends, is slowly eating away at their referrals and margins. Certainly, there are medical centers in some areas that may be the only resource available. Not every city has a Duke Medical Center or a Cleveland Clinic. These hospitals may have had sufficient volumes and referrals, regardless of their ability to stay ahead of a consumer preference curve, and may not have needed to be overly concerned with statistically accurate representations of their brand or market position (although, in truth, the sustainability of smaller regional hospitals has been in crisis for years, due to many factors, social and economic). Most hospitals and medical centers, though, face stiff competition and so ignore public perceptions at their own peril.

The whole notion of hospitals competing with one another to acquire increased referrals and a greater market share of people who are ill or injured is anathema to most people—marketers included. Some physicians and administrators I have worked with will go to great lengths to ensure they never say the "C" word (competition) out loud. When speaking in front of physician groups, I would often steer clear of the concept and talk instead about making it possible for patients to access the right resources at the right time. This was true enough, but all of us knew the subtext. If the patients didn't access us, they'd access some other doctors or hospitals, and the job of marketing was to ensure that that didn't happen. Always acting as ladies and gentlemen, of course. Nothing competitive going on here.

If a hospital, physician practice, or, now, an Accountable Care Organization or an insurance product is to remain viable, it must have patients—preferably nongovernment-paying patients and, in many areas, there are not enough of them to go around. This opens a discussion about the nature of the American medical system that goes beyond the scope of this book, although I'd like to pull together a few observations. No serious academic observer believes our system is really a free market system. Attempts to describe our system require inventing names and definitions that simply highlight its Kafkaesque nature. Marketers must ply their trade in a market that makes no sense in conventional business terms and do so in an environment of tacit competition cloaked in collegial camaraderie and community spirit. Health-care marketers therefore operate in a strange no-man's-land wherein the hospital is committed to maintaining its not-for-profit status, even as it struggles to increase its margins. They are asked to produce and disseminate marketing materials that pretend they are not really marketing materials. Since the government pays a fraction of the true cost of treating Medicare and Medicare patients, marketers must design target markets that resemble gerrymandered congressional districts, aiming materials at commercially insured patients under sixty-five while, at the same time, assuring the public that as a not-for-profit community resource, the hospital's doors are open to everyone. In fact, thanks to the Emergency Medical Treatment & Labor Act, passed in 1986 and widely known as EMTALA, emergency rooms must treat any patient that presents with an illness. The public perceives hospitals as overpriced and executives as overpaid, and they cry bloody murder at any attempt to increase access or reimbursement through laws or taxes, yet when an individual or an individual's loved one is ill, money is no longer an object because without health, you have nothing. Most of the money they are spending does not come out of their own pocket but the pocket of the taxpayer or the insurance company, all subsidized by the commercially insured, whose rates are "cost-shifted" (i.e., inflated) so that the hospital has some slim hope of achieving a sustainable margin in aggregate, the bulk of which monies, in essence, have come from America's industries whose benefit programs pay the bills for most Americans. I defy Apple to sell an iPad to anyone in a market that worked like this.

All of this circles back to my main caveat about discussions with leaders about marketing and positioning. It is essential that marketers do the research necessary to understand the position of the entity they are trying to market. The exercise of distillation and synthesis of this information into a cogent set of statements will clarify your thinking and the thinking of your team. My advice is to discuss with your supervisor the necessity of sharing or receiving approval from the executive group of which you may or may not be a member. I usually favor openness, but your boss may have his or her own thoughts. At any rate, when sharing information of this kind, focus on its utility to the marketing group. Sharing a statement with an administrator that reads something like "Lollipop Hospital is a midlevel neighborhood pediatric hospital that treats children with love and respect and is well-known for its caring and friendly manner" may not satisfy the administrator who believes that her hospital is fully equipped and ready to take on the Children's Hospital of Pennsylvania, despite evidence to the contrary. Under the right settings, conversations can be engendered by this material that can lead to constructive thinking about the advisability of presenting Lollipop Hospital to the public in a manner they will not find credible. It can also lead to aspirational strategies whereby all agree that when Lollipop Hospital opens this or that service and acquires this or that technology or renowned pediatric surgeon, the marketing team can help move the positioning statement to a new space. Sadly, though, it can also lead to the administrator finding the statement unacceptable and insisting on it being rewritten to his specifications, in which case, you have a situation on your hands that, hopefully, the CEO is willing to adjudicate. In fact, dear reader, many times in a marketing career, this exact type of tension will arise, in some cases, on a daily or weekly basis. And now, we are in the realm of organizational culture and we must save that for another chapter.

Once the positioning statement issue is resolved, however that may be, expect that you will use it in your internal work and don't expect anyone on the executive team to refer to it much again, if ever. Some hospitals I know have even dispensed with using these statements altogether. Rather, they've incorporated the analysis into their general brand-management program. These marketers have found that the positioning concept is too arcane, too much like marketing jargon, and smacks too much of overt competitiveness. Whether codified or tacitly understood, in an environment replete with many consumer choices, even for health care, a marketer simply must know how their entity stands in relationship to competing entities.

MISSION AND VISION

At this stage in the process, you have an understanding of the institution's strategies and business objectives and you have an understanding of the institution's competitive market position. Now is the time to compare, contrast, and determine the most effective marketing strategies that will allow marketing to help advance the institution's mission and business objectives.

Health-care marketing departments usually express their mission as growing market share or increasing revenue. This makes perfect sense from a marketer's point of view. My concern with this approach is that it centers upon three problematic factors:

overt competitiveness, focus on revenue, and measurability. Overt competitiveness carries the baggage previously described. To put this concern in a legal context, consider a hospital system that is looking to acquire a neighboring hospital that is failing financially. Such mergers and acquisitions are being reviewed by the Federal Trade Commission (FTC) with increasing assiduity. As the trend in the US for greater consolidation of health-care facilities with larger and larger systems has accelerated, so has the FTC increased its vigilance concerning lack of competition in a given market. Mergers have been denied because memos, emails, and marketing materials have stated clearly that the goal of an acquisition was to increase market share or eliminate a competitor. Don't fall into the trap right off the bat by stating the whole purpose of a marketing department is to do just that.

The emphasis on revenue is a bit more sensitive. Most administrators will expect to see measurable growth in revenue attributable to the marketing program. Difficulties arise in capturing the necessary data. Few hospitals, even today, have the ability to smoothly track an individual's episode of care back to the patients or referring physician's initial decision to choose a particular hospital. True customer relationship management systems that would allow this kind of data gathering are rare in hospitals and often are focused more on revenue from the care episode than on marketing data. So the marketer has two alternatives. One is to build a particular project in such a way that individual tracking is possible for a limited cohort. The other is to retrospectively collect referral or patient inquiry data that corresponds to the time ads ran or other marketing activities ran that can be isolated. Even then, executives are very likely to ask, or rather state, "You can't know which of those patients would have come, anyway, without marketing." That's true, of course; nor can the executive prove they would have chosen the hospital *without* the marketing, but in the end, this is a losing argument for the marketer, not the executive. Measurement will be covered in a subsequent chapter. For now, my advice is to limit promises of increased revenue to selective, measurable projects rather than the whole enterprise.

Hospitals have other reasons for existence besides making money. In evaluating the mission and purpose of a marketing department, my reference is to begin with the fundamental understanding that the job of the marketing department (or, really, any hospital department) is to support the mission *and* business objectives of the organization. Hospital people have a popular, somewhat paradoxical axiom that I first heard in the early 1980s when I worked in Tucson: No mission, no margin; no margin, no mission. Every hospital I have ever worked at has quoted this adage, and I stress it here because it has appeared to me that, as pressures on health care have grown, the truth of the first half of that saying has been muted, and marketers have been pressured to focus on the second. Jim Collins, of *Good to Great,* fame published an excellent adjunct to his bestseller in 2005 titled *Good to Great and the Social Sectors.* I would strongly recommend this book to any marketer—or other executive—in health care or any other not-for-profit. Collins states:

> *A great organization is one that delivers superior performance and makes a distinctive impact over a long period of time. For a business, financial returns are a perfectly legitimate measure of performance. For a social sector organization, however, performance must be assessed relative to mission, not financial returns. In the social sectors, the critical question is not "How much money do we make per dollar of invested capital?" but "How effectively do we deliver our mission and make a distinctive impact, relative to our mission?"*

> —*Jim Collins, Good to Great and the Social Sectors*

Given this reasoning, I favor a simple statement of purpose for the marketing department, for example:

> *The mission of St. Regis Hospital's marketing department is to advance the mission and business objectives of St. Regis Hospital.*

Once this type of statement is accepted by the leadership, it clarifies that marketing will contribute in ways that are intangible to the success of the organization as well as tangible. Make no mistake, the subsequent marketing plan for the organization must include many measures of success, but not every single one of them will be about revenue, although one may argue that they will all increase the value of the organization, as perceived by the public.

PLANS AND TACTICS

Formation of cogent marketing strategies and tactics is one of the most important antidotes to the short-order-cook type of activity that is the bane of so many marketing professionals. When I have been asked to reform a marketing department I have found, to this day, a staff of professionals making goods to order as if they worked at the McDonald's of health-care marketing. I have also found staff creating newsletters or posters or websites for no other strategic purpose than "That's what we do."

Once, I was asked to visit a physician's office to discuss a brochure. He handed me a booklet of some expense that he had edited. Then he asked me, "Why are we doing this?" I was fairly new in the job, and since the content came from the area of which he was the head, the question surprised me.

"I guess I assumed you had asked for it."

"Nope," he said, "I didn't ask for it, and don't have any idea where it came from." After some investigation, I discovered no one anywhere knew why this brochure was being produced. It lived on its own in that strange world of "We've always done it, so we keep doing it."

I can't stress enough the importance and effectiveness of using strategic planning tools to forestall the strong tendencies in hospitals for staff to order up marketing materials the way they might order a STAT imaging procedure. Templates abound in textbooks and online describing how to construct these plans. The critical things to remember are that the strategy has to map to the overall organizational strategy and the consequent tactics have to be doable. Too often have I seen marketing plans for a single service line that ran to dozens of pages with long lists of tactics to be completed in a twelve-month period, only to be followed by an equally voluminous plan for another service line, and then another, and another, all to be completed by the same marketing group in the same twelve-month period.

Often in the process of generating a strategic plan for a service line, the marketing staffers will have a myopic view of their task. A typical brainstorming session among marketing staff will result in long lists of possible tactics. There is a very real tendency to want to do everything possible. What happens less often is serious culling of these lists, partly because internal clients will not be impressed with a short plan of two or three strategies and five or six tactics. The other reason such a plan is created is that marketing staff aren't themselves sure which tactics will be effective, often because they lack the data or the experience to discern among the many available modalities. Worse yet, in organizations where the planning department, marketing department, development department, and communications department are siloed, plans and attendant projects will multiply, overlap each other, and compete with each other for resources, inevitably resulting in confusion among staff and disappointed clients and leadership.

Throughout this text, I have stressed the importance of research and data as underpinnings of strategic marketing. The dark side of depending upon research is the well-known corporate disease known as "analysis paralysis." One department I was asked to improve had, years before, established themselves as the institutional resource for consumer data. While this was an admirable achievement at the time, over the years, extensive, time-consuming research and analysis had become their modus operandi, with the result that the department had acquired the reputation of a bureaucratic "black hole," wherein a request for marketing help would become a process taking many months, eventually producing a plan of fifty pages or more, with a daunting list of strategies and tactics everyone knew were too numerous to complete. By the time I surveyed leadership about their attitudes toward this marketing department, one executive summed up the general feeling by saying, "You should just rename that group the market research department, since that's really all they do."

While his comment was a bit extreme, the caveat is valid. Hone the plans and tactics, resist the urge to drop every possible tactic and medium into the implementation plan, and, as Tom Peters has said, have a bias for action. Despite all the research and academic marketing studies one can assimilate, marketing is part art, or, shall we say, educated judgment, as opposed to a mechanical, completely predictable science. An experienced marketer brings to the table not just knowledge of the facts and figures of marketing, but the accumulated knowledge learned from years of executing strategies and implementing tactical plans in the actual marketplace. This necessarily involves some risk, some failures, and, frankly, at times, a possibility for some embarrassment. Few corporate activities are as publicly visible as marketing. Everyone sees the TV ad, everyone is an expert, and everyone will freely advise you on the mistakes you make, as well as the successes you may achieve. Marketing is not for the thin-skinned or faint-hearted.

THINK GLOBALLY

Developing strategies requires an ability to think strategically. I have found that not everyone possesses this ability. During one session with a department I mentored, a very intelligent and productive staff member—let's call her Christine—was struggling with writing a marketing plan for a service line. One day, Christine confessed that she didn't get my point about being strategic. She said, "I can easily make a list of tactics and match them to a target audience. But when you talk about the strategy thing, is that like the vision thing? Don't we already have the strategies from the leadership team? I don't get it."

Christine had toiled in the vineyards of public relations and marketing for about fifteen years. I had no doubt about her abilities. What she lacked was practice in applying critical thinking based on a synthetic understanding of the organization and the marketplace derived from years of data, focus groups, and retrospective measurement of tactics. You see, the department did not have any of those things. Over the years, random studies had been performed to elucidate one specific situation or another, but the studies were not relatable to each other because they assessed different cohorts with different methodologies and, frankly, a few of them had clearly been tailored so that the results would match executive expectations (not as unusual as you may think). Furthermore, Christine and her colleagues had never been expected to apply critical thinking—I might even say it was discouraged. So now she found herself being asked by a new leader to think strategically and, to be honest, she was frustrated and a bit annoyed with herself and perhaps with me for stressing this amorphous concept.

This notion of thinking strategically about marketing matters, not only in the development of solid and effective plans, but perhaps, most importantly, when a marketing staff person is meeting with a client—in the case of hospitals, an internal leader, department head, physician, or other requestor of marketing services. If marketing staff in hospitals are ever to transcend the order-taker role, they must be able to meet with the head of neurology, understand their situation, gather the necessary data, and then apply all of that strategically, that is, in such a way that when Dr. Corpus asks, "Why are we doing such and such?" or "Why are we not doing this?" Christine can answer with confidence that it may sound great to post billboards on Interstate 70, but here's why they are wrong for this project, why they will have no effect except draining the coffers, and so we are better off doing these other things. This all sounds simple but, over and over again, I have learned that, without sound strategies backing up suggested actions, physicians will lack confidence in the approach, whereas if they see connections among data, strategies, and actions, they have more faith in the outcome, although I will add that physicians in particular are inherently skeptical of marketing, and no matter how much data and strategy you apply, they may insist on doing something "their way." Some of this is simply life in the big city. Yet, again, with good strategic thinking, I have found this kind of randomness can be greatly ameliorated. Furthermore, later in this chapter, we will discuss how we can give Christine the necessary institutional mechanisms that will ensure she is not out there on the front lines with no support.

Previously, we discussed three simple questions that I ask when I am probing about the reason for a specific recommendation. In the same manner, strategy answers the question "How are we going to accomplish our goal?" For example, the goal was to win World War II, the strategy was to invade Europe, the core tactical plan was to do so by crossing the English Channel to launch the invasion, which, of course, hadn't been done since 1066 in the opposite direction. By the way, crossing the channel was not the only option. Others had argued for an invasion from the south, through Italy and on up to Berlin. There are always choices. Strategic thinking means you can assess the data and make an informed choice.

Some staff have shown an inherent ability to see the bigger picture and conceive effective strategies. Most often, staff seem to believe it is something you were either born with or weren't, like having perfect pitch or being able to wiggle your ears. I believe strategic thinking is teachable. So, besides providing Christine with some selected readings about strategy, the main tactic I used with her was to keep asking her how she was going to accomplish the goal of raising our brand preference. "How is the tactic of producing five thousand coffee mugs with the hospital logo on them a strategically intelligent choice?" My point is that it's a matter of practice, practice, practice. Christine may never become the *doyenne* of hospital strategy, but she certainly learned how to ask those questions of herself and come to the table prepared with plans that reflected basic strategic thinking.

The business of coordinating plans, strategies, and tactics across an organization is tricky. Plans abound, departments operate in isolation, and the clients keep requesting more and more "stuff." Hospitals, especially multihospital systems, are large, complex, fast-paced organizations. As chief marketing officer at Mayo Clinic, I was often surprised and perhaps somewhat amused when reporters, visiting physician groups, or even Rochester citizens would tell me that Mayo Clinic was a venerable, old, slow-paced, even monolithic icon—the *grande dame* of medicine that existed in their imaginations as a great medical center that was not quite as cutting-edge as some others. This mythical perspective might have been aided by the fact that, for fifty years, the central building of Mayo Clinic was a twenty-story granite monolith dominating the skyline and looking from the outside like a rather impenetrable block of stone. One half-expected to hear the theme from *2001: A Space Odyssey* and see a gang of protohumans banging bones on stones at its base.

One of my early jobs would be to tour reporters through the Clinic. After a while, their eyes would grow big and their amazement would be palpable. For, in fact, in Rochester alone, Mayo

Clinic employs more than thirty thousand people, and comprises more than fifty separate buildings, housing experts in more than a hundred specialties. These providers care for roughly 350,000 patients a year, or more than 1,000 new patients every day. While the Clinic is a beautiful, college-like campus on the outside where tourists, citizens, workers, and patients and their families stroll or sit in beautifully tended gardens and green spaces (at least, in summer), the truth of Mayo Clinic is that it could not be more fast-paced. Given its extraordinary skill at organization, it is normally a measured, professional, and courteous atmosphere but, behind the scenes, everyone is working full throttle 24-7. Overall, at its three clinics in Arizona, Minnesota, and Florida, and its other owned facilities in six states, Mayo Clinic employs 65,000 people engaged in the most sophisticated medical research, education, and patient care. (Up-to-date information on these facts and much more is available at www.mayoclinic.org).

Why am I telling you all this? Imagine the task of integrating marketing, messaging, branding, internal communications, referring physician relations, government relations, conferences, and other areas across this medical megalopolis. During my twenty-three years there, my colleagues and I were asked to do just that. As the Clinic operations grew steadily in size, intensity, and complexity, medical and administrative departments alike became convinced that, to preserve and enhance the Mayo Clinic brand and to present a cohesive picture to the public and the patient, Mayo Clinic had to elevate its integrative activities.

A later chapter will address the broad issue of integrating seemingly disparate areas such as internal communications, marketing, and government relations. For now, I want to bring us back to the need for critical selection of strategies and tactics. For, even at Mayo Clinic, renowned for its ability to coordinate and build consensus, marketing activities were once siloed, fractious, and, at times, working at cross-purposes. Furthermore, back in the 1990s, the marketing and communications staff were experiencing the kind of isolation alluded to earlier.

At each department I led, I would ask a few questions to break the ice and learn more about what was on the staff's mind. One question I always ask is, "What's the biggest problem facing the department right now? If we could fix one thing, what would it be?"

When I asked this question in my first position at Mayo Clinic, a much younger version of a man who would subsequently work with me for twenty-three years looked up and asked plaintively, "Could you tell us what our priorities are?" I learned, as the years went by, that for every marketing department, awash in multiple projects, each requested by an equally powerful person with an equivalent sense of urgency, receiving from all quarters directives and objectives that pulled them in contradictory directions, the biggest problem was separating the wheat from the chaff or, more precisely, the worthwhile projects from the unnecessary.

POWER AND PRIORITIES

Hospital marketing departments have very little power. Even when a chief marketing officer with impeccable credentials is seated at the executive table, his or her wants and needs for the organization, particularly from the financial perspective, will almost always be trumped by the hospital administrator sitting next to her asking for a new device to save lives or a new piece of insanely expensive IT so the hospital can conform to whatever new regulations have been sent by edict from Washington or the state capitol. For the marketer, this presents a rather curious conundrum. She knows in her bones that her request, which, compared to so many others around the table, is actually quite small, would benefit the organization. Yet how can she compare dollars for marketing against dollars for medical care?

Another related rock to this hard place is the difficulty in setting priorities for the department. Administrators, physicians, and departments have understandable desires to bolster their reputations, perhaps for the good of the institution, perhaps for their own revenue or career (usually a combination of all of the above) and so they come to marketing for a brochure or a department annual report or a special website. The leader wraps her request in the institution's latest mantra about enhancing the brand or getting more patients in OB-GYN or promoting the surgi-center to prevent their rivals across town from taking patients with *their* new surgi-center. To the skilled marketer, this request may be transparently self-serving, yet saying such a thing to a physician or executive is virtually impossible.

No marketing group I've ever led had sufficient political power in an organization to unilaterally mediate such conflicts. Even when I have been armed at the yearly budget wars with reams of data and reports that ring like bells with clarity and power about the worth of the program under discussion, medically minded operationally trained leaders rank those items last on a long list of discretionary projects, few of which can be funded in a given fiscal year.

For a marketing department to have any hope of securing a modicum of necessary funding and developing a workable sense of priorities, it needs operational and medical allies. As we have seen, the marketing department, by now, has written a marketing plan for the hospital or hospitals based on research and honed by experience. Clearly, the plan must be approved at the highest levels.

Presumably, part of the due diligence in creating the plan included numerous interviews with influential leaders from around the organization.

A curious fact is that, after all that, the team may approve the marketing plan in concept and even applaud its good sense, yet at budget time, the team will be reluctant to fund it, even though much of the plan consists of their own requests. If the only advocate at the executive table is the marketing leader, the situation is precarious.

Likewise, assume the marketing leader is experienced and cautiously courageous. She may, in fact, tell the physician requesting the $100,000 department annual report that "We just don't think that sort of book does anything to help our bottom line," or words to that effect. The conversation will be courteous and the physician will disagree and usually make a beeline for the CEO's office. On that hallowed ground, his tone may be less than politic, more in the "WTF?" and "Who is she to tell me anything?" variety.

One critical factor in both scenarios, of course, is the CEO. Without support at that level, marketing has a tough row to hoe. Many marketing leaders I have spoken with acknowledge that the CEO can seem indifferent to the steady stream of requests and petty conflicts among the marketing staff and the rest of the organization. When a CEO is asked to mediate a difference of opinion between two physicians about a marketing strategy, that CEO has been put into a space that she does not want to occupy. No CEO wants to appear to play favorites, pitting one doctor against another. Sometimes the CEO may make a choice between the two alternatives. More than likely, the CEO will push the problem back to the marketing staff and, like King Solomon, ask the marketing group to cut the baby in half and somehow develop a solution that pleases both physicians. This mechanism gets the CEO off the hook but actually pleases no one, since such a solution is always substandard and the outcomes will be substandard as well.

Nevertheless, the CEO is the titular holder of the organization's brand integrity and her support of the marketing plan is paramount. We found at Mayo Clinic that the best solution to the marketing problem described above was to depersonalize the situation. Like any organization, the first working principle is to keep the problem and the solution at the lowest practicable organizational level. These are the staff who know the problem best and who are best qualified to remedy the situation.

Many times, I have had a CEO come into my office brandishing the cover of an annual report or a foamcore board showing choices among two or three styles of type for an invitation to a fund-raising gala. The situation may not have involved a conflict at all. Some staff person, perhaps in marketing, perhaps in another department, simply thought the CEO should have the final say. One CEO said to me, "John, what is this?" speaking of the invitations. "What am I looking at?" I explained it was the typefaces. "Are you kidding? I don't know anything about that kind of thing. Pick one." I did so, started to tell him why, serif versus sans serif, legibility, and so on. He interrupted me. "I don't give a damn about any of that. Just tell Charlene I picked the one you picked."

IMPLEMENTATION

To be sure, some CEOs are micromanagers and want to have a say in virtually every aspect of a marketing piece. Managing such leaders is a full-time job, which we will discuss in the chapter about staff management. Most high-level executives, though, would prefer to have most problems handled at the appropriate level and have only the truly serious issues escalated to high authorities.

The operating principles that have worked the best in my career were:

- ○ Empower the marketing staff
- ○ Empower the marketing leader
- ○ Establish a standing cross-functional operational team to oversee marketing
- ○ Establish a small cross-functional leadership team to oversee marketing policy
- ○ Use the executive team or governing board as a last resort

Such a scheme may, at first, seem cumbersome or bureaucratic. Implemented correctly, it actually saves a great deal of time and anguish, not to mention money, and is the best antidote to the steady stream of random requests from throughout the hospital. Ultimately, this structure is the best method I have found for placing—and keeping—marketing on a strategic path.

Empowerment has become a cliché in the business world. When one uses the word with a group such as I have often worked with, the body language and facial expressions register skepticism and, sometimes, a bit of bitterness. They have been led down this primrose path before and they see no reason to believe anything different will occur if they tread there again. One staff person, Judy, told me her story of the time she responded to Dr. Suture who wanted a special website for his practice. Having been told by the former marketing head that she was empowered, Judy dutifully told Dr. Suture, "No." Marketing couldn't do this for him because he was an independent physician not employed by the hospital and, furthermore, promoting general thoracic surgery wasn't in this year's plan. Judy, a calm, exquisitely well-mannered person, had been as diplomatic as possible. Dr. Suture, not so diplomatically, told Judy what he thought of her rigid obstructionist rules and burned a path to the CEO's office. The CEO called Judy's boss and Judy was told the website would be built by an outside person using Dr. Suture's department funds and that Judy would review and edit the materials, thank you very much.

Empowering staff does not mean giving them permission to exercise independent authority and never mind the consequences. That simply does not work in the health-care setting. Mechanisms need to be in place, such as those listed above, to ensure that the empowered staff person has the backing of the people in the organization who hold the reins of power.

Although Judy's heart and mind were in the right place, the first problem with her interaction was using the word "No." Many people have asked me over the years, "How do you say no to a top-level executive or physician?" The best answer is: you don't, not directly. In a marketing organization that has completed the research, analysis, and planning already described, one would expect that the surgical department was on board with the department and institutional plan. Yet there will always be the Dr. Sutures who missed that meeting or simply didn't give a hoot. Judy listens to his concerns, she explains the planning that has occurred, that the chief of the department has approved the plan, and then, once she ascertains what Dr. Suture is trying to accomplish, she describes alternatives that will give him what he wants in a manner that works within the plan, all without actually telling the doctor, "No, sorry. We can't help you." Although not 100 percent foolproof, this usually placates that vast majority of difficult clients.

Hospitals and health systems depend heavily on a strict hierarchy of command, based naturally on the need for rigorous controls to ensure the safety of patients and eliminate confusion or indecision at critical times. One of the main efforts currently underway to lessen the instance of hospital errors concerns giving permission to staff to "speak up" if they think a physician or other caregiver may be about to make a mistake—in other words, modifying the rigidity of this command-and-control system. Important as this is, it has been difficult to implement, so deeply engrained are hospitals' hierarchical protocols. Ironically, this reliance on hierarchy can be used to marketing's advantage if the marketing leader can establish system-wide processes for review and approval of marketing activities.

The other side of this coin, though, is that marketing, being considered a "staff" function rather than a "line" function, puts the marketing group in a category of activity in which the medical staff and leaders from other provider departments don't always take the rules of the marketing groups seriously.

For this reason, the relationship between the CEO and the marketing leader is critical for the strategic implementation of marketing. A given hospital CEO may or may not have an abiding interest in marketing. I have known both types, those who are indifferent, at best, to the activities of the group, and those who have a sense of its importance and maintain a level of interest commensurate with the time they may have for doing so. Rarely, though, do even interested CEOs consider the activity of marketing to be a priority for themselves.

Management of the brand and reputation of the institution is another matter entirely. While CEOs may not feel their involvement in an ad campaign or a website is warranted, they understand deeply the need to manage the reputation of their hospitals. Interestingly, CEOs often do not see that the competent management of marketing and all its components is a vital aspect of managing the hospital's reputation and brand. Promotions, public relations, brand management, media interviews, fund-raising—for busy CEOs, this can all seem a jumble. It is difficult for them to see the connections. As we shall see, one of my core principles is that these activities—and others like them—should be connected at their core and managed accordingly.

Given the multiple priorities facing the marketing department and the relative weakness of their individual authority, I have found that the simplest and best solution is the appointment of a small interdisciplinary team to handle issues of policy and mediate disputes on behalf of the executive team. At Mayo Clinic in Rochester, we had just such a physician-led committee that assumed the role efficiently and effectively. After some orientation in the basics of marketing, members of the group, consisting primarily of physicians but including the marketing leader and some other key administrators, became, over time, quite conversant with the discipline and were equipped to make decisions in a manner that minimized the individual politics of a situation and spared the CEO from constant involvement in matters not usually worth their time.

The "Case of the Cancer Center Annual Report" illustrates the kind of controversy the committee would arbitrate. It has become common for hospitals to distribute glossy brochures touting specific departments, centers, or institutes. More recently, content is also posted on the hospital's website. Physicians get dozens of these books each year and, as we learned from referring physician focus groups, they are usually ignored. Just the same, Dr. Ward, head of the cancer center at Mayo, wanted to publish a "Cancer Center Annual Report." This would be the first time Mayo Clinic had ever published any such booklet for a specific department. Each year, Mayo Clinic published an annual report for the entire system. Although, as a not-for-profit corporation, they are not required to do so, the philosophy of Mayo is that it is a private trust for the public good and so has a responsibility to apprise the community, its benefactors, and its patients of its financial status and the many social contributions made by Mayo's staff.

Dr. Ward shopped his request around and was politely and frequently told that Mayo Clinic didn't do that sort of random promotion. The hospitals that send out these brochures are generally trying to boost their scores on the physician survey for *US News and World Report's* annual "Best Hospitals" issue. This was Dr. Ward's objective. So he would counter the argument about not doing such a thing with a simple question: "Why not?" When the marketing department said they couldn't meet his request without proper authorization, he was offered the opportunity to make his case at the marketing committee. At that meeting, he showed the many volumes of cancer center brochures being shipped around the nation. He correlated the cancer center scores in *US News* with the hospitals sending the booklets. He made an impassioned plea for Mayo Clinic to try something different.

As is customary at Mayo Clinic, once the proponent makes his case, he leaves the conference room and the committee deliberates. Dr. Ward had made some good points and he had won over some of the committee. In the end, though, his request was denied for a fundamental reason: it would detract from Mayo Clinic's brand. Twenty years of research has shown that the Mayo Clinic brand represents an ideal of integrated medicine and service in the minds of patients. To begin separating out services and promoting them in annual reports seemed to the committee the beginning of a ride down a slippery slope with Mayo Clinic being perceived as a loose confederation of specialty institutes, clinics, and centers.

The marketing department could never have made this decision on its own without serious political blowback of the kind already frequently described. Dr. Ward wasn't happy, but neither was he angry (for long). He had had his hearing and his colleagues and other experts had discussed his proposal with serious interest and had done what they believed was best for the clinic as a whole. The Mayo Clinic culture being what it is, Dr. Ward could accept this without losing face.

Certainly, this type of arrangement isn't foolproof—no system ever is. My experience at Mayo Clinic showed me that having a committed group responsible and accountable for oversight of marketing policies, procedures, and major initiatives is the best method I know of for elevating the respect of the marketing department, ensuring that random ineffective promotions are curtailed, and having the institution buy in to the actions of the marketing team. In fact, what we observed, over time, was that many of the policies and procedures became institutionalized, that is, they formed as much of the fabric of the culture as the edict that all physicians wear suits and ties rather than lab coats. This, in turn, meant that much of the petty bickering that can occur over the color of a brochure or a video on a website fades away over time, and everyone can get on with more important work.

THE FIVE PS

In this chapter, we have examined the issues of marketing health care strategically—to a point. As any business student can recite, marketing comprises the four "Ps" (and sometimes five):

○ Product

○ Place

○ Price

○ Promotion

○ Positioning

For the most part, we have discussed marketing in health care as being almost exclusively concerned with promotion, and some work in positioning that usually comes down to marketing communications activity. I've approached the subject in this manner because that is the prevailing situation in health-care systems today. When I attend conferences of health-care marketing leaders, I watch presentation after presentation about successful or award-winning advertising campaigns, or branding initiatives that are actually little more than naming schemes, and an occasional report on generating increased physician referrals or patient satisfaction that are again mostly driven by promotional activities.

One might ask, "What's wrong with that? What else are they supposed to do?"

My response to these questions is manifold. Within the preceding pages, we examined the historical forces and current attitudes that continue to drive most health-care marketing groups into in-house promotional production teams. We have also reviewed the unique nature of health care as being simultaneously a service and a product, a concept that has as its consequence that mere selling will do little to achieve the goal of increased sales—that is, generating more patient referrals and increasing hospital revenue. We have also delineated the need for CEOs, physicians, and other health-care leaders to look beyond the traditional marketing department for the solutions to the problems that plague them regarding the purpose and intent of marketing health care. The fact that the unsatisfactory performance of many health-care marketing groups can be traced back to decisions made by the very leaders who complain about the underperforming departments remains lost on all but the most enlightened organizations.

Rare is the health-care marketing group that has involvement in pricing. After all, pricing is not actually a free market activity in health care. One cannot assess the consumer appetite to determine what the market will bear. Hospitals don't offer consumers sales or discounts or frequent-flier coupons. Charges, prices, and reimbursement are devised yearly through complex formulae that the classic marketing approach can do little or nothing to influence and are, almost always, handled exclusively by the finance and contracting departments.

The issue of place can, at times, include the marketing group, when health-care systems face decisions about acquisitions or building facilities in a new location. Again, my experience is that the data generated for reports about potential patient demand, needed service lines, and potential financial outcomes often are developed through hospital planning and finance departments with marketing, if they are even equipped with relevant analysts, restricted to a small supporting role.

When it comes to product, my first observation is that no one individual oversees product or service development in health-care systems. Product development in health care is random, behind the consumer curve, and, almost always, limited to repackaging services (e.g., "women's centers") and providing services amenities such as valet parking or gourmet meals. Larry Keely of Doblin Inc. has shown that health care in the United States is not yet a very innovative or transformative industry. To be sure, leaders around the country have declared their commitment to transforming health care. Transformation to these leaders is defined as higher quality at lower cost, which coincidentally increases reimbursement under today's government and insurance company payment mechanisms. Although medical and administrative leaders like to say that their motivation to transform health care is driven by their intense concern for our society's well-being, they also harbor deep resentment that insurance companies, the federal and state governments, and employers have essentially forced them to "transform" by driving down reimbursement. At times, it has seemed that these leaders are oblivious to the fact that with health care consuming almost 18 percent of the GNP and rising, these payers are mad as hell and don't want to pay it anymore. They are rebelling *en masse*. Whether the Affordable Care Act (ACA) is repealed, amended, or remains in effect as is, really is a moot point. Significant transformation must occur, and if health-care leaders cannot manage or lead themselves out of this crisis, unavoidable market forces—and social forces—will do the transforming for them.

I said earlier that marketing could play a substantive role in helping health care achieve true transformation. Clearly, this is not possible with marketing in its current state. My conviction is that marketing in health care needs to be completely redesigned, in essence, transformed, if it is to play a role in the future of health care. Even the word "marketing" does not convey what I believe is necessary for this to be possible.

At Mayo Clinic, I was chief marketing officer to the outside world and chief public affairs officer within the Mayo Clinic walls. The word "marketing" at Mayo Clinic did indeed connote sales and advertising as it does everywhere else. public affairs had a broader connotation of a group concerned with all matters related to the outside world, including not only marketing but government relations and corporate communications. Just the same, for the rest of this text, sometimes I will use the word "marketing" to refer to the broader organization called public affairs at Mayo Clinic, because in every other industry other than health care, marketing does include the five "Ps" and so is the standard word for what I am proposing for health care.

Essentially, my modest proposal is that health-care leaders embrace the concept of brand management in a manner that encompasses the totality of the patient experience, whether within the hospital walls or outside of them. During my time at Mayo Clinic, leaders there did, in fact, embrace and manage to this ideal and still do.

This was not due to anything I did as an individual. Managing the totality of the patient experience is part of Mayo's cultural DNA—always has been and always will be. But, during the second half of the twentieth century, American health care experienced tremendous growth and a series of tremendous changes: Medicare, Medicaid, managed care, Diagnostic Related Groups, an aging population, and mass migration to the south and west. All of these posed potential challenges to the Mayo Clinic model of care, so leaders of foresight and courage began to adapt Mayo Clinic for this sea change as early as the 1970s, well in advance of the full impact of these developments.

By the time I arrived at Mayo Clinic in 1991, the institution was exploding with experiment and innovation. Based in Rochester since 1864, the Mayo Clinic Foundation had opened a Mayo Clinic in Jacksonville in 1986 and another in Scottsdale in 1987. The Foundation was publishing books, acquiring affiliate hospitals and clinics, exploring partnerships with industry, and developing relationships overseas. Just as the venerable Mayo Clinic had always been the world leader in medical research, education, and patient-centered care delivery, now it was becoming a focal point for thinking in new ways about what health care should be, not just for today but for the next hundred years.

So, as luck would have it, I was in the right place at the right time. As my team at Mayo Clinic progressed, we became committed to being participants and even agents of Mayo Clinic's evolution. Achieving the level of involvement we attained in these initiatives was, at times, difficult and even, occasionally, heartbreaking. It was also substantive, exhilarating, and enduring.

It all began with the Mayo Clinic brand.

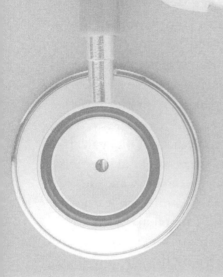

CHAPTER 3

MAYO CLINIC EVOLVES

TRADITIONS

Back in 1991, no one at Mayo Clinic thought the brand needed any "building." Actually, no one used the word "brand" at all. The concept was totally foreign at an institution that was world famous, had more patient demand than could be accommodated, and had been led for 127 years (since 1864) by physicians of the highest integrity. What's more, that culture of integrity, professionalism, dignity, and patient welfare struck me—a mere neophyte by Mayo Clinic standards at thirty-seven years old, with a background in hospital marketing—as pretty much impregnable and immutable. As someone who had a strong desire to make an individual mark, I wondered how that would ever happen at Mayo Clinic. For those first few months, I didn't think much about brand. What I soon learned, though, was that everyone who worked there—and I mean everyone—was completely obsessed with maintaining the institution's reputation. This overriding concern took many forms. First and foremost was the implicit expectation that anyone who worked for Mayo Clinic would strive for excellence every hour of every day. The patient's needs were paramount, and the purpose of Mayo Clinic was clear: to provide the best possible care for patients, to advance medical science, and to educate the next generation of caregivers. By extension, this drive for medical excellence applied to all disciplines—finance, human resources, and, my first group, the Mayo Clinic news bureau.

I was raised as a skeptical—some might even say a bit cynical—New Yorker. Though I left the city when I was seven, my parents, grandparents, and most everyone else in my family were lifelong New Yorkers. I grew up on the East Coast, which I soon learned is as different culturally from the Midwest as cannoli are from "Rice Krispie bars." My first reaction to the institution was its seeming rigidity. Behavior was guided by many rules, most of them unwritten, passed down from generation to generation through mentorship and oral tradition. Always wear a suit. If you leave your office, put your jacket on. Don't chew gum. Don't talk to patients unless it is part of your job. Especially, leave the famous people alone. Treat everyone respectfully. No cursing here.

Stories abounded about the famous founding brothers, Dr. Will and Dr. Charlie, their father, W.W. Mayo, and an encyclopedia of anecdotes and yarns about the many respected physicians and administrators who had walked the hallowed halls. Some of the stories were reverential, others were cautionary, about how to work within a culture that had known nothing but success and growth for more than a century. As one boss said to me in my first week (notwithstanding the "rule" about cursing), "You're director of the News Bureau. Mayo Clinic has an outstanding reputation. Your job is: don't fuck it up."

That was easy enough to understand. Soon, I adopted the posture that Sister St. Joan Willert, the CEO I had worked under at Carondelet, advised: Watch and learn. Don't expect to make any big changes right away. Get the lay of the land.

Nowhere is that more important than at Mayo Clinic, because its cultural topography is highly complex, even byzantine. One spends his or her entire career at Mayo Clinic learning to navigate this highly developed internal world, and one's success at Mayo Clinic is directly proportionate to the degree one can master the cultural game.

Even before I started at Mayo Clinic, when I read some of the preemployment material, I read over and over again the rubric "The needs of the patient come first." I was told this was the sacred value of Mayo Clinic. When I first heard that, skeptical New Yorker that I am, I gently snickered to myself. Already a veteran of two health systems, I knew how often these slogans were bandied about and how rarely anyone took them seriously, except the people who wrote them (usually the marketing group) and the leaders who spouted them. At those other places, these were just pretty words. In actual practice at most facilities, the slogans were seen by staff as little more than corporate propaganda.

When I started working at Mayo Clinic, I received my first enduring lesson about the nature of the culture and, by extension, the brand. I had been quite wrong—the sentence "The needs of the patient come first" was on everyone's lips: in memos, in speeches, in board minutes. It was the touchstone for every decision anyone made. In twenty-three years, I never met anyone at any level of the institution who didn't know those words and what they meant, even now when Mayo Clinic employs roughly 65,000 people around the world. "The needs of the patient come first" expressed in simple terms the compact that Mayo Clinic had made with society as a not-for-profit health-care organization, essentially its brand promise, its reason for being, and our reason for working there.

This famous phrase is actually a simplification of a concept expressed eloquently by Dr. Will in a commencement speech he gave to Rush Medical College in 1910:

As we grow in learning, we more justly appreciate our dependence upon each other. The sum-total of medical knowledge is now so great and wide-spreading that it would be futile for one man to attempt to acquire, or for any one man to assume that he has, even a good working knowledge of any large part of the whole. The very necessities of the case are driving practitioners into cooperation. The best interest of the patient is the only interest to be considered, and in order that the sick may have the benefit of advancing knowledge, union of forces is necessary.

Everything Mayo Clinic does harkens back to that ideal. If, by chance, an initiative is brought forward or comes to life on the fringes of the institution and it cannot be traced firmly and honestly to this ideal, the initiative will gain little support and will fail, if not by direct management fiat, then by starvation, and it will die a slow, silent death. Likewise, a certain type of individual may come to work at Mayo Clinic and will find the idea of a union of forces anathema to their desire to shine as an individual star. Most of the time, after a year or two, the person realizes this is not how life works at Mayo Clinic, and so they will self-select to work elsewhere.

These cultural, historical, and behavioral forces are a significant part of what drives a great brand, even though no one at Mayo, at that time, thought in brand terms. Behavior—performance—is the essence of brand, not advertising, marketing, or sloganeering. Behavior self-regulated through a strong, consistent, transmittable culture—a brand manager couldn't ask for a better starting point or a more difficult culture to change when change was needed.

My final interview at Mayo Clinic had been with the chief administrative officer at the time, Robert Fleming. Few called him Bob. He was known to everyone as Mr. Fleming. I went to his office on the cork-tiled eleventh floor of the Mayo Building, where the top executives sat. His office was nicely appointed but nothing fancy—no one at Mayo Clinic has a fancy office. Mr. Fleming struck me as a cordial, serious man, a quietly powerful person with nothing to prove and no time for extraneous verbiage. We briefly exchanged pleasantries and then he reviewed my resume. After about two minutes, he looked up and said, "What's all this about advertising?"

Gulp. This had been one of the hallmarks of my career thus far. By 1991, most hospitals were advertising to some extent. My teams and I had won awards for campaigns, ad copy, videos, and annual reports. In other words, all the stuff Mayo Clinic mostly abhorred, at least in those days. In 1991, Mayo Clinic was not about to engage in the unnecessary expense and indignity of selling itself. Period. Luckily, I had an intuitive sense of this, and replied, "Yes, Mister Fleming, that's true. I've done a lot of that in my career, but that's not why I'm here. I was brought in to direct the and manage external communications. I don't expect we'll be doing any advertising."

"Good," he said. He stood up, shook my hand. The interview was over.

Did I mention that Mr. Fleming required all applicants to provide their *high school* transcripts? The degree of internal rigor and review was something I'd never seen before. At times, it felt as if a hundred pairs of eyes were watching me, assessing me.

Another anecdote says a lot about Mr. Fleming and the attitude of the people at Mayo Clinic toward ego and self-aggrandizement. Like any sociable person, I remarked upon a rather large crystal bowl that was sitting on a credenza in his office, obviously some sort of award. He said briefly, "Yes, I've had some involvement with hockey and I was given that in appreciation." That was all he was going to say about that. I learned later that the hockey he refer-enced was the legendary 1980 Olympic team that perpetrated the "Miracle on Ice," and that Mr. Fleming had been heavily involved in that enterprise. It was—is—the culture of Mayo to be modest, to be reserved, and to be all about the team, not the individual. This was another key aspect of the brand, which Mr. Fleming personified.

After the first few weeks, I wondered what I'd gotten myself into. Perhaps it was best expressed by a physician with whom I had an orientation meeting a few weeks later. "Welcome to the vortex," he said. Though it sounded odd at the time, soon the truth of that statement became apparent and, as the years passed, the vortex only grew larger and spun more and more quickly. His prediction came true. Mine about advertising, not so much.

SPREADING THE WORD

The Mayo Clinic news bureau had been established in 1984 so that the institution would take the revolutionary step of proactively interacting with the world's media outlets. An additional aspect of this cultural shift, ultimately approved by the board of governors no less, was to allow—in certain carefully controlled situations—the media to talk to Mayo Clinic patients.

For decades, Mayo Clinic had a love-hate relationship with media. Dr. Will and Dr. Charlie built their reputations the hard way—they earned them. They traveled the world learning the latest science and medical techniques so they could apply—and improve on—those advances in tiny, remote, windblown Rochester, Minnesota. As their excellence began to make them famous, newspapers began to carry stories about their "clinic in the cornfields." These stories often contained comments from other physicians who claimed the fame was unwarranted and accused the brothers of being guilty of what would, today, be called "hype." Naturally, this infuriated the people of Mayo Clinic, who knew that the brothers and their colleagues had done nothing more than work, learn, and then work some more.

But the Mayo Clinic had been burned unfairly, and that created a distance between the Clinic and the media that persisted for a long time. Despite this, the truth won out, as it is wont to do, and the Mayo Clinic received extremely complimentary press, even though the stories were few and far between, and often without the direct cooperation of the clinic. When a famous person came to Mayo Clinic, that was news, not that anyone at Mayo Clinic had done anything to generate interest in the media. Quite the contrary, exploiting famous patients—or any patients, for that matter—was considered despicable. Besides, those famous patients came to Mayo Clinic precisely because they knew that matters would be handled discretely.

By 1984, though, the media world had changed and it was impossible to neglect the impact of newspapers, radio, television, and the emerging 24/7 news cycle. Without saying so explicitly, the board was acknowledging that, to manage the brand—that is, the reputation—of Mayo Clinic, the institution would have to step into the sullied world of media, rather than stand idly by and allow the media to create the message without Mayo's participation or control.

I spent five years as director of the News Bureau. Every fourth week, I handled what we called "Press Call," and connected the world's media with the many stories of research and patient care emanating from the institution. No orientation program or set of readings could have better imbued me with the soul of Mayo Clinic and the incredible depth of caring, talent, and scope of activities with which the place continuously hummed.

I had been given the goal of increasing Mayo Clinic's media presence. On the surface, this seemed simple enough. (As an aside, when I told my staff at the Medical Center of Delaware I was leaving to head up Mayo Clinic's News Bureau, one of the more acerbic members of the group said to me, "You're going to be responsible for maintaining the reputation of Mayo Clinic. Boy, that'll be tough.")

I had a terrific group of people to work with (some of whom I worked with for the entire twenty-three years I was there). Like any media relations outfit, we had reactive media and proactive media. Given the volume of requests coming into the Clinic, reactive media took the bulk of our time. Media the world over called every day. We received around fifty calls per week. Mind you, one call from *The New York Times* or CNN or ABC News could result in hours of work that may have to go on for weeks if the story were major, which it often was.

Mayo Clinic took (takes) media relations extremely seriously, far more so than other institutions I have known, except perhaps Cleveland Clinic and Johns Hopkins—although I am sure there are others. Many hospitals, though, hold the media at arm's-length at best, until they want something from them, due in some part to the attitude of insularity so common in health care, and I would say also concern bordering on fear that the media are never interested in truth or fairness and only want to find some dirt that they can use to damage the institution. At Mayo Clinic, even though similar concerns did indeed exist among many leaders there, the overriding behavior was that it was the leader's responsibility to work with the media as much as was necessary to protect and enhance the reputation of Mayo Clinic. Even when the CEO or CAO was not the lead spokesperson, any major story involved them and the relevant leadership extensively to ensure that everything possible was done to convey the right message in the right way.

On one occasion early in my Mayo career, the nation's leading science writer at the time, Victor Cohn of *The Washington Post*, visited Mayo and had lunch with the News Bureau. We talked about potential stories and asked him how we were doing, if there was any way we could improve. I never forgot what he said: "I get hundreds of news releases every week. Most of them are worthless, so I don't look at them. I don't care about who the new chief financial officer is at some hospital in Indiana or about a health fair or a heart run or some other manufactured news events. When I see a news release from Mayo Clinic, I read it, because I know it will be newsworthy. Keep doing that. Send me real news and I will always read your news releases."

He stated clearly a critical "rule" of brand building for health care that is still violated by most health-care organizations on a daily basis. Hospitals present media staff with appealingly safe, low-hanging fruit: fund-raising grip-and-grins, bike rides, bake sales, corporate promotions, community classes—the list goes on and on. These activities are internally meaningful. I have never seen any data to suggest they are meaningful to the patient or the prospective patient. Often, these activities may provide a person with something to do on a slow Saturday afternoon while picking up a free hospital coffee mug. Often, the justification for this type of "marketing" is that it "gets the hospital's name out there," which ranks as the most meaningless marketing objective of all time. They do not increase referrals, brand preference, willingness to recommend, or patient loyalty. They put a hospital in the category of a commodity, where one hospital's refrigerator magnet is just like the other hospital's refrigerator magnet, except one is blue and the other is mauve.

Mayo Clinic eschewed these excuses for news or marketing. By now, many readers may be formulating a rebuttal in their minds that people have said to me many times over the years on any number of topics, not just the success Mayo Clinic has with the media. "Easy for you to say," you may be thinking. "Mayo Clinic has that name, the research, and the famous patients. My hospital doesn't have any of those things, or the budget you probably had, so we do what we have to do."

Let's address the last part first. Throughout my career at Mayo Clinic, our budget for marketing or media or any other public affairs activity was consistently two or three standard deviations below the mean for an institution of that size and yearly revenue. Recall, also, that that budget was intended to market Mayo Clinic worldwide and you can see we had to husband and target our resources just as any hospital does. This is not intended as a whine—Mayo Clinic is financially prudent, particularly in regard to items not related to patient care. I would say appropriately so. I would often hear someone say, "Remember, we are spending sick people's money." A bit crude, perhaps, but it makes an indisputable point.

The second aspect of the "rebuttal" concerns the lack of material available to the local hospital for brand building. The implication is that the stories for the media just fell into our laps and produced themselves. In the midst of a culture of humility as I have described, even when a Mayo Clinic staff person or team had the lead article in *JAMA* or *NEJM*, in the early years, we often found out about it when *JAMA* sent out *their* news release. Two quick points, though—Mayo Clinic had many opportunities to do the kind of manufactured media of which Vic Cohn was so disdainful. Every once in a blue moon, we would have to do it, for whatever political reason. Usually, though, we simply said, "No, that's not what Mayo Clinic does." Second, an infrastructure must be built within the institution to find the news and get it told. I have learned that every hospital has this opportunity.

EXTENSIONS GALORE

The year before I started at the news bureau, Mayo Clinic had distributed around forty-five news releases. The first year I was there, we sent out about 250. As stated, that program remains a fundamental part of Mayo Clinic brand building to this day.

The impetus for a more formal approach to brand building came from a situation that only became clear after a year or so of learning about the many activities of the institution. The first clue of brand confusion and inconsistency manifested itself as differences in approach among the three Mayo Clinics in Minnesota, Arizona, and Florida. The management philosophy at the time of the openings of the two new Clinics was to allow them to develop indigenously, just as the Clinic in Minnesota had done over the last century. As with any management approach, this presented advantages and disadvantages. On the plus side, the clinic administration were free to make any necessary adjustments based on the different market needs and demographics of the new locations. On the other hand, this initiated an era of brand decentralization quite atypical of Mayo Clinic, before or since. For the most part, the medical model was unchanged, except at the time each group of Florida and Arizona Mayo staff physicians admitted patients to a local community hospital. In the case of Florida, Mayo owned the hospital, but it was not closed staff (limited to only Mayo Clinic physicians). In Arizona, Mayo did not own the hospital. In each case, the Mayo staff shared admitting privileges with local non-Mayo physicians. In Rochester, the Mayo staff had admitted to Saint Marys Hospital and Rochester Methodist Hospital from their inceptions, and both hospitals had always been closed-staff facilities. Thus, the situation in the sunbelt states was begun with a lapse of integration that was actually contradictory of the Mayo Clinic brand promise. I hasten to add this situation was long ago rectified and all three locations now own and operate closed-staff hospitals. Before that, though, it presented difficulties in perception. Was the physician treating the person in the bed next to mine a Mayo Clinic physician? He wears a lab coat and has a different name tag. If I am being seen at Mayo Clinic, famous for its "all-services-under-one-roof" concept, why am I driving ten miles to go to the hospital?

The marketing staff at each of the three clinics reported up to three different CEOs, although there was a president and CEO above the other three. Nevertheless, the marketing groups acted quite independently. After a time, the Arizona and Florida marketing groups began to place ads for Mayo Clinic in some of the higher-end magazines. This was the first time in 130 years Mayo Clinic had ever placed an ad for its services. The ads carried a few basic messages. One extolled the virtues of Mayo's model of care, another the excellence of plastic surgery, and a third promoted the executive health program. While there was nothing wrong with the ads *per se*—that is, they were tasteful and discrete—the ramifications were felt widely and immediately in Rochester. Most physicians disliked the fact of Mayo Clinic advertising at all, although a few began to beat the drum of "If they can do it, why can't we?"

Even more significant were the many diversification activities Mayo Clinic had introduced in the 1980s and 1990s. A number had been set up to develop Mayo Clinic's various responses to the rapidly changing and potentially threatening health-care landscape. For an institution as historically conservative as Mayo Clinic, these were bold moves. Many of them were ahead of their time, although today, they would not be considered controversial:

○ *Mayo Medical Services, Inc. (known as MMSI):* Mayo Clinic is self-insured. As the employees and dependents of the growing organization began to reach significant numbers, it became economically feasible for the foundation to administer its own benefit plans by creating MMSI. This group also became the third party administrator (TPA) for other companies, particularly those using Mayo Clinic's insurance products. MMSI also worked in collaboration with other groups at Mayo to provide comprehensive benefit design for outside clients.

○ *Mayo Medical Laboratories (MML):* Mayo Clinic has been renowned for its pathology expertise almost since its inception. In the 1970s, Mayo Clinic laboratories began extending its services for esoteric testing to hospitals other than Mayo's. This organization has grown to be a large, worldwide reference laboratory. Thousands of samples arrive in Rochester each week at a specially built FedEx terminal at the Rochester airport. MML is notable for the excellence of its customer service, which includes partnering with client hospitals to improve their internal labs while providing them with the highly specialized testing that is beyond their scope. MML develops new or improved testing products on a continual basis. MML is the source of many outside partnerships and, as such, presented frequent issues regarding outside companies wishing to capitalize on their relationship with Mayo, sometimes quite literally, by looking for publicity to boost stock prices, which in turn offered some challenges to perceptions of Mayo Clinic's not-for-profit status. (Mayo Clinic *is* not-for-profit.)

○ *Managed Care*: Historically, Minnesota played a big part in the evolution of managed care. While Mayo Clinic is most decidedly not a managed care organization, the Clinic does have certain features that some managed care providers have adopted, notably employed salaried physicians and closed-staff hospitals. As managed care plans were being initiated around the country, Mayo Clinic leadership wanted to ensure that Mayo remained an option for people in these plans. A major part of that effort was building up the contracting department, which became successful at securing contracts with hundreds of payers. Another was to develop health-care plans of its own, which was done at all three sites in the 1980s and 1990s. While these plans no longer exist, they did provide Mayo Clinic with a bridge from the managed care era to the present Accountable Care Organization, Affordable Care Act, and consolidation era. The institution garnered knowledge and experience in the insurance category it could not have gained any other way. At the time these plans operated, though, the brand challenges of Mayo Clinic as a provider alongside Mayo Clinic as an insurer became significant.

○ *Mayo Medical Ventures (MMV, now Mayo Clinic Health Solutions):* Mayo Clinic is highly aware of the considerable value of its intellectual property. Treatment protocols, inventions, devices, and consumer health information are just a small sample of the vast range of innovation and learning that occurs at Mayo Clinic every day. Two Mayo Clinic staff scientists, Dr. Edward Kendall and Dr. Philip Hench, were the first to isolate cortisone and recognize its medicinal effects, and so they were awarded the 1950 Nobel Prize in Physiology or Medicine, along with Polish scientist Tadeus Reichstein, with whom they had collaborated. In the spirit of being a humanitarian institution established for the public good, Mayo Clinic did not patent cortisone. The discovery, as well as all the subsequent profits other companies made from its use, was *given away*. As a retired Mayo Clinic executive, I am proud of this beneficent act. I never saw Mayo Clinic, as an institution, deviate from the ideal of doing first what is best for the patient and society. Yet, even after half a century, the feeling was inescapable that, had Mayo Clinic been able to retain the rights to cortisone, funding for medical education, medical research, and who knows what other breakthroughs or programs would have been assured for decades, if not in perpetuity through potential growth in Mayo Clinic's endowment. As the reimbursement picture grew more alarming, Mayo Clinic decided to establish Mayo Medical Ventures as the operational mechanism through which the institution could capitalize on its intellectual property. Notable examples of this are the Mayo Clinic Healthy Living newsletter, the Mayo Clinic Family Health Book, mayoclinic.com, and many other publications and DVDs. Behind the scenes, MMV handles patenting, production, and distribution of Mayo Clinic inventions and breakthroughs in the medical sciences—everything from improved hip implants to innovations in 3-D imaging. The importance and value of this activity were indisputable. For brand management, though, the activities of this group presented brand challenges Mayo Clinic had never faced before. Considering that consumers revere Mayo Clinic as a noncommercial humanitarian institution, how might their perceptions change after seeing Mayo Clinic publications for sale in a book store, or when they receive a piece of mail—yes, *junk mail*—soliciting subscriptions to a newsletter, replete with coupons and free gifts just for answering the letter and all the other direct mail tricks we are all accustomed to? This from an institution that, for a hundred years, did not advertise, fund-raise, or accept any government money until Medicare forced it upon them in the 1960s. Internally and externally, the potential commercialization of Mayo Clinic was discussed, analyzed, studied, and worried over for years. As the brand management program began profiling consumer attitudes and showed trends in perceptions, this and other information gave all of us a platform for more objective decision making about MMV. In the beginning, though, MMV was a hot bed of out-of-the-box ideas, and some of these would-be products, which must remain proprietary, can only be described as extremely non-Mayo.

○ *Development:* For most of Mayo Clinic's first century, there was no formal philanthropy department known at Mayo as development. This changed when Mayo Clinic established Mayo Medical School in the 1970s. Since then, with the continuing decline in patient care reimbursement, development is a major source of funds to support research and education at the three Mayo Clinic locations. As the development effort ramped up during the 1990s, they became one of the main contact points with patients, families, and other members of the clinic's extended family, thereby becoming an organization with significant influence over brand perceptions.

○ *Mayo Health System (MHS, now known as Mayo Clinic Health System):* During my first week at Mayo Clinic, I met with each of my new staff members and asked them what projects they would be interested in. One person said, "I have heard that Mayo is going to acquire a small clinic in Decorah, Iowa. I'd like to help with that." I'd never heard of Decorah nor did I have any knowledge of Mayo Clinic's plans to build a health-care network in the upper Midwest. I soon learned this acquisition was the first of many to come. Now Mayo Clinic Health System owns health-care systems, hospitals, and clinics in more than seventy communities in Arizona, Florida, Georgia, Iowa, Wisconsin, and Minnesota. As the system grew, so did the brand challenges. Some wondered if these new acquisitions were "Mayo Clinics." Some competitor providers were openly hostile to the "sudden" appearance of Mayo Clinic in their communities. MCHS has been enormously successful and provides care for hundreds of thousands of people each year. During its development, Mayo Clinic had to carefully work out the branding challenges that, at times, went to the core of what Mayo Clinic is in relation to other types of providers.

The point of these programs was not only to prepare Mayo Clinic for a new era in health care but to expand the possibilities of what Mayo Clinic could be. Without using the vocabulary, Mayo Clinic was exploring viable brand extensions. The issues of concern among some of us were centered on how the exciting and multivaried experimentation would affect the core brand.

THE CASE FOR BRAND MANAGEMENT

While members of these groups were carefully managed and just as respectful of the Mayo Clinic reputation as anyone else, these teams acted quite independently of each other and, significantly, were permitted to create separate cultures within their respective groups, separate from the prevailing—some would say overwhelming—culture of Mayo Clinic proper. In part, this was driven by the belief that the activities were not medical care per se. Internally, they were seen not as extensions but as diversifications, an important difference in perspective. Since they did not strictly concern themselves with patient care, medical education, or medical research in its "purest" sense, they were seen as something "other." The attitude was that these activities were experimental, new, and somewhat risky, and may succeed or fail. Regardless of that eventual outcome, to play it safe, leadership did not want these activities closely associated with the valuable Mayo Clinic name. Most of the groups described themselves in more blatant business terms than anyone had ever used with the Clinic before, since they had been given the primary missions of contributing to Mayo Clinic's revenue to offset declining reimbursement for medical care, contributing to the essential mission of conducting research, and providing education whose costs continued to rise and so were particularly threatened by the declines in reimbursement from all quarters. Each of these groups developed vision and mission statements different from the main Clinic, operated under different financial models, and developed into separate business units. The executive management structure also placed these units into different lines of authority. The upshot of all this was an absence—in fact, a deliberate absence— of central coordination among all these divergent groups, in the belief that they would thrive more quickly that way. Besides the internal conflicts these internal mechanics created, the impact on the marketplace soon became confusing, with offerings acting at cross-purposes with each other and continuous debate about whether or not such and such an offering was consistent with Mayo Clinic's reputation (no one yet was using the word brand).

Besides the lack of overall integrated business planning, the other major concern was the approach to the marketplace. Mayo Clinic, again somewhat unconsciously, was now engaged in product development, consumer marketing, and brand extensions into such categories as book publishing, newsletter subscriptions, commercial insurance, and reference lab testing in competition with established giants in each of these fields. Mayo Clinic staff had little to no prior experience or track record upon which to base these new ventures. Of course, some new hires were made to acquire needed expertise, many of whom came from outside of health care and did not always understand or appreciate the Mayo Clinic culture, again seeing that the traditional system would, in their eyes, inhibit entrepreneurial effort. These newly formed groups worked with outside consultants to develop feasibility studies and business plans. For the most part, these were based on the classic health-care assumptions previously discussed: (a) we in medical care know what the people want and (b) if we build it, they will come, especially if it is tagged with the Mayo Clinic name. Little research was done on how necessary or desirable the offerings would be to the consumer or how the offerings would affect consumer perceptions of the Mayo Clinic name.

By the time I had been at Mayo Clinic for a few years, the notion of the vital nature of each group's independence had become part of the accepted wisdom. It was seen as absolutely necessary that they be as removed from the Mayo Clinic bureaucracy as possible. As this attitude gained currency, it grew in strength at Arizona and Florida as well. For all intents and purposes, Mayo Clinic—actually, the parent company, Mayo Foundation—had become a loose confederation of polities—nation-states, if you will—each separate from the other, at times in conflict with each other, governed by independent committees and managed by separate executive groups, and always challenging encroachments from the core Mayo Clinic, commonly called the "practice" and referred to by many in the start-up groups as the "hairball."

Each group was convinced that they were fighting the good fight to save Mayo Clinic from the infernal ravages of health management organizations (HMOs), preferred provider organizations (PPOs), diagnosis-related groups (DRGs), Medicare's coming insolvency, reimbursement shortfalls, rising competition, out-migration from the North to the South, growing consumerism, and an aging population. At various times over the decades, I observed each of these groups in turn wrap themselves in the Mayo Clinic flag (there is one, by the way) and represent themselves as the present saviors of the Mayo Clinic model of care. By extension, anyone who tried to rein in their excesses or call attention to the potential drain on brand equity without proper overall brand management was, at best, someone who simply didn't get it about "business" and the "competitive commercial marketplace" or what it meant to be "entrepreneurial," which was so vastly different from what the practice had to contend with. At worst, those individuals who raised these difficult questions were cast in the role either of Judas or Pontius Pilate, or perhaps Hamiltonian Federalists who represented the "establishment" (Rome, Congress, the "practice") who would destroy their good works through centralization and conformity by forcing them to go through the "hairball."

In the 1990s, a few things occurred that made clear and present the danger such a loose confederation of business units could pose for Mayo Clinic as a whole, that is, as a brand.

King Hussein of Jordan: When a head of state, particularly the reigning monarch of a Middle Eastern nation, comes to Mayo Clinic for care, the news immediately becomes an international event. While King Hussein was in Rochester for successful cancer surgery (a publicly reported event) he was an inpatient at Saint Marys Hospital. At this time, Saint Marys was wholly owned and operated by Mayo Clinic staff. His Majesty was cared for by Mayo Clinic nurses, doctors, technicians, and yes, even us, the News Bureau staff, working (with his permission) to field media calls, deliver statements on his condition, take in faxes from well-wishers, and even sometimes accept enormous bouquets from all over the world. So imagine our surprise when the lead sentence in wire stories that were picked up by all media reported that King Hussein was being treated at Saint Marys Hospital in Rochester. No mention of Mayo

Clinic, nor even of Mayo Medical Center. Despite our best efforts to explain that the hospital was part of the clinic, this terminology confused people, especially reporters who, most of the time, really do try to be factually accurate. "Mayo is the Clinic, right? And he's in the hospital, right?" Sigh.

A rose is a rose, unless it isn't: As mentioned, for a time Mayo Clinic offered managed care plans. One of them, with which I worked closely for a few years, was named Mayo Choice. It had been specially created for IBM in Rochester, the other major employer in the city. One morning, the leadership team of Mayo Choice met with the corresponding team from IBM. Their benefits manager had a spreadsheet in front of him and he began asking about certain charges. "This one, for instance, is for Mayo Choice but the person involved is not one of our employees. And here's another one." After some discussion and review, it was determined that another group at Mayo Clinic, unbeknownst to us, had also applied the name Mayo Choice to a different health plan. Naturally, the accounting issues were resolved ASAP, but the confusion of naming and branding was more than a little embarrassing.

Chiseled in stone: Anyone arriving at the Mayo Clinic in Rochester will notice the artfully landscaped gateway monuments at prominent intersections, with the words "Mayo Clinic" chiseled in stone. Back in the 1990s, though, those signs read "Mayo Medical Center." For more than a century, Mayo Clinic physicians admitted patients to hospitals in Rochester that the Clinic did not own. Over the years, two hospitals emerged as the Rochester clinic's main hospitals: Saint Marys, the first, founded in 1886 and, later, Rochester Methodist. Over the decades, each hospital developed its own culture and pride in accomplishment, just as any successful organization would. By the 1980s, however, health-care economics were such that it made sense for Mayo Clinic to finally assume outright ownership of the two hospitals. As with any merger, this created a sense among some hospital staff of being "taken over" and losing their sense of identity. To help assuage these feelings, the hospitals retained their individual names. To demonstrate a sense of inclusiveness, the three entities together began to be referred to as "Mayo Medical Center." I have been told the name was originally intended to be only internal. Language doesn't work that way, and Rochester was a small town of about seventy thousand at the time, so as the name gained parlance among Mayo staff, it began showing up in the local newspaper and in materials emanating from the Clinic. Then, one day, the stone gateways were constructed and, to my eyes, almost overnight, the words "Mayo Medical Center" were, literally, carved in stone. As the News Bureau director, I began receiving calls. "Is Mayo Clinic changing its name?"

"No," I'd say.

"Then why is it carved in stone?"

"Arrgghh."

I felt like Lucy being quizzed by Ricky on *I Love Lucy*. Ricky: "Lucy, what did you do? You got some 'splainin to do."

Lucy: "Welllll..."

Mayo versus Mayo Clinic: At the risk of being repetitive, I will say again that internal assumptions simply must be tested against external perceptual realities. This notion of a "perceptual reality" drives physicians and scientists a little nuts. For any scientist, perception is often *not* reality. Unfortunately, we in marketing deal with the exact opposite truism. What we share is the requirement to test our perceptions against whatever reality we are trying to understand and, at times, affect. At Mayo Clinic, during this period of rapid and somewhat random entrepreneurial behavior, the belief evolved into a credo that removing the word "clinic" from the name "Mayo Clinic" somehow distanced the purer patient care, research, and education activities from all the other newer activities that were considered far more commercial in nature. Hence, Mayo Health System, Mayo Medical Services Inc., Mayo Medical Laboratories, Mayo Medical Ventures, Mayo Choice, to name a few. As we discovered later, there was only one problem with this bit of accepted wisdom: it wasn't true. Again, as a person fielding questions from reporters and others all day, every day, I soon learned that almost no one considered any of these initiatives to be separate from Mayo Clinic. What this rule of thumb did accomplish was to confuse people. I would even get calls from well-meaning people saying things like, "Did you know somebody put your name on an insurance plan? That isn't you guys, is it?" Besides the confusion and, again, the need to explain, explain, explain, the real concern was the potential for dilution of the brand equity of Mayo Clinic, which we soon began to understand deeply and more objectively is the most valuable brand in health care. No one wanted to see that happen.

By this time, speaking personally, I was rather flabbergasted by the lack of internal consistency represented by the operational issues mentioned above, which grew steadily more frequent and more widely visible. What was even more troubling was the enormous conceptual inconsistency represented by the language of diversification, product, business, and, later, brand and reputation, which betrayed an even deeper, more irrational willingness to suspend belief in the obvious: that these diversifications or extensions or whatever one called them were bound, sinew and bone, to the very Mayo Clinic practice from which these groups aggressively distanced themselves—until they needed the Mayo Clinic name. Ironically, even as they fought for what was essentially brand independence, they fought just as hard to use the Mayo Clinic name on their offerings, in tacit recognition that without the collective wisdom and actions of the physicians, scientists, and other caregivers who are represented by that name, there would be no newsletter subscribers, no reference lab engagements, no benefactors, no clinics in Arizona and Florida at all. For five years, a few of my colleagues and I, while working closely with these groups to help them succeed, began also to discuss the need for Mayo Clinic to address these inconsistencies and conflicts before something serious happened to the Mayo Clinic name that could not be reversed.

In 1995, three of us—myself, director of the News Bureau, which by this time had also grown to include marketing communications, Kent Seltman, then marketing director, and Shirley Weis, recently recruited two years before to lead Mayo Medical Services Inc. (MMSI)—developed a white paper describing the situation, along with an expression of the urgency we felt about the need for Mayo Clinic to address these issues by considering a professional brand management program.

As far as I know, this was the first time anyone had called Mayo Clinic a brand. As I have shown earlier, Mayo Clinic carefully managed its reputation, mostly by fulfilling its three-shield mission with work of the highest quality and integrity, and by carefully managing media relations (through a physician-led committee known as Patient Affairs). What little other brand management there was, at that time, was the provenance of the powerful Medical Industry Relations Committee (Med-Rel). As the name implies, Med-Rel's main job was to manage relationships between the Mayo Clinic staff and outside companies. Much of their agenda concerned managing contracts and other details when physicians or other staff were approached by industry to serve on boards or provide their expertise as consultants. They also reviewed news releases about Mayo Clinic's collaborations with outside partners such as IBM or GE. The News Bureau reviewed such releases as well and sometimes wrote them. This could be a tricky business, since every firm Mayo Clinic ever worked with wanted to enhance themselves by association with Mayo Clinic's enormous brand equity. The trouble would arise when these releases violated Mayo Clinic's iron-clad nonendorsement policy. Occasionally, this could reach a boiling point in partner relationships. A few times, a vendor or partner would ignore Mayo's concerns and send out a release, or later post something online, extolling the virtues of this special relationship.

This, invariably, created quite a stir within Mayo, with the Med-Rel chair often having to call the offending firm and ask for a retraction or correction, usually with the involvement of Mayo's legal department. It did happen a few times that the breach in trust would lead to a permanent break. In any case, many partners were left bemused by Mayo's obsessive concern about the use of their name. Fundamentally aware of the asset Mayo Clinic had in its name, the institution was protecting it the best way they knew how, mostly by simply saying, "No."

Such a program of name-use management is necessarily a component of a complete brand management program. Unfortunately, many health-care leaders even now believe that this is all there is to brand management. Recall our earlier discussion concerning internal assumptions about branding and the marketplace needing to be confirmed or refuted, based on a robust research program. As brilliant as the Med-Rel membership may have been, they were essentially making subjective decisions based on their own experience and judgments. Much of it was akin to common law, built on precedent, yet still fundamentally an internally focused process. They believed they knew Mayo Clinic and knew what was best for Mayo Clinic and did not feel compelled to ask "outsiders" their opinions about such matters very often. As the years went by and the brand program matured, the accumulated data and consequent understanding about Mayo Clinic's brand attributes, strengths, and positioning gave this committee a very strong platform upon which to base subsequent decisions and policies, particularly where the aforementioned diversification activities were concerned since, as these took flight, they became a primary source of brand information for people worldwide.

Other than this committee, no other group had oversight of the Mayo Clinic brand. Fortunately, in response to our white paper, senior leadership agreed with the need and appointed a task force to take a serious look at establishing a brand management program.

CHAPTER 4

MAYO CLINIC AS A BRAND

CONFUSION

In the beginning, as described earlier, not many people at Mayo Clinic had ever heard of brand management let alone knew how to build a program. Many of us knew that brands were managed carefully and aggressively at companies like P&G and Coca-Cola. None of us knew of any formal brand management programs among health-care providers, although there may have been a few fledgling initiatives. The collective experience and knowledge of our nascent Brand Management task force was that hospitals managed their reputations just as Mayo Clinic had done, through media relations and, in the case of hospitals other than Mayo Clinic, by advertising. In the mid-1990s, I'm not sure many hospitals had progressed to the point of seeing themselves as a brand or a collection of brands. Moreover, as far as we could tell in 1995, almost no health-care center could claim to be a national or international brand on the order of Mayo Clinic.

If a team is charged with managing the public affairs and patient perceptions of a hospital in, say, Wilmington, Delaware, they will certainly be presented with some brand challenges. When I worked at the Medical Center of Delaware, the hospital leadership decided to start charging for parking at their new suburban hospital in Newark. This immediately caused a statewide furor because Delawareans remembered a promise had been made that the suburban hospital had sufficient acreage to allow for free parking. A bill was introduced into the state legislature to stop the parking charge program. My boss and I went to the state capitol to plead the hospital's case for needed revenue. In the end, our pleas fell on deaf ears. The backlash grew so pervasive the leadership saw no recourse but to reinstate free parking. I don't know if parking is still free. The point is that the decision to charge for parking was made, again, from a purely internal perspective, and the concept of brand did not enter the conversation. This tempest in a teapot was all about action-reaction, with articles in the newspaper and unflattering talk swirling around that very small state until hospital management had to change their minds or risk incurring further damage.

Such a problem at Mayo Clinic could and, at times, did make national news. Even in 1991, Mayo Clinic was an institution that already operated Mayo Clinics in three states and was acquiring hospitals in others. As time progressed, it became obvious that a decision to offer free parking in one Clinic would quickly result in the other two Clinics wanting to know why, and patients at the other two Clinics asking administration why they had to pay for parking in Arizona if they didn't in Jacksonville.

Furthermore, with the expanding development department and the new Mayo Medical Ventures distributing materials that were reaching millions of people each year, the scope of Mayo Clinic's brand was decidedly national and international. Mayo Clinic was becoming even more famous the world over. But famous for what?

GO MIDWEST, YOUNG MAN!

Indeed, famous for what? This is not an idle question, and so, at this point in our story, we need to take a short diversion. Before I came to work at Mayo Clinic, I knew virtually nothing about it. My view of the country resembled that famous *New Yorker* magazine cover by Saul Steinberg, with the coast exaggeratedly large and the great gap in the middle a vast nothing one simply had to fly over to get to the other coast. As a child, since I was an avid reader, I did remember reading a biography of the Mayo brothers as children, part of a series of biographies of the childhoods of famous Americans. My primary vision of the Clinic was an illustration in this book of the brothers' father, William Worrall Mayo, performing surgery on an injured farmer in the farmhouse kitchen, the farmer lying on the kitchen table and Will and Charlie Mayo, ages twelve and eight, respectively, assisting in the procedure. What I knew of Minnesota I garnered from watching the *Mary Tyler Moore Show*. So I knew it was rural and it was cold. To a kid from Queens, it all seemed a bit Wild West.

Years later, I graduated Brown, moved to Tucson, Arizona, got a job at a weekly newspaper, *The Green Valley News*, and soon met a reporter there, Jennifer, who became my first wife and the mother of our two sons, Carlo and Alex. As fate would have it, Jennifer's father, a well-known radiologist, had served at Mayo Clinic from 1946 to 1956, first as a fellow and then on staff. Now, in the mid-1970s, he was one of the founders of the largest radiology group in Tucson at that time. Jennifer and I moved around a bit after we married, first to Miami and then to Seattle. In 1980, we came "home" and settled in Tucson. The fates intervened again, and I landed my first hospital job as the first, and only, publications specialist for St. Mary's Hospital, the original hospital of the Arizona Territory. This hospital had a Western and Mexican flavor. We were in a barrio and not far from the city limits and the uninhabited portion of the Sonoran Desert. The pace of business back then can only be described as ambling, except in the practice of medical care, which, of course, must always move STAT when the situation demands it. This contrasts with health care today, everywhere, where the pace is a flat-out sprint from morning to night, for medical and nonmedical personnel alike.

They set me up in a windowless room on the administrative floor with an IBM Selectric typewriter facing the small break room that housed the constantly frequented coffee machine. Since I was responsible for every publication, whether the weekly employee newsletter, the monthly employee magazine, the quarterly development magazine, the physician newsletter, and every other brochure, flyer, pamphlet, or what have you, I pounded away at that Selectric relentlessly. At first, VPs refreshing their coffee would stand in my doorway and say, "Slow down. You're making us look bad," or "You're gonna break that thing." Soon though, they were stopping by my office to give me things they had written, even memos or letters, and asking me to "clean it up." They'd say, "Give it to La Forgia. He can fix it," or "Hey, John, can you make this sound good? You know how to use those fancy words. Thanks, man."

I know, it sounds like an old western movie where the nerdy city slicker sets up shop as a printer and letter writer and the townsfolk come to him and ask him to write love letters or condolences. It actually had that flavor to it. I have found that most anyone can compose an adequate business letter. (Pursuant to your communication of the 4th I would like to remind you of our conversation of the 5th pertaining to the delivery of the 9th, blah blah blah) Few people, though, feel they have the skill often called "a way with words." In my career, I have been surprised by the value intrinsic in having a bit of a way with words.

Of course, as I became more deeply immersed in my new job and the operation of a hospital (my first hospital lunch conversation revolved around an interesting brain surgery one of my lunchmates had participated in) I would come home and tell the family about my day. Often, I'd bring the Selectric home too, because I had so much writing to do and, now, so many coffee buddies (yes, I'd close the door but one can't be completely antisocial) that I had to work nights to meet all my deadlines. That was how I learned John Lennon had been murdered, watching *Monday Night Football* as I typed away, TV and Selectric on the dining room table, papers strewn all about, and Howard Cosell intoning that it was a sad day, a tragedy in New York—John Lennon was dead. Disbelieving, Jennifer called a friend at the news desk of the *Arizona Daily Star* and confirmed the story. I didn't get any more work done that night.

I worked for St. Mary's and then the parent company in Tucson, Carondelet Health Services, for ten years. So, for ten years, I would bring home news of a project I was working on or an initiative Carondelet was planning and, for ten years, my father-in-law would say in his distinctive Cape Town accent, "John, you should see what Mayo Clinic is doing in that area. I'm sure they have experts in that field." It could be video, conference planning, or anything else. Mayo would be a leader in that aspect of health care. He never lost his adoration of Mayo Clinic. During those ten years, he would tell me stories about what it was like to work there in the days of Dr. Chuck Mayo, Charlie's son, and some of the medical giants of that era. He clearly missed it and, until the day he died, he believed the Mayo model of physician-led, consensus-driven, patient-centered health care was the proven model that the rest of the country should adopt.

Having never been within a thousand miles of Rochester, I was content during that time to let my projects and my growing department move along without consulting Mayo Clinic. When I was ready to move on from that position in 1989, having plateaued, as they say, I finally asked him to connect me with his good friend Jerry Brataas, who would introduce me to some people there and show me around Rochester.

As Jerry drove me around, I tried to imagine myself living in this tiny community of sixty thousand people. The leaves were turning, and the air had that crispness I always associate with new beginnings. Carefree high school kids in letter jackets ran around downtown after school. Mayo Clinic dominated the town center, more like a university campus than a typical hospital. When I had time between meetings, I walked through the nearby neighborhoods and passed "row after row of the prettiest little homes you ever saw," as the lawyer says to mean old Mr. Potter in *It's a Wonderful Life.*

Inside the Mayo Clinic was just as neat and tidy, and serious, and a tad boring, at least in terms of decor. I always thought of the environment as beige on beige. Coming from colorful Tucson and an office with Herman Miller furniture I was surprised to see beige vinyl wall coverings, white Steelcase desks, and, in 1991, almost no desktop computers. Only a few of the staff had them for "desktop publishing." The "professionals" were in the offices along the walls, surrounding the "secretaries" who worked in a large open pool. I felt like I'd stepped back in time.

Everyone I met, though, it must be said, was as nice, helpful, polite, and seemingly sincere as any people I'd ever met anywhere. A couple of years after I got the job, my mother came to visit. After a day of "doing Rochester," my mother, the native New Yorker, said to me, "Johnny, everybody here is so happy all the time."

"Yes, Mom. They call it 'Minnesota nice.'"

Unfortunately, at that time, Mayo had no suitable positions for me, so my family and I moved to Wilmington, Delaware. I worked for the Medical Center of Delaware (MCD), a multihospital system and I must admit that, though I liked the people well, living back on the East Coast did not inspire me. It felt like I had taken a giant step backward in life after my western adventures. Once again, all the radio station cover letters began with the letter "W," just as they had when I was a child. I just knew I was on the wrong side of the Mississippi.

About midway through my year at MCD, I got a call about a job at Mayo. It was a level below what I was doing, so I turned it down. Then, in the fall, I received another call about directing the news bureau. This appealed to me, so I flew out to Rochester in already-cold November, interviewed with about a dozen people (including Mr. Fleming), and eventually landed the job, just as my obligatory year with MCD was coming to an end. Those first few years were a tough adjustment. My wife and I flew to Rochester in January to find a house. As the real estate agent drove us along snow-covered streets to look at snow-covered houses while it snowed, I glanced at the temperature indicator mounted on the inside roof of her car. "Does that really say negative twelve?" I asked. "It's twelve below zero out there?"

"Oh yes," Ann said. "It's the middle of January. We always get a few weeks of below-zero weather around now."

CULTURE ON STEROIDS

My first workday at Mayo Clinic was March 4. By then, it was snowy, mushy, cold, then sunny, then warmer, then colder, then snowy again. Toward the end of the month, I noticed a distinct change in the office atmosphere. I asked Karen, my administrative assistant, if she noticed anything. "Half the office is empty," I said. "Everybody else seems kind of fidgety. What's going on?"

"It's spring," she said. "This is the first really nice day we've had since September."

Clearly, I had landed on an alien planet. A tiny town with, at that time, not much else besides Mayo Clinic, IBM, and a lot of hotels, motels, boarding houses, and truly mediocre restaurants to serve the bulging population of patients and their loved ones. Not even a Starbucks (yet). At work, there wasn't much socializing, and everyone worked hard, all day, every day, because there was so much to do, and everyone was committed to doing everything the best they could, all the time. I'd never seen anything like it. The whole operation was incredibly impressive. If I needed something from purchasing, I got it in no time. If something was broken in the office, it was fixed immediately. If I asked someone for help—from someone I'd never met before—I got the help I needed immediately. Once, my boss's boss called me and asked for something. It would take a bit of time. I was busy, so I figured I'd do it tomorrow. A couple of hours later, Bob called back. "Do you have that for me?"

"You wanted it today?"

"Yup, pretty much." I did it right away and learned that was the culture of Mayo Clinic. Get it done. Now.

For a couple of years, I wondered when, if ever, I would understand this corporate culture in this, to me, alien region of the country. That all did happen, eventually, through some events that I will save, since they illuminate subjects covered in a later chapter. For now, suffice to say that, after four years, I found myself sitting around a table with some of Mayo Clinic's most illustrious physicians and administrators planning a Brand Management program for one of the most famous brands on the planet.

This would be my first true immersion into the Mayo way of doing things that my father-in-law Andre had said so much about. The process is subtle, collegial, and, in a strangely positive way, insidious. After a certain amount of time participating in this style of governance in which no one possesses ultimate power, nor wishes to act as if they do but prefers to discuss as equals the pros and cons of whatever issues arise, politely, intelligently, and thoroughly, the behavior starts to get under your skin. By the time I'd been there five years or so, I'd clearly drunk the Kool-Aid.

The white paper Kent, Shirley, and I had presented on the need for brand management had evolved from a growing understanding of Mayo Clinic's direction, combined with knowledge and experience each of us brought to the table from our different backgrounds. No one of us would ever have implemented a program like that by ourselves, or just because the CEO said, "I like it. Let's do it." Mayo Clinic just doesn't work that way, a fact that I soon came to see was one of the institution's essential strengths. Any potential programs of sufficient size and scope, such as brand management, had to be studied, discussed, and approved by leaders all around the institution, not just our task force. This process of consensus is another force that keeps Mayo Clinic at the top. Earlier in my career at Mayo, I had drafted a brochure about using patient information in research studies. The brochure was intended to explain to patients how the research benefitted humanity and reassure people that all information was anonymous, while also explaining the choice they could make to opt out of the program, thanks to a new law passed by the Minnesota legislature requiring this option (this was before the Health Insurance Portability and Accountability Act(HIPPA)). I was given a list of ten or so physicians who were to review the draft. A few weeks later, I had a stack ten inches high in my inbox. One of the physicians had given the brochure to his entire staff of fifty or so physicians to review. I showed my boss, who laughed and said, "That's Mayo. Everybody has a say."

Naturally, the top leadership of Mayo Clinic knew how the culture operated and so put mechanisms in place to assure that a project had the best chance for success. Sometimes this would even involve appointing the most vocal opponent of a project to the committee reviewing it. This seems in stark contrast to so many organizations in and out of health care. There, the CEO usually has considerable unilateral authority. Projects devolve on an individual or a team who are expected to bear the burden of garnering acceptance and pursuing implementation on their own, while other leaders, more or less, observe from afar or contribute in snippets of email or perhaps just through the grapevine. They don't feel any sense of collective ownership of the initiative, living as they do in a siloed business unit, concerned with matters of more immediate importance to them . In the current era of the American health-care industry, there is much consolidation taking place, but very little true integration. Few institutions can claim to have the level of deep, meaningful integration across all business units that Mayo Clinic has attained.

I knew the executive team was appointing the members of the Brand Management task force. I wanted very much to be a part of the program. I felt passionately about the subject and believed I had something positive to contribute. Still learning the culture, I wasn't sure if I should apply to be part of the group or if that would be taken poorly as a sign of o'er-weening ambition. At that time, a person would be sitting at their desk and receive a memo, more or less out of the blue, stating they'd been appointed to a committee, and if they were willing to serve, asking them to please contact the committee's secretary. The process, to me was, somewhat arcane. Later, I became one of the executives appointing people to these committees but, at this time, I had no idea how the process worked.

My then-boss, Robert Smoldt (the aforementioned Bob), chair for planning and public affairs, gave me a suggestion I never forgot. Bob suggested I write a modest email to the CEO and simply say that I was very interested in the brand project and would be willing to help out in any way he saw fit. Happily, this suggestion worked well. Over the years, I would make the same suggestion to many of my staff as they worked their way through Mayo's complicated culture and structure. My intuition about overt ambition proved true as well. Many times, I observed a new person come to work at the Mayo Clinic, full of "piss and vinegar," talented and ambitious, determined to make their individual mark and to use the same political skills and aggressive behavior that, ironically, brought them to a level that attracted Mayo to them in the first place, only to watch them last a year or maybe two before they left in complete frustration. Their style demonstrated to others that they were more interested in their own careers than in the project, the team, the good of the institution, or, most importantly, the best interest of the patient. This last, Mayo Clinic's Occam's Razor, that the needs of the patient come first, seems so simple in concept yet, in execution, often confounded many people's individual sense of how one gets ahead or even how one does one's best work, when the touchstone of success was not one's own individual contribution but one's ability to somewhat disappear, melding into the team and the institution as a whole for the greater good, without regard for immediate individual reward. As I was absorbing this culture, at times, the whole thing seemed very Zen to me. By not using power overtly, one attains more power. By disappearing into the group, one becomes a stronger individual. And so, it would prove, time and again, during my time at the Clinic.

As stated, there were bound to be quite a few opponents of a formal brand management program and more than a few skeptics who would ask if such a program were even necessary. Although highly advanced in terms of best practices in all disciplines, Mayo Clinic staff have an aversion to adopting the latest business school fad or implementing a program just because all the other hospitals, or all the other companies, are doing it. Mayo Clinic prefers to think for itself, which at times can appear to the outside world as a touch of arrogance and, admittedly, a few times has meant that Mayo, so state-of-the-art in just about everything, may be slower than others to acquire a technology or start a certain program, because they don't see the effort or expense as necessary or proven. This is not due to a lack of knowledge or interest. Mostly, the attitude is one of concern that, by taking on the latest fad, be it Six Sigma, experience officers, or what have you, the Clinic ran the risk of damaging a highly successful culture that, as of 2014, was 150 years old and going strong. And so it was with brand management. No one knew if it would be right for Mayo. No one would support it just because it might be what everyone is doing these days. The rationale had to be Mayo-centric and patient-centric. People will ask how this program helps Mayo Clinic do a better job. They will ask, "How does this program help me do a better job for my patients?"

The answer could not be, "Let's try it and see." The rationale had to be clear and well documented and, even then, the task of getting from approval to implementation was fraught with obstacles.

Another aspect of this same balance of forces is that Mayo Clinic, with a highly articulated bureaucracy of committees and subcommittees, is simultaneously highly unstructured and organizationally loose. During my tenure, the institution grew to a size and scope that necessitated implementing some additional structure around administrative practices. The path to a project's approval, though, or the manner in which one might advance, or how one would implement a major organizational change such as brand management is generally almost completely unpredictable and, for the most part, is different for each new initiative. Therefore, a major skill for any Mayo staff person, and particularly the top leaders, is the ability to navigate this ambiguity by developing an acute sense of Mayo Clinic "street smarts" that includes the aforementioned modesty, considerable networking, negotiating, and a patience and persistence not everyone possessed. Many times, staff would be in my office venting about the slow, tortuous process they had been going through to make "something happen." Our discussions would center on figuring out who to talk to next, which group to address, how to reframe the proposal, whether to make it a limited pilot, reduce the budget, and take other actions until we could gain a foothold, and then see what could develop. Once, Dr. Noseworthy, Mayo Clinic's CEO from 2009 to 2018, addressed a meeting I was in by drawing a picture of a green sapling on a whiteboard in the Mayo 11 conference room and explaining how we had to plant these saplings and nurture them if we were to develop the next generation's Mayo Clinic, since it was so easy at Mayo Clinic for someone to stomp on it, or pluck it, or just let it die of neglect.

The yin and yang of these paradoxical forces was extremely powerful, and we were to discover that their interaction manifests itself in mysterious ways as the Mayo Clinic brand, in a manner none of us before 1995 would have described in the same language, born of the shared understanding our brand studies provided.

THE TASK FORCE

The newly created Brand Management task force got off on the right foot, thanks to some wise choices made by the executive team. First was the inclusion of the CEO on the committee, Dr. Robert Waller. His seat on the committee ensured that the entire organization could see that he supported going forward with this analysis and would be included in the deliberations. Given the nature of the many diverse organizational energies previously described, his support was essential, and it never wavered. Given that Mayo Clinic is physician-led, having the physician leader at the table was even more critical. A comprehensive brand management program eventually becomes part of an institution's DNA. Seen from another perspective, you could say that everyone at Mayo Clinic knew that a brand management program had the potential for meddling with their business—in fact, everyone's business. With all the growth of the many new diversification entities Mayo Clinic had nurtured during the previous couple of decades, no one doubted that a brand management program could foment rebellion in some quarters. The necessity for strong CEO support of a brand program is now considered axiomatic. To this day, Mayo Clinic's successive CEOs have taken on ownership of the brand as one of their key accountabilities.

A second decision that aided the brand management effort immensely was the appointment of Dr. Scott Swanson as chair of the task force. Dr. Swanson, a surgeon who served on the board of Mayo Clinic in Arizona, is a whirlwind of energy, enthusiasm, insight, and decisiveness. The task force could not have had a better leader. Despite his many other duties as a practicing surgeon and board member, he became deeply involved in the initiative and quickly made himself an expert in the field. My good fortune was to be the secretary of the task force, which meant he and I worked side by side for a number of years. At Mayo, being a committee secretary means helping set agendas for the group, writing and distributing minutes, and being the organizing administrator for the effort. Working with Scott made all this happen with great efficiency and was also a lot of fun.

Third, the task force was assisted by having membership from all three Mayo Clinic boards and a few key leaders, both administrative and medical, from some of the diversification activities. The institution could be assured that the interests of the various entities would be represented. For an institution based on consensus decision making, this was vital to eventual buy-in of the program if it were eventually established.

When we gathered as a task force for the first time, we agreed we needed to be educated about the whole subject of brand and brand management. Accordingly, we sought out an expert, and found him in the person of Professor Kevin L. Keller, then on the faculty of USC and now a chaired professor at the Tuck School of Business at Dartmouth College. Dr. Keller—or should I say Kevin, since he always insists we call him by his first name—visited Mayo soon after we contacted him and presented a day-long course for the task force we dubbed Brand Management 101, a course that, with his permission, is still being taught to new members of various relevant committees around Mayo Clinic. Given Kevin's credentials and accomplishments, among them having written *Strategic Brand Management*, the core textbook on the subject, and coauthoring *Marketing Management* with Philip Kotler, you'd be excused if you expected him to be a serious, slightly pompous, academic kind of person. Nothing could be further from the truth. Kevin is certainly brilliant in his job and as academically rigorous as they come, but to quote Lewis Carroll, he also is a "beamish boy" with boyish good looks, a ready smile, and a great sense of humor. He spoke to a Mayo Clinic assemblage of management once and, in the process of answering a question from the audience, he said, "You know, this isn't rocket science, and I ought to know—my father *is* a rocket scientist." (Sorry Kevin, I hope this doesn't ruin that line for you now.) His infectious charm and modest demeanor suited the Mayo staff perfectly, a group all too familiar with outside experts coming to Mayo Clinic with an attitude. Besides his educational work, Kevin also consults and has worked with some of the world's leading brands, such as Nike, Disney, Starbucks, and a host of others. This working knowledge of the field also impressed our team, since even the physician leaders at Mayo who have significant administrative duties continue to practice their specialties and treat patients during their workweek. Kevin applies his field knowledge and experience deftly and was able to help us place Mayo Clinic on the brand map, so to speak, as far as what kind of brand category we were dealing with, and he also helped us develop an action plan for getting from investigation of a program to implementation. By virtue of his assistance with this project, which lasted for about two years, he has become a permanent part of Mayo Clinic's extended family and continues to consult occasionally for Mayo to this day.

Kevin hammered home a concept that we also gleaned from our readings in David Aaker and other sources: that the brand is not owned by Mayo Clinic but is owned by the consumer. It exists in the public "consciousness" as a great amorphous neural network of fact, factoids, rumors, misinformation, imagery, news stories, family folklore, and actual experience with the institution. This was not an easy concept for most Mayo Clinic staff to accept. Certainly, such an axiom might apply to politics or consumer goods or the type of celebrity represented nowadays by the Kardashians. Mayo Clinic, we thought at first, had to be different. Steady, constant, Mayo Clinic had been true to itself and its mission forever. The medical, educational, and research outcomes spoke for themselves, as did the happy by-product of that good work, financial stability, and continuing patient demand. How could the Mayo Clinic reputation be subjective, emotional and—if this were all to be believed—so vulnerable?

To men and women trained as physicians and scientists, the prospect of the Mayo Clinic name and reputation hanging on the whims of an unpredictable public seemed more than a little dangerous. As Kevin would say, that's exactly the point. Great brands have come and gone. Mayo Clinic, as a very mature brand, needed to have a better understanding of the actual nature of its brand and also track the dynamic nature of those perceptions, the perceptions of millions of people, all over the world, having countless millions of interactions with this thing called Mayo Clinic, by virtue of being treated there, or hearing a news item, or looking up a disease on Mayo Clinic's website, or hearing the story of a friend or relative who went to Mayo Clinic for care. Getting a proper handle on all that loomed as a daunting task.

Besides, as I said earlier, just about everyone at Mayo Clinic believed they knew what the institution stood for and would have been quite happy to tell you. "The needs of the patient come first" would be the starting point, and then they'd tell you about being the world's first integrated multispecialty group practice of medicine, with the world's first fully integrated medical record, and the three-shield mission of patient care, education, and research, with salaried physicians who do not acquire increased compensation via productivity and only order the tests that are necessary or the procedures that are medically justified. The truly well-informed might quote the Dartmouth Atlas, that showed how effective Mayo Clinic is at providing extraordinary care without driving up costs unnecessarily, and how good it would be for the country if more health-care providers followed Mayo's example.

As the task force was soon to learn, some of these statements, while all true and often discussed in the hallways, cafeterias, offices, and surgical lounges of Mayo Clinic, indeed formed some of the components of Mayo Clinic's brand. Some of these statements, though, however true, did not enter into the brand picture at all.

ASK THE CUSTOMER

Before we understood the meaning behind these assertions, we spent a few weeks engaged in the classic business tactic of bench-marking. We knew we were the caretakers of a mature historical brand. We knew the brand was multistate and multinational. Since the 1980s, the brand had experienced significant extensions into categories well beyond "health-care provider," among them the areas of insurance, publishing, digital commerce, fund-raising, and mergers and acquisitions. Using these parameters, we met with a variety of companies outside of health care who could give us guidance on navigating the intricacies of those types of brand issues, including Marriott, 3M, Harvard, and Disney. As we acquired excellent information about setting up and managing brand programs from our gracious hosts, we also began to see that, just as health care marketing is *sui generis*, a thing unto itself, so too did the shape of Mayo Clinic's brand begin to emerge as an entity all its own, with characteristics similar to a family-owned legacy brand such as Disney, or with multiproduct branding issues as at 3M, or hospitality and service concerns such as Marriott, yet, still in all, possessing a culture and a mission so unique as to defy traditional categorizations. Again, it was not easy for members of our task force, some of whom had begun their careers at Mayo Clinic when it was one relatively small clinic in the tiny remote town of Rochester, Minnesota, albeit even then world-renowned, to wrap their minds around this new Mayo Clinic, on the cusp of emerging as a multibillion-dollar, multinational conglomerate of numerous business entities in various product and service categories that were growing in influence at a steadily increasing rate.

To put this into perspective, since its integrated medical record system was instituted at the beginning of the twentieth century, Mayo Clinic has issued a "clinic number" to each individual patient in consecutive sequence. Each time that individual came to Mayo Clinic, the number is used for registration and all medical records regarding that person, throughout their lifetime. So, based simply on the clinic numbers, we know that by 1995, Mayo Clinic had issued more than five million such numbers, each number representing a unique individual. Five million people experiencing Mayo Clinic over the course of about a century. With the emerging internet, five million people could experience something about Mayo Clinic, good or bad, in five minutes, maybe five seconds, all over the world. Managing this brand would indeed require something more than removing the word "clinic" from Mayo Clinic.

The time had come to field a major brand study, the first in Mayo Clinic's history. We decided that we required an understanding of Mayo Clinic's core brand as a starting point. Additionally, we needed to know how the brand had been affected by the opening of the Clinics in Arizona and Florida. Were perceptions of Mayo Clinic changed by these moves? Did patients and visitors to either of those two clinics have a different brand experience from the one in Rochester?

This question had been discussed even before the two new clinics were built, although without using the language of brand discipline. Considering the enterprise in Minnesota had grown more or less organically from its roots as the Mayo family practice over the course of a century, no one was quite sure what patients would think about a Mayo Clinic built *de novo* in such different regions of the country. In Rochester, a great deal of institutional lore centers on the "Midwestern work ethic." One hears this phrase all the time in Minnesota, not just at Mayo, and I'm the first to say the people there are industrious, dedicated, and as mentioned earlier, possessed of "Minnesota nice." Would these new Clinics in the Southeast and the Southwest have equivalent values? Or would they take on a culture and hence a brand all their own? These questions were debated ever since the respective openings in 1986 and 1987 and were still important conversations at Mayo Clinic at the time I started there. An in-depth brand study could provide some important resolutions to these nagging issues.

We also hoped to learn how the various extensions and diversifications had affected brand perceptions. How did people feel about Mayo Clinic operating insurance companies? Did reading the Mayo Clinic health living newsletter provide a brand experience consistent with what people experienced as patients? Did all the solicitation for subscription renewals, book sales, and other commercial ventures diminish the stature of Mayo Clinic or enhance it?

Since the categories of Mayo Clinic's enterprises had expanded, we decided to have focus groups with a number of differing audience types, including patients, people who had never been to Mayo Clinic, and people who only had experienced Mayo Clinic through one of its other offerings, such as the newsletter, referring physicians, and, critically, employees. Having employees participate would enable us to test internal perceptions against external perceptions of the brand. The typical employee opinion survey would not get at the same kind of information as the brand study. We knew that if employees' perceptions of the Mayo Clinic brand matched the outside world's that would be good news for all. If not, that would put a much more complex and difficult challenge before us.

We chose a variety of locations as well, considering the broad sweep of Mayo Clinic's reach. Each year, patients from every one of the fifty states and more than a hundred other countries visit Mayo Clinic for care. For cost as well as logistical reasons, we focused on the United States, choosing key markets for each of the Clinics and other parts of the country that were representative of large referral populations or users of other Mayo Clinic products.

We engaged a firm from San Francisco, BRG, which, at the time, was among the world's leading groups doing this type of research and worked closely with them on development of the discussion guide and eventual deliverables. Although Mayo Clinic staff are generally skeptical of outside experts, as mentioned earlier, we could not have fielded this study on our own, despite the fact that Mayo Clinic has substantial expertise in patient-oriented research surveys and consumer market research. This particular effort required special expertise.

None of us had ever participated in an in-depth brand study such as the one conducted for Mayo Clinic in 1995. Task force members observed the focus groups as their schedules permitted. Sitting behind the one-way mirror, watching people from all walks of life describe Mayo Clinic in terms no one had ever heard before, provided each of us with an experience we'll never forget. Some of what we heard and saw was a revelation to all of us. As BRG had told us beforehand, this sort of research project was designed to elicit responses from various levels of a person's awareness and understanding. In other words, if you ask someone, "How would you describe Mayo Clinic?" chances are the respondent would talk about doctors, hospitals, famous patients, and other top-of-mind items that don't say much about a brand except the obvious aspects. If, however, you say to the person, "If Mayo Clinic were a human being who could walk into this room right now, what sort of person would they be?" you evoke a very different type of response that compels the focus group participant to delve into a different part of their brain altogether, reaching into their precognitive selves to gather feelings, memories, and associations, most of which they'd never before articulated, to create a picture for themselves and for us of this unknown thing, the Mayo Clinic Brand.

Other techniques in the focus groups included giving participants crayons and asking them to draw a picture of Mayo Clinic.
They also played word-association games and made collages from
a pile of random photographs cut out of magazines. These sessions
were four-hour affairs, twice a day, along with some scheduled in
the evening to accommodate referring physicians and others who
couldn't make an earlier meeting time. By the end of this process,
we had an enormous amount of material to synthesize, analyze,
and interpret.

Along with our sense of wonderment regarding some of the
stories, drawings, and collages people invented to describe Mayo
Clinic was a certain sense of disbelief that this kind of activity, much
of which was frankly childlike, could produce anything useful for
Mayo Clinic's future decision making, which, after all, was the
whole point of engaging in this study on brand management as a
whole. Our doubts receded as, over the course of observing dozens
of focus groups, definite themes emerged. Besides the kind of new
"data" that we garnered from this exercise, we also found other
reasons to feel genuine affection for the many people who had come
to Mayo Clinic for help and, in turn, had agreed to participate in
these focus groups to help Mayo Clinic figure itself out in this new
way. Time and again, people said they were honored to be asked,
privileged to participate, and would do anything for Mayo Clinic.
Speaking as a retired staff person, it is impossible to tell anyone
that you worked for Mayo Clinic and not hear that person or the
person next to her say, "Mayo Clinic saved my father's life," or,
"If it weren't for Mayo Clinic, I wouldn't be here." A study we did
some years after this initial research determined that fully one-third
of the people in the United States either had been to Mayo Clinic
or knew someone who had been treated there. These brand focus
groups provoked much story-telling about Mayo Clinic episodes of
care that touched all of us profoundly.

With people being asked to draw pictures of Mayo Clinic or describe the institution as a human being, inevitably the participants would loosen up after the first exercise and the room would be filled with animated conversation. As they say in my former home state of Hawaii, the people who gathered were anxious to "talk story" about this institution that had played such a large part in their lives. Also, as you might expect, adults exhibiting their crayon drawings and describing imaginary people sometimes made the room fill with laughter. I remember one woman in particular who was describing the Mayo Clinic in Rochester as a tall, distinguished, handsome person, who cared for his patients and his family with extreme expertise balanced by a sincere humility. She went on for a bit and then finally exclaimed, "What can I say? He's every woman's dream man."

On the other hand, once in a while, someone wasn't so kind. When Mayo Clinic expanded beyond Minnesota, some physicians in Florida and Arizona were not all that happy about having to compete with what they perceived as the eight-hundred-pound gorilla. One referring physician, when asked to hold up his drawing, revealed a picture of a devil, complete with horns and pointed ears. Now, from the perspective of more than twenty years, history has shown that Mayo Clinic's presence did not diminish anyone's practices, and the markets in Arizona, Florida, and, now, even Minnesota are more competitive than ever, by which I mean that the current state of health care in the United States has done quite a bit to level the playing field. Additionally, that same historical perspective shows that Mayo Clinic's presence in a market grows that market, attracting patients from all the states and many other countries, and also, by extension, benefitting the location's economy as a whole. Back in 1995, though, this wasn't as clearly seen, and some physicians in the focus groups strongly expressed their resentment, tinged with a bit of fear. Overall, though, the findings were remarkably positive, and twenty-five years of brand research since has shown that the brand remains in extraordinarily high esteem among the vast majority of Americans.

TRUTH TO POWER

After the focus groups were concluded, BRG spent a few weeks trolling through hours and hours of video, stacks of collages and drawings, reams of flip charts, and pages of copious notes. Once they had made a preliminary draft of their findings the task force reviewed them, and after a few edits and re-edits, we felt we had a solid presentation for our executive leadership.

As I have mentioned, Mayo Clinic had only recently expanded into new states and new market categories. In 1996, the state of the union was still evolving. Governance was more of a confederacy than a united nation, the philosophy of loose reins still ruled, and the culture of business unit independence was still in its ascendency. As part of a long-term plan to bring these disparate groups closer together, the executive team, which consisted of the CEO of Mayo Foundation, the three Clinic CEOs and other top leaders decided to begin an annual meeting of the executive team, the three clinic boards, the heads of research and education, and other important executives. The group totaled around sixty people, if my memory is correct. The group was to meet at the Mayo Clinic in Scottsdale, Arizona.

I have a special fondness for Arizona since, as I mentioned earlier, Tucson is where I feel my life as an adult began. Furthermore, my son Alex was born there, and I spent many years there learning to love the unique environment of the Sonoran Desert and the incredible beauty of Arizona as a whole. And, of course, Arizona has some of the best Mexican food anywhere outside of Mexico.

Ironically, the first time I had ever had a personal interaction with Mayo Clinic was in Scottsdale. When that Clinic opened in 1987, I was working at Carondelet in Tucson when my father-in-law, a former Mayo Clinic fellow and staff physician, received an invitation to attend the opening ceremonies. Andre offered the invitation to Jennifer and me, and so we drove up to Phoenix and then way out east on Shea Boulevard. Back then, the area between the edge of Scottsdale's development and the Clinic location was miles of undeveloped desert and Jennifer and I thought for a while that we'd gone the wrong way until we saw, somewhat isolated against the mountain backdrop, the modern—and I would say architecturally beautiful—desert version of Mayo Clinic. We listened to the speakers, we read the brochures, and then we toured the facilities.

I was visiting from St. Mary's in Tucson, the first hospital established in territorial Arizona back in 1880. My office was in a former hospital room in a stone block structure built in 1950 painted a desert pink, with an atmosphere more like the kind of hospital you'd see in a classic *film noir*, rather than the kind of sophisticated institution we were now touring. Everything gleamed. The décor was muted desert tones; paintings and sculptures were all around. Our guide took us through a desk area, then a hallway of patient rooms, and then we paused to review a typical Mayo Clinic exam room. Our guide explained that, in Rochester, these exam rooms doubled as the physicians' offices, but in Arizona and Florida, with new construction, leaders had taken the radical step of providing separate offices for the staff. She also told us the history of the system of desk registration, the hallways that radiated like spokes from the central desk, the coded lighting system beside every exam room door indicating the status of that room, for example, a patient is waiting, the doctor is in, or the patient is ready to move on. A light blinked if the patient had been waiting longer than a certain amount of time, so the desk attendant could check on the patient and the situation. The whole system, first implemented in the Rochester Clinic when they opened a new building in 1914, was devised by Dr. Henry Plummer, a physician hired by Dr. Will Mayo back in the early twentieth century, and of whom Dr. Will said,

"Hiring Henry Plummer was the best day's work I ever did." Our guide explained that Dr. Plummer was an eccentric genius, given to absent-mindedness, yet brilliant in his specialty of pathology and also his avocations of engineering, architecture, system design, and many other fields and he was responsible for the integrated medical record as well as many other innovations still in use today. Even the exam room's organization, complete with a specially designed exam table, the physician's desk, the changing area, and the built-in sofa where patients waited with their loved ones to hear the news, dire, hopeful, or otherwise, was the same as existed in Rochester and in Jacksonville, although naturally modernized and refined.

We also toured the many amenities typical of a Mayo Clinic facility, including the patient cafeteria, pharmacy, outdoor eating areas, and various exhibits on Mayo Clinic's history. Outside, the grounds had been landscaped in a manner appropriate for the desert, with a nature walk through the undeveloped areas, a feature that especially impressed me, knowing as I did of the fragility of the Sonoran environment and the rapidity with which it was being destroyed.

Finally, we toured the auditorium, appointed with a stage, television screens, and the capability for video conferences with Rochester and Jacksonville. Little did I know then that, during my career at Mayo, I would spend hours each day in such conferences. Overall, I was amazed at how Mayo Clinic had all the latest technologies and could afford to install the type of facility that most hospital administrators only dreamed of. Nowadays, much of this capability is more common, but in 1987, it was a rare thing. And now, not even ten years later, the brand management task force and I would be flying to Arizona to be part of a presentation of highly controversial material about the very essence of Mayo Clinic to a group of people who had never met in the same room before, that room being the auditorium I had envied and admired.

Many of those in attendance brought with them that healthy Mayo Clinic skepticism, not just regarding the enigmatic agenda item called "The Mayo Clinic Brand," but about the whole intent of this meeting. Wary of what could be another step toward increasing "federalism," some leaders came prepared to ensure that "state's rights" would endure, that the confederacy would remain loose, and the freedom to operate mostly independently would not be curtailed. Again, time has shown that this was fighting the tides of history, not to mention efficiency and intelligent brand building, since Mayo Clinic is now very much a united entity with strong centralized leadership modeled on Mayo Clinic's core value, and core brand attribute, of integration. In the late 1990s and early 2000s, though, this was all yet to be determined.

Into this environment, we brought a PowerPoint presentation with collages made from pictures cut out of magazines, quotes about "dream men," and drawings that looked, for all the world, as if they had been executed by eight-year-olds.

To be brief, the presentation was a disaster. Our hearts went out to the brave representative from BRG whom we had chosen to make the presentation. It was clear within minutes that we had committed a tactical blunder of the first magnitude. Bad enough that our task force was presuming to tell multidecade Mayo Clinic veterans what *their* Clinic was all about. To have an "outsider" give this presentation, however expert, articulate, or well-intended, was simply setting her, and ourselves, up for failure. The whole event went over like the heaviest of lead balloons, complete with, seemingly inevitably, some technical difficulties with PowerPoint and the playing of video clips.

Our presenter gamely pursued her prepared remarks, to little avail, as she was consistently interrupted, almost from the get-go, by physicians asking questions such as "How do you know that?" or "What was the *n* of this group?" or "How reliable are focus groups anyway?" and the real kicker, "What are we supposed to do with all this?" When she finished, visibly shaken but at least still standing, our task force chair, Dr. Swanson, took the stage to field the *really* tough questions, including, "Who's going to be in charge of all this?" and "Why are we creating another unnecessary bureaucracy?" and "Why do we need these people to tell us what we should do?" People were kind of angry, and I will confess I heard a few leaders raise their voices and I remember hearing "bullshit" and "hell no" spoken out loud a few times, something that, after nearly twenty-three years at Mayo Clinic, I can attest is an extremely rare occurrence, especially at a public forum such as this.

In that distinctly Mayo way essential for anyone who would lead Mayo Clinic, Dr. Michael Wood (then CEO) and Dr. Swanson remained calm, patient, and reassuring. They explained this was information for a later discussion, that nothing had been decided about any program, and that much work remained in front of the task force regarding if and how we would put brand management into place. Most importantly, they made the point several times that the leadership in the room would have ample time and opportunity to review, comment, and participate in the decision making about any eventual program, which would probably be a pilot. Finally, the angry mob was placated and became, again, a dignified assembly of physicians and executives at one of the world's most distinguished organizations.

Learning is a painful experience, I find, and the most important lessons hurt the most. Privately, I felt stupid, crushed, and wondered if I had just witnessed my own career suicide. Dr. Swanson, on the other hand, in the meeting after the meeting, expressed a realistic optimism, urging us to remember this was new stuff for Mayo, and Mayo takes a while—sometimes a long while—to adjust to new stuff. As the years went by, I used to counsel my staff about this phenomenon, saying, "Remember, there's time, there's geologic time, and then there's Mayo time." Patience and persistence win the day at Mayo Clinic, as I learned time and again.

We all consoled our BRG presenter, who was understandably disappointed about how it had all gone down, although being an experienced consultant, she recovered quickly. After all, it wasn't her fault, but ours, as we readily acknowledged. The lessons we took from that imbroglio would stay with me for my entire career, although at times I would make similar mistakes—that is, pushing Mayo Clinic to make a great leap forward only to have the body politic push back, insisting "Not so far, not so fast, but thanks." Nonetheless, change happened, as it must, and as it did for Mayo Clinic in due time.

Fortunately, my boss, Bob Smoldt, was a consummate Mayo Clinic strategist and himself a patient and calm individual who had navigated these waters many times before. Before the meeting proper, he had arranged for Dr. Swanson and me to meet with him and the CEOs of the three Clinics to give them a heads up about the presentation and to feel them out about their potential reactions.

Those meetings had been less cantankerous, although just as tense. I recall the CEOs listening impatiently, not wanting to waste time with a lot of business-school mumbo jumbo. In my career, I have found physicians, in general, to be practical, get-to-the-point personalities, at least on the job, and especially at Mayo. Studies have shown that many physicians barely listen to what the patient says beyond the initial complaints, and often follow their own thoughts regarding diagnosis and treatment, even as they conduct their examinations while the patient is still speaking. This is not to say they are uncaring or disinterested. It's more about their experience—they already know what to do—and their time—they don't have any. Now, at Mayo Clinic, I found the physicians generally good listeners, and they are famous for spending ample time with each patient. Our own studies over the years steadily confirmed that patients appreciated that the physician actually connected with them, answered their questions, and thoroughly explained their situation and their options. In business, the physician leadership tended to jump almost immediately to tactics and desired outcomes, once they felt they had grasped the gist of a proposal, not unlike how they might assess a patient's case fairly quickly and become most concerned about what to do for them, rather than have a lengthy discussion about abstractions or whys and wherefores. To my mind, this meant they sometimes dismissed the possibility that a business proposition such as brand management might require some deeper thought and discussion. They failed to see the nuances of brand building or consumer perceptions and, frankly, seemed unable to view any discipline other than medicine, and perhaps finance, as worthy of serious inquiry. After all, as Kevin Keller said, these ideas are hardly rocket science, or, in physicians' minds, not even science at all, just a mass of random, subjective opinions and attitudes, like politics or cable news, that did more to cloud or distort a problem than help solve it.

So the meetings with the CEOs were somewhat ambiguous and the full meeting was anything but, or so I thought, because, much to my relief and surprise, our task force was not disbanded, nor were we asked to change direction. Instead, a week or two later, when the executive committee had met privately, we were permitted to move forward and asked to come back in a few months with a full report and recommendations for the future.

Why this occurred, I cannot be sure. In many meetings, whenever there is a strong political subtext, leaders, not only those in health care, need to take a public position on behalf of their constituency, then, in the background out of the public eye, they can wheel and deal or even change their vote so long as they can maintain their public stature as defender of the realm. My sense, without any proof, is that some of that disastrous meeting consisted of this kind of showboating. I do believe, and subsequent events bore out, that the business entity leaders were threatened by this brand management initiative. Over the years, I saw many programs officially approved by a leadership group, only to watch them die a slow death due to inaction and passive resistance from the rest of the organization. Proposals at Mayo Clinic have been plagued with this sort of death by a thousand cuts. I've seen this happen at every hospital I've ever worked at. I don't know about other industries, but I suspect it is common. Health care, historically, has been unique in the sense that the CEO usually lacks direct authority over a physician or physician group. The relationship has been complex. Physicians, historically, possessed a great deal of individual power and autonomy and have been able to just say no as they chose, with little a hospital administrator could do about it except plead, persuade, or pay. As discussed in previous chapters, this balance of power is shifting rapidly, much to the chagrin of physicians, as hospital systems consolidate and acquire physician groups as financial partners or even outright employees.

THE BRAND REVEALED

At any rate, at Mayo Clinic, the collective power of the consultants, as staff physicians are called at Mayo, remains formidable, able to derail a project or policy change through overt action, or more commonly through covert tactics, usually something as simple as ignoring the damn thing until it goes away. Consequently, making any substantive change at Mayo Clinic requires garnering the support of legions of people, not unlike waging a campaign in the public interest or changing a public or government policy through grassroots actions, such as Mothers Against Drunk Driving (MADD) or antismoking laws.

It was just such a campaign that turned the tide on brand management for good.

After the dust settled, the task force gathered for the tedious work of assessing Mayo Clinic's current branding situation. This involved an audit of all branding activities across the enterprise: product, service lines, facilities, benefactor recognition, hospitals, campuses, and the rest. After the brands were collected, the names along with their disparate logos and other aspects of visual identity were organized into a brand schema, eventually a chart showing a hierarchy of master brands, sub-brands, and extensions, arranged by service or product category. When we finished this task, weeks later, we had a large, poster-size exhibit with more than 150 product and service names in at least a dozen categories. Placing these products and services into their appropriate slot on the chart was not an easy task. We invited the leaders of these groups to give us a description of the kind of activities they were engaged in and what they were being called. These meetings also gave us an opportunity to talk with them about the rationale for the project and to solicit their suggestions on how the program could best work for them. They also readily shared their concerns about the loss of control. Then, our task force, augmented by staff from marketing, communications, and public affairs, assembled and reassembled the brand hierarchy to reflect discussions occurring at the task force. The final result could not have been a more dramatic representation of brand confusion and—one might almost say—the brand management incompetence that Mayo Clinic was exhibiting to the world.

One of the constant rebuttals I have heard about the previous statement can be stated simply: "So what?" Individual business leaders will point to their own bottom lines or project successes with pride and make the case that "messing" with their name or logo or their brand organization, such as it was, would cause their own products to lose market share. Some even made the case, more emotionally than rationally, that their particular initiative would outright fail if this brand management fad forced them to alter their approach to the market in any way.

Another common rebuttal was the already-classic canard about the terrible, horrible, fearsome, demonic Mayo Clinic hairball, lurking in the background, ready to pounce at a moment's notice, worse for business than a plague of locusts or a stock market crash. To this would be added their favorite weapon of mass destruction: "What do you know about insurance, commercial publishing, retail laboratory services, fund-raising, or running a business?" Many times, this sort of brick was thrown through the brand management window. At Mayo, the hurler of the brick usually caused themselves more damage than was done to the task force's glass house, for the task force had one absolute, a guiding light that, at times, seemed lost on those who had been given the charge to grow their independent revenues quickly and dramatically: Our task force existed a priori for the good of Mayo Clinic as a whole. Now, no one desired to do any damage to any of the individual entities. In fact, a corollary to the previous working principle also emerged as we deliberated: The stronger Mayo Clinic was as a complete and comprehensively integrated brand presence, the stronger would be the individual businesses. We sometimes wondered how the individual units had lost sight of the dependence they had on Mayo Clinic and its brand equity. These were entities that fundamentally depended upon Mayo Clinic's brand excellence and intellectual property, without which they would not exist.

At the time these principles were first articulated, we had no factual proof. How could there be, given the state of the Mayo brand at that time? No data were being collected tracking the effect of these activities on the core brand or on the perceptions accruing each day about the separate entities. Here, again, we come to the importance of data in the management of these programs. Without it, one simply engages in endless circular debates based on intuition and emotion. Eventually, we amassed the data necessary for intelligent decision making. At the start, we had that first brand survey and not much else.

As we analyzed our first sets of data and spoke with the various stakeholders, a story arc emerged that began to cause some of us concern. A small family Clinic in the upper Midwest develops a sophisticated method for delivering an integrated model of care unlike any other organization in the world. For 120 years, this Clinic operates in a highly consistent fashion, aided by being in a small, remote town in Minnesota, a geography that virtually forced everyone to get along, since they lived in the same neighborhoods, ate together at the clinic, their kids attended school together, and, sometimes, they even married each other. This close-knit community managed the brand experience through mentorship and osmosis. As a result, the Mayo Clinic became the stuff of legend, the kind of brand that just about everyone in the country knows about and reveres. Then, in the 1970s and 1980s, for many good reasons, Mayo Clinic engaged in a series of potentially disruptive changes, each individually managed and with only small amount of attention given to the effect on the Mayo Clinic brand overall. After twenty years of change, the brand is becoming confused in the minds of consumers. The even more intense internal contradictions and confusions begin to leak into the media and the public conscious, as well as into the mouths of competitors. If left to its own devices, this brand that took more than a century to build could be damaged irreparably in a relatively short time.

And what a brand it was and is. While the task force sorted through the morass of names, products, services, and political mine-fields, we also retooled the presentation from BRG in a manner that would allow us to present the findings around the institution. Kent Seltman and I were deputized to modify the slides and make the presentations. Dr. Swanson joined as his surgical and travel schedule allowed.

By the time we finished our tour, Kent and I had spoken to more than a hundred groups across the institution, in Arizona, Florida, Minnesota, the Mayo Health System, at physician department meetings, at committee meetings, at administrative conferences either in person or on video, in massive lecture halls and in small gatherings. We even had the opportunity to present to the board of trustees, where the likes of Barbara Bush, Jim Barksdale, Hugh Price, and other luminaries were in attendance. No matter what group we presented to, the results were always the same: fascination and pride. The techniques used to discern this information were new and interesting to these audiences. More importantly, the study validated what many associated with Mayo Clinic knew in their hearts to be true. By the time we finished, the room positively glowed with the strength of the group's collective pride in Mayo Clinic. We always stayed late for the many questions. People couldn't seem to get enough of finally having a deep understanding of Mayo Clinic's public standing and brand essence.

Here's why: The study showed that Mayo Clinic was one of the strongest, most respected brands in the world, which also meant the brand was extraordinarily valuable, both intangibly in terms of reputation, but also tangibly as a material asset. BRG said they'd never seen anything like it. We were all at a loss to find another brand that had quite the same level of unblemished success. The brand promise of Mayo Clinic was distilled to one word: "Answers"—answers to questions you might ask your doctor, answers about the best method for treating an illness, and answers that often amounted to discovery when a patient, after making the rounds of physicians and hospitals in their hometown or elsewhere in search of a definitive diagnosis, would come to Mayo Clinic frustrated, scared, and on the brink of despair, only to have the team approach of Mayo's excellent caregivers come together and identify the elusive infection, the undiagnosed metabolic syndrome, or the one-in-a-million condition that few specialists had ever seen outside of Mayo Clinic. The brand study showed that this sort of experience was shared by thousands of people, filling them with awe and gratitude and, as is so much a part of human nature, a strong desire to tell others—everyone they knew—about the remarkable experience of receiving medical care at Mayo Clinic. A subsequent study we fielded showed that, on average, each patient who had a positive experience at Mayo Clinic told forty-four people about it, much higher than the usual rate for word-of-mouth marketing. Considering that Mayo Clinic, in Rochester alone, sees more than three hundred thousand unique patients each year, with patient satisfaction percentage rates in the high nineties, that is positive word-of-mouth reaching millions of people every year.

The umbrella term, "Answers," comprised a number of core attributes. Chief among them were leadership, wisdom, dedication, integrity, and teamwork. We showed the representative materials and quotations from focus group participants that elucidated these concepts. For leadership, one person drew Mayo Clinic as a castle, saying, "Mayo is the gold standard. It's at the top of the heap." For wisdom, a person described Mayo Clinic staff as serious, dignified, and sophisticated without being patronizing or pompous. "Sophisticated but humble," she said. "Quietly competent."

Dedication went beyond devotion to the profession of medicine but encompassed the core Mayo Clinic value of putting the needs of the patient first. One person's drawing was a simple circle with a patient in the center. "They don't stop until they find the answer," this person said, repeating a theme we heard often, that Mayo Clinic leaves "no stone unturned" in their quest for a solution.

Other distinctive attributes were named but, for proprietary reasons, I won't get into those details. It should be no surprise though that Mayo Clinic's two most distinctive attributes are integrity and teamwork. In a world of retail medicine, mall clinics, and the ongoing melding of providers, payers, and the government, Mayo Clinic has stood out as an institution of integrity, making decisions for the patient's benefit, not for profit or individual glory. Mayo Clinic was seen as noncommercial. "The business element is taken out of Mayo," one said, "which gives me greater faith in their diagnosis."

Since Mayo Clinic founded the notion of an integrated group practice and honed the mechanisms of integration, audiences found it especially satisfying to see that the focus group members recognized this quite clearly. "Mayo is like a well-conducted symphony that works harmoniously."

Another said, "What makes Mayo unique is that you see a team of doctors. Doctors are even questioned by their colleagues. Everything is continually evolving, efficient, thorough, and collaborative." These words accompanied a picture of a building, with a number of stick figures inside, and a caption: "All under one roof. All communicating."

Some of what few negatives we found centered on the concept of exclusivity, which has plagued Mayo Clinic for decades. Since Mayo Clinic is known by the general public for treating celebrities and presidents and is seen as being the best, with only three locations, mythologies have grown up around these circumstances. Some people think you cannot get an appointment at Mayo unless you have an "in" or are referred by a physician. Neither is true—anyone can refer themselves and make an appointment. Others believe Mayo is not covered by insurance—also untrue, as many hundreds of insurance plans have Mayo Clinic in their contracts.

The brand study was able to show that the core Mayo Clinic brand attributes were perceived consistently across the three Clinic sites, which was a bit of a surprise, especially to some long-time Rochesterians, who harbored a conviction that there could only ever be one real Mayo Clinic. In my early days at Mayo, the sites in Arizona and Florida were often referred to as satellites, much to the annoyance of the staff at those sites who were equally convinced they were providing the same Mayo-quality care Rochester always had. Anyone who has visited either of those clinics recently knows they are Mayo planets in their own right, not mere satellites of the original. Back then, though, the two newer sites were considerably smaller than Rochester, their research and education programs were fledgling endeavors, and the physicians admitted patients to community hospitals they shared with non-Mayo physicians. None of this was consistent with the model in Rochester, fueling the internal disparity in perceptions. Our study showed that the public saw things differently. Mayo was Mayo, they believed, as well as experienced and, in fact, the public thought the three Clinics were even better integrated than they were at that time. Nowadays, the three Clinics operate largely as "one clinic in three sites," a rubric that captured the imagination of leaders and staff a bit later on. The original brand study did compel people to revisit their attitudes, and I believe helped drive a zeitgeist at Mayo Clinic toward comprehensive integration of all activities.

The study also examined brand extensions, using the simple dichotomy of what was "permissible" and what was "impermissible" for Mayo Clinic to engage in. This proved especially useful in future decision making, and a bit painful when applied retrospectively. Mayo Clinic had embarked on a number of extensions via Mayo Medical Ventures, and this group had a long list of "out-of-the-box" ideas and even some controversial irons in the fire regarding additional forays into new business categories that could earn additional revenue for research and education. Our task force members were quite interested to see whether some of these proposals would pass muster with our focus groups.

The exercise began with the moderator leading the groups through a series of somewhat obvious "permissible" and "impermissible" options that helped participants grasp the nuances underlying the choices. No, it would not be permissible for Mayo Clinic to operate a consumer laundry service. Yes, it is certainly permissible for Mayo Clinic to brand a new-and-improved hip implant or imaging device developed by its own physicians and scientists. (Good thing, since this had already been done!)

The discussion grew more nuanced and more animated when the subject turned to branded food items or health supplements. Should Mayo Clinic brand vitamins? Should Mayo Clinic have its own brand of aspirin or acetaminophen? What about food that helped lower bad cholesterol or combat childhood obesity?

Because of the unwavering trust people have in Mayo Clinic's name, at first, they found appealing the idea of a line of Mayo Clinic vitamin supplements, health supplements, advanced medicines, special foods, even home medical equipment. Upon deeper discussion, a few doubts emerged and, after a while, the groups reached consensus on a number of principles or caveats that stood Mayo Clinic in good stead for years to come.

The groups started from the premises that they had already established, that Mayo Clinic represents "the best of the best for all things health care": innovation, trust, humanitarianism, noncommercialism, and also "something special," the fortunate synergy of operational effectiveness, extraordinary expertise, and caring individuals—a culture, in short, that was priceless and irreplaceable. I have heard it called the "secret sauce," "our legacy," "the Mayo Way," and once, in a wonderful YouTube video, years later, a patient said that he had visited "Planet Mayo" and detailed his experiences from the vantage point of having seen and done something that did not exist anywhere else in the known world. Clearly, anyone who had experienced this did not want it to be compromised in any way.

Based on this research and our own deliberations, the task force ultimately recommended that Mayo Clinic should not enter a product or service category that was already crowded and commoditized, such as vitamins, health supplements, and the like, unless Mayo Clinic had discovered or invented something to set that product wholly apart from the dozens of other similar products on the market. We explained that, since Mayo Clinic's primary mission is to contribute to humanity's health and well-being, products and services from the institution should fall under those auspices. Any product or service branded Mayo Clinic must truly include a significant and substantive contribution of Mayo Clinic intellectual property. Simply putting the name on a bottle of aspirin because it will help sell the aspirin is impermissible.

Contrary to the original thinking at Mayo Clinic at the time Mayo Medical Ventures was established, our study found that consumers saw the institution's book and newsletter publishing operation as brand consistent. They welcomed the introduction of Mayo Clinic expertise into the crowded and confusing area of consumer health information, with studies contradicting other studies week to week, and no one sure who was benefitting on the side from which proclamation. They trusted Mayo Clinic to cut through all that clutter and tell them the truth. Nor did they have any qualms about paying for this information, especially when they learned that all proceeds benefitted continued medical research and education. This proved so compelling an argument that, eventually, the activities of Mayo Medical Ventures became seen as a vital part of Mayo Clinic's core brand, not something to be distanced from the main medical activities of Mayo Clinic. Sometime after this initial work was completed, two important changes were made: the words "Mayo Clinic" were used on their products, not just "Mayo," and a tag line was printed on the product indicia stating that proceeds from the sale of this product benefitted advanced medical education and research at Mayo Clinic.

We all found it gratifying that the Mayo Clinic culture was so strong that the brand held consistent not only geographically across the three main sites but also across health information, fund-raising, and other categories. One exception was perceptions of the non-Mayo hospitals being used in Arizona and Florida. Patients wanted to see Mayo having their own closed-staff hospitals as they do in Minnesota, and as they do now in Arizona and Florida. Although people cannot always articulate the technicalities of the Mayo Clinic model of care, they know the experience well and they can sense intuitively and experientially when it isn't quite right.

The most controversial finding of the study concerned the category of insurance. As mentioned earlier, each Mayo Clinic site was operating insurance plans of various types: fee-for-service, health maintenance organizations (HMOs), and others. Internally, these were seen as necessary experiments and, should the managed care phenomenon of the 1990s take hold and shut Mayo Clinic out for geographical or financial reasons, Mayo would be able to compete with these plans on its own terms. As we all now know, this did not pan out. Many of us remember being in the audience watching the movie *As Good as It Gets*, released in 1998, when the female lead, Helen Hunt, launches into a tirade of frustration about how her HMO is jacking her around and, as far as she could see, only existed to ensure that her ailing child did not receive the medical care he desperately needed. Audiences all over the country exploded in spontaneous cheers and applause. As I sat in the theater in Rochester, I knew at that moment that managed care as it had been perpetrated was doomed.

Our focus groups expressed these views, sometimes just as vehemently as Helen Hunt. They hated managed care and told the focus group leader one of their main reasons for loving Mayo Clinic was the freedom of choice they enjoyed. The less Mayo Clinic resembled managed care or any kind of insurance plan, the better. They felt Mayo Clinic might be the last bastion of the type of medical practice, where, as one person put it, "My doctor is doing what's best for me, not for his income." Another person, expressing her deep hope that Mayo Clinic would not become involved in insurance (even though it already was) put it this way: "I could never be sure if my doctor was acting out of concern for me or out of concern for the bottom line. This would be a real problem of trust."

To its credit, the leadership of Mayo Clinic did not stop the task force from reporting these findings across the institution. I learned later that this was typical of the institution's belief in transparency. Many hospitals would be very surprised by the degree to which Mayo Clinic is honest about things, not just with other leaders or physicians but with the entire staff. Interestingly, most hospital people and many others view Mayo as a mute monolith, partly because of their historic media shyness and, as already mentioned, partly because the main Mayo Clinic building in Rochester for fifty years was, in fact, a twenty-story granite "monolith." Keeping secrets from employees fit the paradigm some had developed about Mayo. My experience with Mayo and other hospitals has been that Mayo is far more forthcoming with its staff. Other hospitals are more guarded, secretive, and incommunicative to their staffs. Later, we will discuss Mayo's approach to corporate communications, including many examples of how this transparency may, at times, have caused short-term pain, yet, in the end, redounded to Mayo Clinic's and its staff's benefit.

The presentation of this information regarding insurance products upset many people, particularly those who were leading and implementing the programs. At meeting after meeting, Kent and I were challenged to justify our findings. In typical Mayo fashion, the fundamentals of the study were called into question, and we were asked repeatedly if this meant Mayo Clinic was going to shut the programs down. We explained that one study would not result in large, expensive program investments being terminated and that, in branding and product development, there are many paths to brand "worthiness." One of my early brand mentors, Mitch Seltzer, put this concept to me very simply: "Branding is all about execution." We'll delve into that later in the story. For now, suffice to say this idea was lost on the insurance proponents, who thought we were just being evasive about the possible end to their programs.

We weren't being evasive. Kent and I had no inside knowledge about leadership's plans in response to the study. The medical director of the insurance programs, politely incensed, sat next to me after a committee meeting one day and regaled me with stories about satisfied members, schooled me on the nuances of managed care and the need for Mayo Clinic to be in the game, and said that if Mayo were to cancel these programs, it would be far more damaging to the institution's reputation than whatever was happening now, of which he was completely skeptical, since his plans had thousands of members and we had only spoken to a handful of people in focus groups (which everyone knows are sketchy, easily taken over by an opinionated loudmouth, and have no statistical validity). Each time this subject came up, he challenged me to quantify the brand risk, make it real for him, which was, in a sense, asking me to prove a negative, since nothing yet had happened with the plans that had been publicly damaging.

As he talked, my mind tried to absorb the totality of the situation. Here I was, about ten organizational levels below this physician, a physician who was world famous and brilliant in his specialty, having a conversation in which it appeared that what I said mattered. Granted, by now, I was in my early forties and we've had presidents of the United States who were that age when elected. Nevertheless, perhaps simply as a byproduct of my own personality, I had a rather strong sense of anomie at this moment. *How did I get here? Why am I having this conversation? What do I say to this man?* I've never been paralyzed by these metaphysical reflections, although I have them often, particularly when I am sitting at the grown-up table after many years of being at the card table with the green vinyl cover and the folding legs at our big Italian family dinners. Being a child of the 1960s certainly fueled this fever. Never in my wildest dreams, when I was a long-haired, earring-wearing undergraduate at ultra-liberal Brown University, could I have predicted that I would be sitting in a suit and tie in a conference room in cold-as-hell Rochester, Minnesota, debating brand management with a world-renowned neurologist. Yet here I was.

I've never lost that sense of wonderment about my career— or my life, for that matter. My experiences at Mayo Clinic only expanded that sense of awe and occasional *anomie*. All of the above adds up to a feeling that has carried me through many tough situations like the one I was facing now. It wasn't about me, in any way, shape, or form. I just wanted Mayo Clinic to do the right thing, and I just wanted to do the right thing by Mayo Clinic.

The conversation with the director of the insurance program presaged many similar confrontations about branding, marketing, and the totality of Mayo Clinic presence and activities that I would have for the next fifteen years. Many times during those years, I reflected upon the days when I studied French Symbolist poetry at Brown or, later, educational theory or rhetoric at the University of Washington. My sense grew that those studies, some quite obscure, in a peculiar fashion, prepared me perfectly for the discussions, confrontations, and decisions that I would be a part of once the brand management program became a permanent part of the Mayo Clinic.

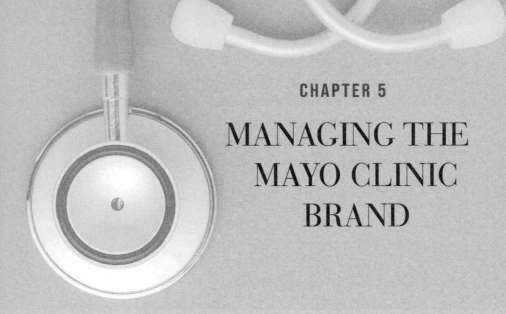

CHAPTER 5

MANAGING THE MAYO CLINIC BRAND

RESISTANCE

On a day in Rochester, when a blizzard hit and the wind chill dropped to twenty below, Fahrenheit, the administrative director of Mayo Medical Ventures met with me to discuss brand management. I knew she was not happy. A few weeks before, the executive committee had formally approved the establishment of a brand management program, with a high-level committee that included most of the members of the task force. I stayed on as secretary. My visitor didn't care about that. What bothered her was that the committee had been formed at all.

We exchanged a few pleasantries, talked about the horrible cold, and then, as was her style, she got right to the point.

"Of course, you know, none of this brand management stuff applies to us."

She was dead serious, but then, she always appeared dead serious. Sally was the kind of person who seemed, on the surface at least, to live and breathe for her job, with no outside perspective about it. At this time, I didn't know her very well. Later, I learned, as with most things, there is more to a person than meets the eye, and I found out that her intensely businesslike demeanor masked a rather likable, intelligent, and witty person who had a healthy sense of the absurd about life, work, and people. But that came later. Now all I saw was daggers in her eyes and a bearing that communicated clearly that she would fight this new initiative to the death.

"Why do you say that, Sally?" I asked.

"John, Ventures isn't Mayo Clinic. We're completely different. We create commercial products that have to compete in the real world against professional, established companies that want to eat our lunch. We can't be saddled with the brand standards and naming conventions and logo restrictions of a conservative health-care provider like Mayo Clinic. We won't be able to compete. We have to be able to be creative and nimble, not hounded by bureaucracy."

In a word, I was nonplussed. She outranked me. She'd been at Mayo about five times longer than I had. I knew she had powerful allies on the executive committee and even answered to a separate board, among whose members was my own boss. All those circumstances paled in importance, in light of this particular exchange. Here it was, sooner than I expected, and in a manner that I hadn't expected: a direct, fierce, thoughtful, and angry refusal to cooperate.

It hit me as we spoke—lucky me, I was now the brand czar. I'd never heard that term until they made me secretary of the committee. I'm not really the czar type. My preference is to talk through issues, look for common ground, maybe find room for compromise. Yet, increasingly with this new responsibility—which, by the way, I did as part of my regular job as chair of communications, not as a new job—I came to see that I had somehow acquired a certain amount of power.

Not that all that much actual authority was embedded in my brand position. At Mayo, power rarely accrues to an individual on a grand scale, unlike what I have observed at other companies. Most health system have CEOs or hospital administrators who seem to hold regal sway over just about everything in their facilities. Not at Mayo. Once, one of the Mayo Clinic CEOs I worked with opened up to me about his frustrations. This was a person one would easily perceive as dynamic, forceful, and able to push through any agenda item he chose. He said, "I can't do anything around here. I'm like a weak mayor with a powerful city council. People think I can just wave my wand and make things happen. Not here I can't."

He exaggerated a bit. He accomplished a great deal during his tenure, moving Mayo Clinic a long distance along that spectrum from its recent increased fragmentation to enterprise-wide integration, from State's Rights to Federalism, so to speak. It took time, though—not to mention the many battle scars he earned.

What I represented to Sally was an initiative with a powerful committee overseeing policy and another entity, the brand operations team, soon shortened to the brand team, managing day-to-day implementation, both of which she wanted to avoid completely. True, I was not administrative leader for brand management, yet I actually didn't know at this juncture that what I said in response to Sally was really true.

"Sally, as far as I know, brand management applies to everyone and everything at Mayo Foundation. That's my understanding."

Sally was having none of it. She battered me with specific potential applications of brand policy on book jackets, newsletters, DVD jewel boxes, media program concepts, you name it. I had few answers, except to say, "Yes, all of that goes to the brand team for review and approval and, if you're not happy with the decision, you can take it to the brand committee."

At that, Sally stood up and left abruptly with a curt, "Very well. Thanks." Although I did confirm that the brand management program did indeed apply to "everything," it soon became evident that that was easier said than done.

BRAND MANAGEMENT TAKES HOLD

The task force, and then the committee, had decided not to follow so many other companies by creating a special position for this function, often called director of Brand Management or Vice President of Brand. That kind of autocratic power centered on one individual would have sunk the brand ship on its maiden voyage. The central idea behind the committee and the brand team membership was inclusiveness.

This was especially critical when applied to the brand team membership. In my opinion, the brand team was a brilliant stroke of collective genius on the part of the Mayo leadership. This team comprised representation from all the affected areas: the three Clinics, the health system, development, Mayo Medical Ventures, Mayo Medical Services Inc. (MMSI), graphics, publications, media, marketing, and communications. The members were managers, supervisors, and staff, each of whom had direct responsibility for areas that would be directly affected by brand management policy.

This forum became a mechanism through which issues could be discussed candidly and decisions made by group consensus. Those who needed to had the opportunity to plead their case. A member of my staff chaired the group, so as to keep it completely at the operational level.

At first, the team and the committee did garner a reputation for creating a bureaucracy and a certain amount of autocratic control. Given the chaos that the group needed to rein into some kind of order, this was probably inevitable.

Years later, the department chair for cardiology asked to meet with me. Wanting to be more aggressive in promoting his cardiology practice, his frustration had reached the boiling point. We met on the twelfth floor of the Siebens Building, which was then the executive suite, in a small sunny conference room with a panoramic view of Rochester and the hills beyond. Even Rochester can be green and beautiful in the summertime.

We sat facing each other at the table, *mano a mano*. Dr. Hind had a long list of grievances and dove right in. Every item he described began with "Here's another thing we can't do because brand won't let us." I listened in amazement. Most of what he said was complete news to me. No one in my group had made any sort of decisions of the type that he said stymied him. I wasn't even aware of them.

"Dan, I don't know what's going on. Most of what you're talking about is just fine to do. I don't know why you all got the idea this would be any kind of brand problem. Who's telling you this?"

Dan looked perplexed. His ire still high, he searched for answers and to regain his momentum. He really wanted to market his practice. Cardiology had been perennially number two after Cleveland Clinic in the widely despised and obsessively monitored *US News and World Report*'s hospital and specialty rankings. Not one person at Mayo Clinic believed that ranking was accurate, especially the cardiologists.

"I don't know, really. I don't know anyone's name. I get this from the other cardiologists. They bring me materials from Cleveland Clinic or some other hospital and say, 'Why can't we do this kind of thing?'"

He wasn't just talking about brand in terms of names or logos; he was talking about the whole manner in which cardiology and, by extension, Mayo Clinic was presented to the world. Most of my colleagues in health-care marketing will tell you that cardiologists are always among the most assertive specialties about wanting their practice marketed. Dan had a long list of requests and felt he'd been thwarted by the brand bureaucracy. After we talked for a while, I had the uncanny realization that no one in particular had denied any of these activities or made any decisions about them. Certainly, I hadn't. It dawned on me that the institution was doing it to itself. In ten years, Mayo Clinic had evolved from an institution in which nobody ever uttered the word "brand" into an institution where the word was constantly a part of the internal conversation. It was all brand, all the time. Although I'd observed this evolution with a certain amount of pride, other consequences weren't so splendiferous. True, Mayo Clinic had internalized the idea of being a brand. Just about all the policy matters or strategic initiatives that came before the board while I sat with them mentioned brand in some manner, usually in the sense that such and such an item was sure to enhance Mayo Clinic's brand equity or was consistent with our brand values and attributes. I saw "brand" used repeatedly as a touchstone in many conversations and the business side of the house appreciated having the brand quantified and valued as part of their dealings with the outside.

This meeting with Dan, though, pointed out the most serious downstream consequence of our success. Mayo Clinic was policing itself, far more restrictively than some of us in brand management expected or intended.

My executive colleagues and I had observed this organizational characteristic before at Mayo Clinic. Let's call it hypercorrection, which is actually a concept from linguistics. Hypercorrection is what compels people to say, "Mom took Carol and I to the store," when the actual correct grammar would be, "Mom took Carol and me to the store." After years of being taught to say, "He and I," not "Him and me," in many situations, the person overcorrects and uses the "and I" construction, even when it isn't necessary, because they apply the "correction" to everything they say.

Mayo Clinic staff were overcorrecting like rabid schoolmarms with a two-inch grammar text. Suddenly, it seemed, everyone was a brand expert. After my meeting with Dan, I tuned in to conversations and asked my staff to help me understand the phenomenon—and modify the behavior. After a time, it seemed clear the staff were mostly motivated out of a desire to protect what they had learned was one of our most precious assets. The dark side was no one wanted to hassle with what they perceived to be a painful process of review and approval, and so they just stopped themselves in their own tracks before they had to run the painful brand gauntlet.

How had we gotten to this brave new world? Once the brand committee was established, we set about taking care of business in what the Supreme Court might have called "all due deliberate speed." Within the first three years of the group's existence, we systematized 150 brands and then eliminated many that were out of sync with the naming conventions we had developed. The key working principle was that our naming had to make simple sense to the public and had to be easily implemented internally. Another working principle referred to the enormously important brand attribute of integration. Different logos for different hospitals, different color schemes for divergent specialties, on and on it went, with all of it needing to be brought together into a coherent whole.

Even though the membership of the committee included some of the busiest, highest-ranking leaders at Mayo Clinic, they devoted an extraordinary amount of time to these first few years, sometimes meeting for two hours, and for full days or half days when we needed a longer retreat to accomplish our work. The beauty of this involvement was that, after a time, even those physicians who had been somewhat skeptical of this invasion of "social science" into the world's most famous temple of medicine, evolved into brand mavens, capable of discussing for twenty minutes whether Mayo Clinic should use the word "center" or "institute," or neither, if we were to be true to our brand promise of integration. We sometimes joked this was the modern version of asking how many angels could dance on the head of a pin, yet at the end of our labors, we knew we had accomplished something good and lasting for Mayo Clinic.

The other invaluable asset of having this kind of committee at this level was the obvious message communicated to the rest of the institution: that these issues were damned important and not to be downgraded or trifled with. As my conversation with Dr. Hind made clear, that had been accomplished.

While the brand committee was setting policies and procedures, the brand team was implementing them in efficient and collegial fashion. People loved serving on the brand team. This was where the brand came to life. A steady stream of real-world examples and requests passed through the team and, over time, a body of common law became manifest that guided the team and the rest of the institution.

"Dan," I said, "I see what's happening here. The culture is policing itself. In fact, people are overdoing it. Most of what you want is totally doable. Let me talk to the staff. If things don't loosen up, just give me a call."

There would be many such calls for the first years of the brand implementation program. At first, the whole mass of decisions and changes that had to be made seemed insurmountable, but over the first five years, many decisions were finally made and, by the early 2000s, we all decided that the brand committee had served its function and could be disbanded. The structure was changed so that I would be the chief brand administrator, along with my other duties as department chair for public affairs, and I would be partnered with a board-level physician. We would adjudicate the tough issues or bring them to the CEO's or the board's attention as needed. This happened about six times a year. Most of the work was handled by the brand team. Brand management had become a part of the fabric of the institution. Just as no one at Mayo Clinic would dream of floating a bond without going through finance or hiring a physician without working with the personnel committee, now, no one—well, almost no one—would dream of engaging in any activity that could affect the brand without the appropriate review and, if necessary, background research to assess the positives and negatives of the initiative's overall brand impact.

CONSEQUENCES

Below are some of the most significant accomplishments of the brand management program, many of which addressed issues raised in previous chapters.

MAYO VS. MAYO CLINIC VS. MAYO MEDICAL CENTER

One day, in the early 1990s, I crossed the street on my way to the Mayo Building. As often happened, when I got to the corner, an older couple stopped me for directions. Since all staff wore business attire and name badges, we were easy to spot. The woman asked, "Excuse me. Where is Mayo Clinic?"

I pointed to the twenty-story building behind them. "It's right there," I said. "That building is where you need to go."

Why the trouble? The sign in front of the building said "Mayo Medical Center. Mayo Building." It didn't say Mayo Clinic, anywhere on campus. Anywhere.

Hard as it may be to imagine, for most of the 1990s, Mayo Clinic struggled with its own historic name. Some thought that the term "clinic" connoted a small physician practice and didn't do justice to the large, multistate provider it had become. For a time, the term Mayo Medical Center gained prominence. This name, meant to be inclusive of hospitals as well as the outpatient practice, was favored by a number of members of the board of governors of Mayo Clinic in Rochester.

Once our brand research program kicked in, the confusion about Mayo, Mayo Clinic, and Mayo Medical Center became manifest. As mentioned earlier, the leadership had adopted the notion that leaving the word "clinic" off the name of a consumer product or insurance offering somehow inoculated the core practice—that is, the core brand—from any taint of commercialism or lapse of integrity. Contrast this notion, which posits the importance of the word "clinic" with the idea that, to truly reflect all of Mayo's activities, one needed to remove the word "clinic" and use the name Mayo Medical Center. It's amazing where reliance and insistence on internal assumptions (prejudices?) can lead a person or an organization.

The internal conflicts over all this grew more intense as the two clinics in Arizona and Florida grew in patient volume and national prominence. For many different reasons, some staff in Minnesota insisted the clinic in Rochester was the only true Mayo Clinic. Some of these attitudes can be attributed to the relatively short time the new practices had been operating, with small research and educational components that, at that time, were dwarfed by Rochester's century-old preeminence. Another factor was simply a matter of status. Rochester physicians had been vetted over a number of years before gaining a coveted spot on the Rochester staff. Some believed that the newer Mayo Clinics had brought in physicians more hastily with the idea of growing the practices quickly. In the eyes of these Rochester veterans, the upstart clinics were satellites, not yet worthy of the name Mayo Clinic.

All of this devolved into a convention which showed that the parent company, then confusingly called Mayo Foundation or Mayo Foundation for Medical Education and Research, had three primary entities: Mayo Clinic Scottsdale, Mayo Clinic Florida, and Mayo Clinic, or, sometimes, Mayo Clinic Rochester. The Rochester advocates insisted that the Rochester practice should only be called Mayo Clinic. And so it went.

This head-spinning over naming continued for years. I recall at least two sessions with the board of governors of the Rochester clinic presenting brand research findings along with my physician partner, Dr. Patricia Simmons, at which we both politely pleaded with the leadership to dispense with the term Mayo Medical Center and use the internationally known and understood name Mayo

Clinic. That this was resisted surely puzzles anyone not intimately involved with the internal politics of Mayo Clinic at that time.

Names carry enormous symbolic significance. Mayo Clinic— that is, the entire organization—struggled throughout the 1990s with its identity, structure, and governance. Looking back, one can easily see these conflicts as necessary, some might say inevitable, growing pains as the institution evolved from a large single-state practice into a multistate, multibillion-dollar health-care provider. Interestingly, the same physicians and executives who might have decried the expenditure of time and resources on branding or marketing became passionate advocates when the issue of these naming conventions arose. Often, the groups I attended could easily spend half an hour or more debating the possibilities. The members would ride the circuit, so to speak, visiting all the options, their consequences and the political ramifications, and, when they had ridden the full circle, they'd fall back into their Aeron chairs, frustrated and defeated. Once or twice, someone would say, "Can't you guys figure this out?"

Eventually, we did. By the end of the 1990s we had accumulated enough data to be able to state, unequivocally, that Mayo Clinic was the name to use. We found that consumers did not hear "small outpatient practice" when they heard the words Mayo Clinic. Those two words communicated in efficient fashion everything that a major modern academic medical center comprised: research, education, inpatient care, outpatient care, wellness—you name it. The words Mayo Clinic were a single unit of meaning. People didn't split hairs about clinic or hospital or newsletters. It was all just Mayo Clinic.

This was driven home around this time when the clinic in Arizona decided to construct its own hospital on its Phoenix campus. By an accident of history, there wasn't any convention for naming hospitals at Mayo. The two hospitals in Minnesota had been acquired by Mayo in 1986 and came with their own historic names, Saint Marys Hospital and Rochester Methodist Hospital.

The Jacksonville practice owned its St. Luke's Hospital, but it too had been acquired along with its historic name. The Arizona facility would be the first Mayo hospital entirely built from scratch. So what should it be called?

The marketing group conducted focus groups in the region and came up with a name I am certain would never have occurred to anyone within Mayo: Mayo Clinic Hospital. As soon as we heard it, its intuitive simplicity and brilliance were obvious. No one within the institution would have thought to pair "Clinic" with "Hospital" in that manner. Yet consumers overwhelmingly favored and understood that name, because they saw Mayo Clinic as that single, all-encompassing unit of meaning. Years later, the newly constructed hospital on the Jacksonville campus was also named Mayo Clinic Hospital.

The tide eventually turned as the mass of evidence accumulated. One day, I was driving to work and passed the stone sign at the entrance to the Mayo Campus. Seemingly overnight, the words had been changed and it now read "Welcome to Mayo Clinic." And, as if to seal the issue forever, the half-billion-dollar complex constructed as the central focus for patients and visitors to Mayo Clinic in Rochester—which was named the Gonda building after its major donors—had at its entrance points, in giant stainless-steel letters, matching the canopy designed by architect Cesar Pelli, the words "Mayo Clinic," becoming the only building on the entire campus to have those words emblazoned on its façade. Every day thereafter, I looked at those words and sighed with relief.

LOGOS

Logos are the bane of a marketer's existence. They generate strong emotions in many people. Staff associate themselves with the hospital or company logo the way many Americans identify with the Stars and Stripes. The logos are on their name tags, on patches on their uniforms, watermarked on their paychecks (or electronic paystubs), and, often, are scattered around the facility on posters, statues, and even sometimes stained-glass windows. Take away the logo, they feel, and you rob them of their heritage, their identity, and, I have been told, the "soul of the place."

In my career, I've been involved in many mergers, acquisitions, product launches, partnerships, and other situations that called for some kind of modification to a logo or creation of joint letterhead with two logos, or some other manipulation. These requests have, more often than not, descended into contentious and, sometimes, acrimonious discussions that, at times, transcended reason, logic, or business necessity, centering instead on ego and sentiment.

My first exposure to this odd reality occurred when I was a relatively young department head at Carondelet in Tucson, Arizona. I originally worked only at the century-old St. Mary's Hospital in the previously described west side of town. Now, in the mid-1980s, this hospital was merging with the other Carondelet hospital on the recently developed and relatively more affluent east side of town, St. Joseph's Hospital. Although both hospitals were owned and operated by the Sisters of St. Joseph of Carondelet, with a common central leadership headquartered in St. Louis, the word on the street was that St. Joseph's was being "taken over" by St. Mary's. Part of that takeover meant a promotion for me, from director of media and communications at St. Mary's to corporate director over both hospitals. Needless to say, hostility ensued, as always happens with mergers. There are always winners and losers, either actual or perceived, which, for most people, amount to the same thing.

My group was charged with developing a logo and corporate identity for the new corporation, Carondelet Health Services. My personal experience with branding at this time was zilch. We also were not flush with cash, being a not-for-profit Catholic hospital group, so our in-house designer, Sister Rosalynn Russell, used the letters *C, H,* and *S* and superimposed a hand-drawn, stylized fleur-de-lis, the symbol of the order, which had originated in France. We selected a simple gray stock for the letterhead, made some mock-ups of business cards and such, and presented our materials to the board.

This was my first ever presentation to a board of any kind. My team and I sat along the wall in the peanut gallery as the directors discussed the graphics. What ensued astounded me. To my surprise, the conversation went on for more than an hour. Every minute detail was evaluated. Was gray the right color? Should St. Mary's and St. Joseph's keep their own logos? What about the treasured history of St. Mary's as the state's first hospital? At one point, the assembled leaders of Carondelet Health Services passed around the Pantone ink sample book, evaluating shades of blue. The only question I was asked concerned the cost and time frame for implementation, which, by most standards, was pretty small.

Looking back on my young self, new to this kind of logo mania, I am sure I was a tad unfair, because I thought the whole thing was a colossal waste of time and money. That a group of people whose salaries exceeded mine by a multiple of ten or twenty would delve into such trivia was something I had not witnessed before. Since then, I have seen it too many times to count.

Finally, the group agreed on a black CHS fleur-de-lis logo and a shade of gray for the paper stock. St. Mary's and St. Joseph's were allowed to keep their individual logos and colors.

Naturally, chaos followed. Which logo went where? When was it CHS and when wasn't it? What evolved without any formal guidelines was the use of CHS for corporate staff and, at this time, I learned about the deep-seated emotions concerning logos and corporate identity. My CHS colleagues and I were corporate. We were suits. We were unnecessary overhead. We wore gray name tags with black lettering emblazoned on them. The hospital people called us "gray badgers." My staff began putting their name tags in their pockets or purses whenever they visited one of the hospitals to avoid the glares and snubs.

It's been a long time and I am sure that all this has been worked out many times over at Carondelet. I learned that the idea of identity was real and charged with potent forces. At every health-care facility I've worked with since then, these issues were always front and center. Since the trend throughout my career has been hospitals becoming systems, each company struggled with legacy logos, inconsistent branding, vocal opponents of change, and equally vocal advocates for the necessity of change.

In the mid-1990s and early 2000s, Mayo Clinic faced a multitude of these conflicts, large and small. As the brand committee and brand team implemented the branding standards, it wasn't long before the logo issue reared its ugly, dangerous head.

The Mayo Clinic logo is three shields with the words "Mayo Clinic" either stacked above the shields or strung alongside. The official Mayo color is a particular PMS shade we dubbed "Mayo Clinic Blue." In the 1990s, the logo had the word "Mayo" (not Mayo *Clinic*!) above the shields, all in lower case, as was fashionable in the 1970s. Many of us wanted to replace this logo with something more contemporary and reflective of the institution Mayo Clinic had become. The symbol was dated, awkward to use, and did not translate well to the emerging digital communications media. Furthermore, although the words "Mayo Clinic" were widely known, our studies showed that the public did not recognize the three shields as the institution's logo and had no idea what they represented. Since the Clinic had done almost no advertising, the logo was rarely seen outside of the campuses of the three clinics, so the logo had made no impression on people's minds.

Even more compelling to those of us in the branding world was the reality that Mayo had used at least ten different logos in its long history. No one even knew for certain how or why the three-shield logo was developed, or by whom. My colleagues in the division of systems and procedures, who oversaw printing and graphics, did extensive research into the logo history and found:

> *According to oral tradition and some documents in the Mayo Clinic Archive, the inspiration may have occurred at a social gathering. It seems that sometime in the early 1970s, Dr. Brian and Sonja Dawson hosted a party in their home. Dr. Dawson was of English ancestry, like the Mayo family, and guests admired the academic insignia on display. The suggestion arose that Mayo Clinic should have a similar crest or coat of arms. Someone—accounts vary—apparently sketched a design on a cocktail napkin. Unfortunately, that napkin has not survived! It is interesting to note that an early concept for the tri-partite design focused on William Worrall Mayo, M.D., and his sons, William James Mayo, M.D., and Charles Horace, M.D., rather than on the three activities of Mayo Clinic. Just how the napkin design found its way into the Mayo Clinic committee system is not clear, but in 1973, the shield design was approved as a symbol of the institution—first as a single shield with three sections, which soon evolved into three separate shields linked together.*

For the brand team, all of this added up to a case for change. When we broached the subject with senior leadership, we were summarily disabused of that notion. The logo had by 1995 become "sacred." The three shields stood for the brothers and their father; for patient care, education, and research; and now even the three Mayo Clinics. It could not be replaced, any more than you could put a miniskirt on the Statue of Liberty. After some discussion we did get approval to modernize the symbol and have it redrawn professionally. The lines were thickened and the shields made proportionate, and the words Mayo Clinic were typeset in capital letters. The Mayo blue PMS color was "codified" and a handsomely printed manual of approved colors, logo types, typefaces, graphics styles and other matters was distributed throughout the organization. Now a similar manual is posted online.

This didn't stop what seems to be the inbred human desire to distort, adulterate, mutilate, and otherwise deface the logo they ostensibly revere. During my time at Mayo Clinic we had requests to put the logo on a hot air balloon, on bike helmets, in multiple colors as long as it wasn't blue, and animated in videos with varying degrees of manipulation and "dazzling" digital effects. The medical school students made shirts with a version no one had ever seen, as did other departments until word got out that a committee had to review all such materials. We would remind these creative proponents of the dictum adopted by the executive committee, "thou shalt not trivialize the Mayo Clinic brand." While this would restrain the production of rogue materials, many resented having their imagination and individual creativity suppressed, especially the in-house graphic artists, who were given a design grid with strict instructions on what could and could not be published.

Another aspect of the logo standardization that made us few friends was the ban on outside companies creating Mayo Clinic materials without our consent. One can go on eBay and still find Mayo Clinic ashtrays, Mayo Clinic shot glasses, and other similarly inappropriate paraphernalia. Letters went out to vendors and merchants telling them these products had to be withdrawn. Again, most vendors complied with little fuss, and the Clinic did give them help in acquiring the approved materials.

At first the logo battles arose on a daily basis. One by one the various business entities were brought into compliance—a word they all hated, by the way. Naming conventions were adopted across the organization, along with graphic standards and, later, digital media guidelines. Most names included the words Mayo Clinic, contrary to previous practice, with the Mayo Clinic name and shields prominent as the master brand, and the other entities named alongside, endorsed by the master brand. For fund-raising, a manual was prepared in collaboration with the development department to ensure that the Mayo Clinic name featured prominently in any naming opportunities. Additionally, any research papers published by Mayo Clinic would always place the Mayo Clinic name first, and then the name of the business entity or clinical department responsible for the research. The effect of this was to prevent something being published that would read, hypothetically, "The Tom Jones Research Center has developed a cure for Alzheimer's disease," when, yes, the research had been funded by Jones, hence the center's name, but the research was actually conducted at the research facilities of Mayo Clinic in Jacksonville. So, the news release, and the citation, of such developments always listed Mayo Clinic first, and, emphatically, not Mayo Foundation, Mayo Medical School, Mayo Cancer Center, and so on.

ONE BIG HAPPY

The two most contentious and longest holdouts were first, the two Clinics in Arizona and Florida and, second, the two hospitals in Rochester. These entities used logos, graphic standards, and other branding practices that indeed seemed sacred to them, although no apparent business logic suggested their importance, nor could any alternative logic persuade them of the importance of using the developing Mayo Clinic enterprise-wide standards. They would base their arguments on their individual histories, on presumed consumer awareness, and on supposed harm to the business performance if anything were changed. Consumer research conducted over this time period effectively nullified each of these arguments. Consumers didn't know or didn't care that Arizona used an earth-tone palette or that Florida used a tropical one. What consumers cared about universally was that they were going to Mayo Clinic and, by extension, would have been most comforted knowing that Arizona and

Florida were one and the same with Rochester, although separated geographically. As is so often the case, the resistance seemed based more on ego and a stubborn desire for autonomy from the mother ship than any solid business proposition. One could argue the steadfast retention of historical symbols and practices was actually counterproductive.

Eventually, as the tide of reintegration swept across Mayo Clinic in the early and mid-2000s, leadership, more or less, demanded that the two newer Clinics adopt the Mayo Clinic enterprise standards so as to present one, whole, fully integrated multistate presence to the public. I am not aware of a single negative consequence of this move, nor of any concerns from the consumer about the transition. Both newer Clinics continued to draw patients—in fact, even more than before.

As for the Rochester hospitals, the issue was complicated by two seemingly insurmountable obstacles. One, the multimillion-dollar way-finding system across the sprawling campus of Mayo Clinic in Rochester used the names Saint Marys Hospital and Rochester Methodist Hospital, even after the stone signs were changed from Mayo Medical Center to Mayo Clinic. Second, when Mayo Clinic officially acquired Saint Marys Hospital from the diocese in 1986, they agreed contractually to maintain the hospital's catholicity. As mentioned earlier, these names actually increased confusion among patients, who frequently asked if the hospitals were part of Mayo Clinic or not. The nomenclature also confused journalists, who often reported that such and such famous person was being treated at Saint Marys Hospital in Rochester Minnesota, without a single mention in the news item of Mayo Clinic. Other issues concerned reporting of quality measures, in-house equipment, and a number of other items that would cause the two hospitals to be listed individually on various reports and rankings, even though the way Mayo Clinic practiced medicine belied the hospitals' individuality. The truth is that the two hospitals are fully integrated into the entire practice in such a way that one could almost say the Mayo Clinic had a "department of inpatient services" that functioned within the entire medical practice. Since this model was so unique and counterintuitive to just about everyone outside of Mayo Clinic, the names simply worked in reverse benefit and seemed to signify that Mayo Clinic had two separate hospitals in Rochester. These lost opportunities troubled many of us, and we began looking for solutions. This took a number of years, since the mechanisms of negotiating change, slow moving enough at Mayo Clinic, are even slower in the Catholic Church.

As awareness grew of the unintended consequences of presenting a nonstandardized identity to the world, a tipping point came one year when National Instiues of Health (NIH) published its annual list of institutions receiving research grants. There was Johns Hopkins at the top of the list, as they were almost every year, followed by other major medical centers. Mayo Clinic was listed, to be sure, but so were Mayo Clinic Rochester, Mayo Clinic Arizona, Mayo Clinic Scottsdale, Mayo Foundation, Mayo Cancer Center, Mayo Medical School, and, if memory serves, either one or both of the two Rochester Hospitals. Had all of these entities applied for grants under the name Mayo Clinic, the institution would have placed in the top five of grant-receiving institutions. As the research department made clear, the fragmented reporting obfuscated the size and scope of Mayo's major research commitment, putting future funding at risk and, by the way, making it appear as if the University of Minnesota was the state's premier medical research engine, which wasn't accurate by any measure.

As mentioned, the 2000s saw a resurgence of the internal force to integrate across the Mayo Clinic enterprise. Successive CEOs, CAOs, and other leaders developed mechanisms to integrate shared services, prioritize, and approve capital projects as one entity rather than many, and engendered cross-pollination of staff among the three clinics and the burgeoning Mayo Health System to foster collegiality, familiarity, and spread the Mayo culture through mentorships and partnerships. Probably the most significant cultural change was the creation of a clinical practice committee (CPC) for oversight of medical practice throughout the enterprise. At Mayo, the CPC is the most powerful and important internal governing body after the board of governors. When I started at Mayo Clinic, each of the three sites had its own CPC. As reintegration progressed, a clinical practice group was established that met quarterly to exchange ideas and "get to know one another." This baby step evolved into a CPC that eventually had other CPCs reporting to it. Successive medical chairs of the CPC played pivotal roles in leading the now $10 billion entity known as Mayo Clinic from being a family practice in Rochester, to a somewhat fragmented yet successful collection of practices and other entities and, ultimately, into a worldwide integrated provider delivering the same brand promise across multiple states and products.

Integrating clinical services is the most significant and most difficult of the changes necessary to truly deliver on the brand promise of a fully integrated system. Even at Mayo Clinic, where integration and consensus decision making are as natural as breathing, various groups, particularly medical department leaders, resisted this change. For many good reasons, physicians are acculturated to be autonomous, to think for themselves, and take the consequences if necessary. Although Mayo physicians share those characteristics, they are a bit muted by the desire to perpetuate a system of interdependence and shared knowledge—the classic learning organization—that has proven adept at meeting patient needs in a superior way. It took years, and courageous leadership on the part of the CEOs and a number of other top leaders, to bring the medical staff leadership of the three Clinics together and insist they develop structures to facilitate and enhance a permanent mode of behavior to create, say, not three departments of cardiology but one, or one department of neurology, and so on. Anyone can imagine the political fallout from this development, yet, after a number of years of small steps, Mayo began creating specialty councils that were led by one of the three department chairs (or more if the health system participated), and became responsible for joint planning, budgeting, and decision making about practices, procedures, and capital procurement. I am not familiar with too many other institutions that have pulled this off, especially an institution that has the consensus-style governance of Mayo Clinic, which sometimes requires years of persuasion, negotiation, and the occasional executive push to bring major initiatives about. I am personally convinced that this type of medical integration is the cornerstone of being a truly integrated system. Many systems say they are but, in truth, they are merely amalgams of separate institutions, with perhaps some central oversight of budget or human resources practices. Truly, though, I cannot understand how a system can call itself integrated if its physicians each practice in different ways at different institutions, rather than working together to develop the highest standards for all.

How brand research motivated, instigated, or validated this activity is impossible to quantify. Having been present at the creation, I know that all the data analysis, presentations, and conversations we had at leadership groups for twenty years about consumer expectations, frustrations, and hopes for the future of health care played a major part in bringing the institution to a realization of the true meaning of integration. Ironically, this true meaning resembled, in no small way, the original integration practiced in Rochester when the Clinic was a small cadre of excellent physicians, other caregivers, and their families working together and socializing together in that remote snowy town on the northern plains in the first part of the 20th century. When I think of the isolation of the place and relative obscurity of the location—except for its name—and the mythology that grew up around the Mayo method of practice, it reminds me of a medical Manhattan Project, with thousands of people laboring together to perfect the art and science of health care and its delivery, while the rest of the country proceeded down a quite different path, to the anarchic and troubled system we have today.

I witnessed Mayo Clinic emerge from a chaotic time of reinventing itself to a new self-awareness of Mayo Clinic as a national and international presence and force. Branding became more than naming—it became the process for understanding, meeting, and exceeding consumer expectations and it pointed the way for the strategic path Mayo Clinic needed to take to anticipate and innovate in order to meet the needs of patients and families as they manifested themselves in years to come. Branding as an essential aspect of strategic planning, decision making, and operational implementation had arrived.

With this as a backdrop, essential clarifying decisions were made. The three clinics would be known collectively as Mayo Clinic. The name of the legal corporate parent was amended to read Mayo Foundation for Medical Education and Research, doing business as Mayo Clinic. When referred to individually, the clinics were Mayo Clinic in Arizona, Mayo Clinic in Florida, and Mayo Clinic in Minnesota. Entities that had previously dropped the word "clinic" from their names dropped it back in. Grant proposals were to be submitted by Mayo Clinic. Finally, the words "Mayo Clinic" would be placed in front of the hospital names (in Saint Marys case, with the approval of the Bishop) and the two areas around the hospitals would be called Saint Marys campus and Rochester Methodist campus.

I knew we had made major strides on the day we were able to change the graphic elements of the pages of MayoClinic.org to the standard Mayo blue. We were a long way from the days of the fragmented institutions of the previous decades, although there was still much to be done in other areas of branding and operations.

CHAPTER 6

THE MEDIUM IS
THE MESSAGE
IS THE BRAND

LESSONS IN CULTURE

In 1993, Bill and Hillary Clinton launched their ultimately fruitless attempt to reengineer the American health-care system. Although President Clinton mentioned Mayo Clinic in a State of the Union speech as a model for the nation, just as President Obama did twenty years later, many Mayo Clinic leaders were deeply skeptical of what they knew of the plan and harbored grave concerns that the proposed arrangements could easily place Mayo Clinic out of network for patients within the borders of whatever administrative districts were developed. My media and marketing team knew all this, yet we couldn't suppress our happiness that Mayo Clinic was getting that level of national attention.

Not everyone shared in the glee. Some months before, I had a conversation with Bob Smoldt, a very influential leader and, at the time, the chair of the department of planning and public affairs, who spent a great deal of time working with state and federal government officials and other policy makers. He and the CEO at that time, Dr. Robert Waller, had been participants in the now-historic Jackson Hole Group that many say was the birthplace of managed care. To be sure, Mayo Clinic leaders did not support the manner in which managed care was ultimately implemented. A bedrock of Mayo Clinic's approach to health care is patient choice and, as we all came to see, managed care practitioners gained reputations as gatekeepers who limited access and choice. Typical of Mayo, though, was the sense of obligation to be part of a group as important and potentially influential as the Jackson Hole project, so as to speak on behalf of the provider, the Mayo Clinic model of care, and, most importantly, on behalf of a patient's right to choose the doctors she needed when she needed them. In later years, even Paul Ellefson disowned what managed care had become, expressing his extreme disappointment in an op-ed in *The New York Times*.

As I got to know more about Mayo Clinic's delivery system and model of care and became more familiar with Bob Smoldt and Dr. Waller, I came to a couple of conclusions: (a) Mayo Clinic was a model of health-care delivery and efficacy that the nation should adopt and (b) Dr. Waller and Bob Smoldt knew more about health-care policy and delivery systems than anyone else I'd ever met, heard of, or read about.

So, one day, Bob and I were walking to a meeting through the crowded underground pedestrian walkways that Mayo calls subways. I'm six feet tall, but Bob is taller, leaner, and lankier—a guy from Grundy Center, Iowa, with an aw-shucks country demeanor that belies a seriously astute mind and an erudition that clarifies any conversation in the rare moments when he chooses to speak his mind. As I double-timed my steps to keep up with his loping stride, I blurted out that I thought Mayo Clinic *should* present itself as a model for the country. Bob turned to me and smiled and actually slowed down a bit.

He rarely gave a flat-out yes-or-no answer but, this time, he said, "No, that would not be a good idea. People will say we're doing it for self-serving reasons. We've been told many times in conversations with government leaders or other providers that the Mayo Clinic model would never work in their state or their hospital. Salaried physicians, integrated records, being physician led, asking physicians to do patient care and research and education—not all providers want that, and they think it will cost too much. They think we're expensive, even though all the studies show that, in the long run, we aren't. We learned many years ago that it's best if we let others present Mayo Clinic as a model. It doesn't work if we do it. It's just not who we are."

As the debates wore on about the Clinton health-care plan, Bob and Dr. Waller worked quietly through Mayo's government relations staff to influence the process when possible. They kept such a low profile that some Mayo staff wondered if they were doing anything to prevent what many of them saw as the looming Clinton health-care catastrophe. Mind you, with more than three thousand physicians on staff, Mayo has individuals of just about every political persuasion, even some who would endorse national health care *a la* Britain or France. The official Mayo stance, though, is that all Americans should be covered, but not by a single payer and certainly not by the government, which manages Medicare.

At any rate, Bob had given me a valuable lesson in Mayo Clinic's innate humility, which, as I have said before, can be seen by outsiders as aloof or even arrogant.

The reform debate came to a head for me one day when Bob called me to say that Hillary Clinton wanted to come to Mayo Clinic and host a live television program from our auditorium about the need for health-care reform. This was to be part of a national barnstorming campaign the First Lady was embarking upon to drum up support for reform. Bob, Dr. Waller, and the other board members huddled over this invitation in the "executive suite," on the eleventh floor of the Mayo Building for a couple of days. My then direct supervisor told me they weren't sure how to handle the request. Many Mayo leaders, at that time, were quietly opposed to the Clinton plan. There may have been more than one Republican on the board, although I don't know for sure. People at Mayo rarely discussed personal politics. My boss did not like the idea of Mayo Clinic being used for political purposes, regardless of the issue, and was hoping we would politely decline. Perhaps the University of Minnesota would be a better venue. As it was, Mayo had a standing policy never to allow its facilities to be used for political gatherings. Rochester being the small city that it was, Mayo Clinic had, by far, the best facilities for such meetings and we received frequent requests. The policy was ecumenical and consistently applied, regardless of the worthiness of the cause. Besides, Mayo Clinic was (and is) a not-for-profit foundation. Any action that implied Mayo Clinic was taking one side or the other in a political debate could be harmful to that important status. Not to mention, Mayo Clinic had substantial benefactors who had close ties with one or the other political party. The board of trustees was populated with both prominent Democrats and Republicans, people like Barbara Bush and Tom Daschle. This was done as a matter of policy for fairness and balance of opinion.

Obviously, the request from the First Lady was supercharged with conflicting internal political tensions. As News Bureau director, although aware of these machinations at the highest levels, I was more concerned about how we would pull off this production with what looked to be about three weeks' notice, according to the schedule we received from Mrs. Clinton's aides. This effort would fall on the shoulders of my entire team, as well as our colleagues in media production, printing, audio-visual, facilities, and other departments. Producing an hour-long program with patients, families, policy experts, video lead-ins, PowerPoints, and all the other accoutrements in a professional manner would be a mammoth effort for us. Maybe CBS News could do it in a couple of weeks, but that's their main job. We're a medical center, not a TV studio.

Let me give you a sense of how Mayo Clinic handles such matters. A few years before, when I was as new as I could be at Mayo Clinic, I received a call from a prominent reporter at *The New York Times*. This person had broken the story about the excessive salaries and perks given to the leaders of the United Way at that time. Now he was investigating the salaries of the CEOs of other prominent not-for-profits, including Dr. Waller's. I told the reporter I'd get back to him and went next door to my supervisor. I asked him what I should do. He said, nonchalantly, "Just give Bob [i.e., Dr. Waller] a call and ask him." Frankly, I was a bit stunned. It was like he had said, "Just call the President of the United States and ask him." At many hospitals where I have worked, the CEO is remote, hard to reach, often protected by the administrative assistant, not just from outside callers but from internal people as well. One boss I had gave his subordinates explicit instructions not to contact the CEO without going through him, a corporate vice president, first.

Here I was, at the world-famous Mayo Clinic, and I was just going to call up the leader of one of the greatest institutions on earth and just say, "Hi." I'd never even met him. "How do I do that?" I asked my boss, rather stupidly.

"Use this number. It's his pager. We have direct-dial pagers. You dial this number, he picks up, and you're connected."

Dr. Waller was a legend by the time I'd gotten to Mayo. He'd been president and CEO for years. He was tall, white-haired, extremely dignified, a complete gentleman in everything he did. He spoke with a careful, slightly southern accent that made him seem Lincolnesque. He was universally respected, both as an ophthalmic surgeon and as a leader. He had led what was known as the diversification committee back in the 1970s and 1980s that led to all the innovations mentioned in previous chapters.

I picked up my phone, took a breath, and dialed his number. I still remember it; I called it so many times afterward. Within seconds, I heard, "This is Bob Waller."

"Hi, Dr. Waller. This is John La Forgia, the new director of the News Bureau. I have something I need to ask you.

"Well, yes. Hello, John. I've heard good things about you from Bob Smoldt. How can I help you today?"

I gave him the lowdown on *The New York Times* inquiry, the background about the United Way angle, and then I asked him what he wanted to do.

I waited for a second. Then he said, "John, what do *you* think we should do?"

His simple question spoke volumes to me about the kind of man he was and the kind of place Mayo Clinic was. I didn't hear his question as a test of me, or as an executive practicing some feeble tenet from Management 101. What I heard was a sincere request for my opinion, my "expert" opinion. I answered by saying we should give the reporter the information he sought, since I was confident that Dr. Waller's salary would appear reasonable and appropriate in and of itself, and especially when compared to other nonprofit CEO salaries.

Dr. Waller listened carefully, then said, "Well, John, let's do exactly that."

One of my colleagues calls these "Mayo moments." Something happens at a meeting or you see a Mayo staff person helping a family in the subway, and you experience the Mayo history and culture of respect and service in a gesture or an exchange, and you feel like there couldn't be a better place to work or better people to work for, and it's all for the people we serve.

During my time at Mayo, I found the culture of integrity and accountability most visibly on display during times of issues management and crisis communication. The leadership never threw the problem back at the "PR flack." Everyone with a stake in the issue or the crisis came together, instantly, worked together tirelessly to do the right thing by Mayo and by the patient, time and again. First, as the chief Mayo spokesperson, then also as the brand chief, and finally when I was responsible for all of Mayo's public profile, I was never made to feel I was hanging out there alone, only one slipup away from losing the best job I ever had. On the contrary, even when I made mistakes—which happened a few times, let's be honest—my superiors used these as moments to counsel me, not berate or threaten me. We were all there to help each other be better.

The Hillary Clinton program was not the main focus of my energies in 1993 until the day I got an unexpected phone call from Bob Smoldt. Usually, his phone demeanor was rather jovial; he would joke around for a minute or so, asking me how I liked the latest Vince Gill CD, knowing full well I didn't much like country music. Another of Bob's phone personae, though, is a more serious, controlled, even slightly conspiratorial tone, as if he were calling you from Langley and the head of the CIA was sitting next to him, so he had to choose his words carefully and speak in a hushed tone. When I picked up the receiver, serious Bob said, "Say, John, could you come up to Mayo Eleven and stop in at Dr. Waller's office? We'd like to visit for a while about this Hillary Clinton program."

"Sure, Bob. When do you need me?"

"Oh, right now would be good." Click.

As I walked across the campus and rode up the elevator of the Mayo building, I wondered what they wanted with me. I wasn't in trouble—I hadn't spoken with anyone about this program except to say what a lot of work it would be. I figured they were going to tell me what they'd decided and either have me write a diplomatic letter explaining why we couldn't participate or tell me we were going to do it and "Here's what we need from you and your team." I knocked on the door, prepared for either outcome.

Even though I'd been at Mayo for two years, this was my first meeting in the president's office. Dr. Waller's office was neither large nor ornate. Basically, he had the same style office with the same simple furniture and decorations as any other Mayo Clinic executive. As I stepped into the room, the area seemed shadowy—very film noir. I glanced around and saw Dr. Waller, Bob Smoldt, and eight or nine of the highest physician leaders—I assumed mostly board members—all in dark suits, white shirts, dark ties, staring at me with serious expressions. Four of them were squeezed shoulder-to-shoulder on a small sofa, the rest in chairs pulled into an arc at the center of which they seated me—the hot seat, facing the jury. Dr. Waller spoke, saying they'd been having trouble deciding how to handle Mrs. Clinton's invitation for all the reasons mentioned earlier. Then he said, "What do you think we should do?"

That was not the question I was expecting. Although I was surprised, I was even more surprised when I realized I knew exactly what I wanted to say. I composed myself for a few seconds, then said, "Dr. Waller, I think we should do this. The debate is far from over, and we don't know the outcome. If the plan fails, fine. We all go back to square one. But if it succeeds, then I have to think it would be a very bad thing for us if we have insulted the First Lady of the United States by refusing to let her come to Mayo Clinic for this broadcast. From what I've learned of the program itself, I don't see how it can hurt us. Besides, we'll get some national attention and maybe, while she's here, you and Bob and some others can meet with her about reform."

Bob said, "Say, that would be good if we could have a meeting with her. I like that approach."

The others didn't say much, Dr. Waller thanked me, and I left. Oddly, I didn't feel I'd just killed my career or anything like that. In fact, I felt that I had done my job and the board would do what it would do.

Shortly thereafter, word came down that the board had approved participation in the First Lady's road show and wanted me to be the project manager for the program. I was relieved and also a bit happy, since I sincerely believed it was the right decision for Mayo Clinic. My colleagues in the News Bureau rose to the occasion splendidly, as they always did. Nothing is better for a media relations team than a high-profile "crisis" with an impossible deadline.

We did what any similar team does with a major project—we assigned areas of responsibility to each of the staff, we worked late nights and weekends, we stressed and debated, and we forged ahead over all obstacles.

My group at Mayo Clinic went on to handle innumerable crises, both positive and negative, and, as far as I was concerned, they became the best crisis and issues management group in the country. I always look back on the Hillary Clinton episode as the time when the team came together.

It's been a long time since I read Goethe's *Faust*. Some don't realize that Goethe's version of the story doesn't stop with Faust's damnation but continues into a second book in which Faust atones for his sins by becoming a benevolent leader. One passage describes a community threatened on all sides by flooding. The citizenry must work together at all times to keep the waters at bay. They are happy. They share purposeful work and they must rely each upon the other or they will perish.

It's not a stretch to say that this consciousness propels Mayo Clinic. Everyone treasures this unique institution and is devoted to its perpetuity. The News Bureau group thrived on those moments when we were in the center of it all, working together to help Mayo Clinic survive a crisis or manage a major public event.

Given the board's initial reluctance to do the program, we all felt a bit of responsibility to make sure the show went well and that no harm came to Mayo Clinic because of it. I have to stress, though, that this motivation was internally generated—that is, no one, not Dr. Waller, Bob Smoldt, or anyone else ever said anything to imply that we or I would be toast if Mayo Clinic was somehow tainted by this event. We had all made the decision together and we all shared the responsibility.

By contrast, when I held a previous position at a different institution, an issue arose that demanded the CEO's attention, at least in my judgment. I didn't know the man well, being somewhat new, and he epitomized the distant executive who spent all his time with donors and board members. I called him and explained the situation and he literally said to me, "You're the PR guy. You handle it." I did, but I never lost the bitter taste in my mouth from that brief insulting exchange. When I incorporated that moment into many other aspects of the institution I was working for, it all came together, so to speak, as to the place's dysfunction.

Again, the level of shared accountability at Mayo Clinic is unique, in my experience, and is one of the primary reasons for its legendary success. Just about every company will claim to operate based on values such as mutual respect and teamwork. In the nonprofit world, at least, CEO's love to say that their employees are a family. When push comes to shove, though, these value statements fade as though written with invisible ink. Something goes wrong and people are blamed and scapegoated and made to pay. Am I saying Mayo Clinic never fires anyone? Of course not, but only when it is absolutely necessary and only after due process occurs, often taking a number of months. In such an environment, people are not fueled by fear—they are inspired.

I'm sure it's clear, by now, that the program went off without a hitch, although my memory may have glossed over anything too painful. Years later, one of my staff unearthed a photograph of me talking with Chris Gade—at the time, a young man in his twenties—now a father of two and still rising to new heights at Mayo Clinic. Chris is one of the most productive and capable people I've ever known, and he may be one of the few people on the planet more intense than I am. In the photograph, we are both looking at each other, intensely, as if we were planning an invasion or the safe return of Apollo 13.

We had spent quite a bit of energy preparing for a media onslaught. To be sure, about thirty media showed up, but it was rather anticlimactic, considering we'd expected about a hundred or so. I still remember the woman from Clinton's camp assigned to manage the media representatives. We had laid out a buffet to feed the group before the airtime. Shortly before zero hour, this staffer, a petite person, stood up on a table and shouted, "All right, listen up. All of you come over here and let me tell you how it's gonna work." From there, she yelled out the rules of engagement like a drill sergeant hammering at new recruits. My group was astounded, since the "Mayo way" was to be polite, respectful, nice, even to journalists.

I spent a lot of time with an aide named Andrew who had worked on the Clinton presidential campaign. He told me stories of President-elect Clinton reading him drafts of his first inaugural speech in their hotel suite. Later, he got a job at the US Commerce Department compiling media briefings for the secretary, which meant his day started at 4 a.m. I learned this was typical of these young staffers to presidents or members of congress. They kept inhuman hours and schedules that could only be termed chaotic, 24/7. With an event like this, my group would live that life for a month or so, and we would find it exciting and meaningful but, ultimately, exhausting. After the "crisis" passed, we'd have a respite, of sorts, getting back to our normal fast-paced routine. These government staffers lived that life every day of their jobs, and I admired them for their dedication. Over the years, as Mayo Clinic grew more and more famous, and larger, and present in more and more states and business categories, we would look back on the 1990s as a halcyon era of relative peace. In the twenty-first century, we seemed to be handling a crisis of a more or less serious nature almost daily.

Finally, the big show was broadcast. My staff and I stood at the rear of the auditorium, watching the show and stealthily drifting back and forth between the program and the food next door. We were winding down and, since we'd produced most of the program, it held little surprise for us. As the hour wore on, we knew we were in the clear. Nothing controversial was said that could taint Mayo Clinic in any way. Mayo Clinic's senior leadership had their meeting with Mrs. Clinton and her staff. Tomorrow, it would all be in the past.

As the crew struck the set, people filed out of the hall in orderly fashion, per Secret Service's direction. I walked up to the edge of the stage and saw Mrs. Clinton greeting the audience members. In situations with celebrities, I usually keep a respectful distance. I always imagine the level to which these public individuals must be besieged by people who want to invade their space, shake their hands—touch the hem of their garments, so to speak. As they filed past, I watched the line weave past her and then, abruptly, she was standing alone. She said to me, "Don't you want to shake my hand?" Of course, I was happy to shake the First Lady's hand and we chatted briefly about the program. I told her who I was and what my position at Mayo was and she expressed her gratitude. Even in our brief encounter, she struck me as a smart and confident woman who was quite earnest about trying to improve the American health-care system.

Later, my group gathered at a Rochester restaurant for a strike party. We had a couple of drinks and congratulated ourselves. We also made a few jokes about how the level of work we put into the production did not result in an equal level of national coverage as we had hoped. In my mind, though, that was secondary, even tertiary. Mayo Clinic had come out of it all just as nonpartisan and pristine as it had been before all the hubbub. My other source of pride was in my staff's handling of the situation and how the whole event had drawn everyone closer, in a manner that had not quite manifested itself in the previous two years. We had become a team, and I was confident we could do amazing things in the coming years.

A few days later, I received an interoffice envelope that I could see had come from Dr. Waller's office. When I opened it, a white piece of his personal stationery slipped out. He had handwritten a thank-you note to me that read, in part, that Dr. Waller was not only grateful for my hard work and expertise but for my *judgment*. To this day, more than twenty years later, this is the most treasured item of recognition I have ever received, more meaningful to me than awards from professional societies or gifts for lasting twenty years with the same company or even, on an emotional level, the promotions and raises I received over the years. Dr. Waller's note was a model of how a leader should recognize an employee. It was short, it was personal, and it was specific. For the rest of my life, I would remember that a man as respected and admired as Dr. Robert Waller, CEO of Mayo Clinic, had valued me for my *judgment*. With that letter in my hands, I felt I had finally arrived at Mayo Clinic.

BEING THE BRAND

There are many ways to manage the message a company sends out to its constituents. Those of us in health-care marketing are asked almost daily to write a speech, compose a media statement, draft a news release touting some internal achievement, or post something on the Web on behalf of a physician or some other service provider. Most of the time, these proponents come forward with the expectation that the outside world has been waiting in keen anticipation for their news of the latest internal promotion or department reorganization. "Theresa Holbein, formerly head of Medicaid accounts receivable, has been made project manager of Ricardo Hospital's conversion to ICD-10." This is not news for the world. It is important to a few people inside the organization and a few outside the organization. This is not messaging about the organization in a meaningful way to customers. Often, senior leaders have pet projects or even serious interests in one health cause or another and expect the marketing and media staff to "get something going" on the subject to "tell people what we're doing."

In moderation, these "little" projects may seem justified. After all, we are helping the community, we are building our brand (maybe). I have done my fair share of health fairs and runs and walks and the like. What I've learned over the years is that, for most hospitals, even Mayo Clinic when I first got there, these events and messages and the expectations surrounding them were random, subjective, and fragmented, since they floated in an anarchic space without the benefit of any connection to a comprehensive understanding of the institution's brand, positioning, and true differentiation. Therefore, all the effort and expense were generally ineffective, a waste of time and money that could have been put to better purposes.

My deduction, after more than thirty-five years, is that the behavior of every employee, but in particular the leadership in setting the tone and parameters of that behavior, is more important than any focus-grouped statement or Clio-winning TV spot. Behavior creates the experience of the patient or the customer in a meaningful, lasting, usually emotional way that the patient never forgets. The type of culturally consistent behavior I'm talking about doesn't simply arise out of the goodness of people's hearts. At Mayo, it is purposefully managed every day. Now that Mayo Clinic is more than 150 years old, the culture, in many ways, propagates itself and new staff learn much from osmosis and mentorship. All the same, Mayo has grown tremendously in the past twenty-five years and cultural management has become more important than ever. It can be a rocky and, sometimes, humorous journey.

One day during my first year at Mayo Clinic, long before we had a brand management program, a beloved, somewhat whimsical staff physician asked me and my team to help him organize and promote something called "Be-Bop Day." *Be-Bop Day?* I soon learned that the city government was hoping to encourage Rochester commuters to walk, ride a bus, or carpool to work. The Be-Bop Day event would consist of the mayor, Dr. Waller, and a few dozen other Mayo and civic dignitaries donning bike helmets and be-bopping to work *en masse*. Our physician sponsor also requested that we purchase blue helmets for the riders and have the Mayo Clinic logo painted on them.

Now, on the face of it, this was a worthy cause. Mayo Clinic occupies most of downtown and, every day, thirty thousand people from the region report to work, making parking a rapidly diminishing asset. Even though Mayo Clinic has built surface lots and ramps, the average employee, as of my retirement date a few years ago, was waiting twelve years for an on-campus parking space. Mayo also subsidizes bus passes, provides shuttle transportation to and from more distant parking areas, and makes many other attempts to help solve the congestion problem.

So Be-Bop Day was for a worthy cause. My team and I were a bit perplexed, though, wondering how this type of event fit into any kind of context about what Mayo Clinic was, is, or wanted to be. Recall that, on my first day on the job at Mayo, the first question my staff asked me at our first meeting was "What are our priorities?" A staff that was fielding requests from *The New York Times*, CBS Evening News, *60 Minutes*, not to mention dozens of other media around the world, was going to be diverted to arrange and participate in Rochester's landmark Be-Bop Day.

Mayo Clinic may be a large and successful organization, but the management is just as careful about adding full-time employees as any other company. In other words, it wasn't as easy as it may seem for me to ask for "an extra person" to handle all the Be-Bop Days or Heart Runs or whatever else of that ilk might cross the marketing path each year. A book called *Chase's Calendar of Events* shows that every day, week, and month of the year is designated as a special period of recognition for something in health care—hospital week, nurses' week, doctors week, breast cancer month, lab tech day, boss's day, among many others. If my department fulfilled all of the requests for support for all these recognitions, they would do nothing but that, year after year. This is marketing?

Although Be-Bop Day raised these questions in some minds, we had little chance to stop it. Dr. Waller had given his okay, and he was not one to go back on his word. We made the posters and the flyers and placed the stories in the employee newsletter and wrote the media advisory inviting the media to watch us all ride our bikes to work. Around 7 a.m. on a chilly spring morning, about twenty of us gathered with our bicycles and our helmets and rode five blocks along Fourth Street to a parking spot for our vehicles, with the media taping and photographing along the way. The sponsoring physician had managed to persuade someone in the graphics section to affix a Mayo logo to his helmet, even though we'd asked him not to do that. In our minds, it trivialized the brand, even though that particular brand rule ("Thou shalt not trivialize the Mayo brand") had not yet been promulgated.

We glided downhill, all smiles and laughter, then locked up our bicycles and went to work. I doubt that Be-Bop Day made much of an impression besides letting people watch the exceptionally dignified Dr. Waller ride his bike to work.

Our staff soon forgot Be-Bop Day ever happened until the following spring. The city wanted to conduct "Son of Be-Bop." We drew straws, Mike O'Hara was the victim, and then, for the third Be-Bop Day, Mike volunteered to take care of it again, because he's that kind of guy. Mercifully, that was the last year for Be-Bop Day. By then, even the city realized it was a waste of time.

Some of you may be wondering why I would spend precious pages talking about something as inconsequential as Be-Bop Day. Be-Bop Day is but one example of hundreds of such events my various teams have had to spend their precious resources on, usually with no measurable outcomes, almost always at the behest of someone who thinks this is how Mayo Clinic or whatever hospital can "be a good citizen" or "get our name out there" or "get us some publicity" or "enhance the brand."

There are better ways to do all these things, ways that are measurable, cost-effective, and in keeping with the brand. For me, Be-Bop Day and events like it were not uncommon at the community hospitals I had worked at, but to see the world-famous Mayo Clinic expending its time and brand equity in such a manner was a shocker.

You see, when it comes to enhancing a brand, especially a brand as precious as Mayo Clinic's, and particularly when it comes to preserving and enhancing the talents and morale of my staff, no matter what the organization, I can be quite a curmudgeon. Far too often, physicians, administrators, and CEOs have sought out groups like mine to plan an executive's retirement party or put together a humorous video ("It won't take you long"—Wanna bet?) or stage the umpteenth health fair in the local shopping mall.

Many times, the proponent will tell me it will be "fun." It's as if they were saying, "Marketing groups, well, you know—aren't their jobs all about fun stuff like TV and magazines and advertising? They're not saving lives or managing finances or anything really important. They can do that kind of stuff for us. Why else are they here?"

Over the years, I adopted a slogan for myself: I don't do fun. I'm not going to wear a funny hat or a red nose or jump out of a cake for some inane purpose when I should be doing meaningful work.

A SEAT AT THE TABLE

By the time the third Be-Bop Day came around, my team had also been involved in the Hillary Clinton program. We had worked with *Good Morning America* and Dr. Tim Johnson on a long piece about Mayo Clinic, we had worked with *60 Minutes* and Lesley Stahl on a long segment about the great neurosurgeon Dr. Thoralf Sundt, and we had handled a number of crises, including a murder-suicide at Mayo Clinic's Saint Marys Hospital. Our group was acquiring respect and being appreciated for our abilities and our performance. It was becoming more apparent to leadership, and to us in the news bureau, that something was changing. We would never have said this out loud, but it was dawning on us that we were becoming more important.

This emerging status in the organization did not come about by executive fiat or by my whining to my boss about how I should have a "seat at the table." It happened because of Mayo Clinic's slow but steady emergence into the big wide world of late twentieth-century marketing and communications, and the need for a highly skilled team of professionals to manage the many complex moving parts at the intersection of this world and the expanding global presence of the Mayo Clinic Enterprise.

A number of factors fostered Mayo Clinic's success in communicating and managing its message during this time. As far as I know, these precepts are still followed today:

1. Every member of the staff considered managing and communicating Mayo Clinic's message to be one of their highest priorities.

2. As the brand program evolved, it provided deeply researched, verifiable information about a host of trends and attitudes affecting Mayo Clinic that helped leadership and the staff hone and target messages effectively.

3. As the media world changed into a 24/7 news cycle with digital media, global communications, and then social media, Mayo Clinic had the courage to adapt quickly and effectively to use these new modalities.

4. When a crisis arose, Mayo Clinic leaders and staff came together immediately and worked tirelessly to follow best practices to weather the storm and, when necessary, accept accountability.

Be assured these precepts were a manifestation of the Mayo culture—I am not implying that I or my team invented these norms. I do believe my group, due to its excellence and our acceptance at leadership tables, helped Mayo Clinic adapt those behaviors for a new era.

THE NEWS BUREAU

Aside from word of mouth, media relations have always been the backbone of Mayo Clinic's marketing. From the time when the brothers Mayo became renowned for their surgical skill, and the Clinic for its revolutionary approach to group practice and health-care delivery, news stories have tracked the institution for its innovations and, certainly, for its famous clientele. At times, the brothers were stung by accusations of grandstanding or hucksterism. These proud men who had done nothing more than revolutionize medicine through hard work and diligent application of what they learned took umbrage with these mischaracterizations. A culture developed of wariness and a fair amount of distrust toward the media. This attitude took hold for decades, giving Mayo Clinic the reputation of being an impenetrable fortress that hid dark secrets behind its granite walls, with kings and presidents and movie stars walking from appointment to appointment and being whisked in and out of the city through shadowy secret passages, with no one the wiser. Inevitably, reporters at the local newspaper, Rochester's *Post-Bulletin* (known locally as "the PB"), an afternoon paper of all things, spent a great deal of their time trying to cross the moat, ram the gates, and tell the world about the goings-on of the *real* Mayo Clinic.

My predecessors were just as committed to ensuring that none of those "kids" would ever breach our defenses. After all, one reason the world's VIPs came to Mayo Clinic was that they could count on the strictest confidentiality and have their medical issues taken care of in an atmosphere of dignity and comfort. This is a rare thing, even more so in this day and age, and it is a promise Mayo Clinic still keeps.

A word about calling the reporters "kids." Not all of them were, of course, but since Rochester is a very small media market and, in those days, was even smaller, many journalists found their first professional jobs in Rochester, would stay for a year or two, and then move on to a bigger market. By contrast, Mayo Clinic is an institution with turnover so low it is usually under 5 percent in a given year. Many staff stayed thirty, forty, or even fifty years. So I would have the experience of setting up an interview with, for instance, the surgeon who operated on King Hussein of Jordan, who had been practicing for decades, with a reporter who might be twenty-three years old and often knew nothing about health care, science, or Mayo Clinic. We often wondered how Mayo Clinic's history might have been different had W.W. Mayo decided to settle in what became a major media market, like Minneapolis, or San Francisco, or Chicago—although, by the time I was at Mayo Clinic, we had regular inquiries from those markets and many others around the world.

It wasn't until 1984, with the creation of the news bureau, that Mayo Clinic would allow any media access to patients—that is, media access through Mayo's official infrastructure. For years, thousands of patients, after treatment at Mayo, have gone home and, besides telling all their friends and families about the wonders of Mayo, would write a letter to their local newspaper, or pen a column, or even appear on local TV shows. Now sometimes patients blog their journey through Mayo in real time on the Web. Even Garrison Keillor of *Prairie Home Companion* fame felt compelled to write a piece about his experiences for *Time* magazine.

When I was asked to work at Mayo in 1991, it was for the express purpose of expanding its media presence. As mentioned earlier, in 1990 Mayo Clinic had sent out about forty-three news releases. After my first year, the team had sent out more than two hundred. The obstacles we ran into seem almost quaint now, except that they represented a sincere sense among many Mayo physicians that participating in a media story was contrary to the Mayo Clinic tradition, medical ethics, and, less obviously, might subject them to ridicule from their peers, or worse, that particular disdain from a colleague that Garrison Keillor describes so well in his descriptions of Midwestern culture, that consists of a quiet look of disapproval, a whisper to a colleague at lunch saying, "Did you see Joe Hudson on TV last night? I guess he's pretty special these days." Dr. Hudson would hear about these comments through the grapevine and would then decide to lay low for a year or two or maybe forever, rather than have to cope again with that powerful social censure. By the time I retired in 2013, I observed, for the most part, that attitude had finally loosened its grip. It was a whole new world and a new generation of physicians was becoming more in tune with social media, the internet, and the need to have a strong public presence. Like any hospital in the United States, Mayo Clinic would receive inquiries days and evenings from journalists seeking status reports on patients brought to the ER for a car accident or some other trauma. The evening and weekend press call duty was shared among the fifteen or so professionals in the division of communications, of which the news bureau was a section. For daily press call, four of us in the news bureau took one week on a four-week rotation. During the other three weeks, we would continue working on stories and projects from our week on press call.

Many of the requests required considerable planning, preproduction work, and, ultimately, working closely with journalists on-site doing interviews and shooting B-roll. In between all this, despite being fundamentally the media relations team, we were also responsible for marketing communications, news releases, and, of course, other duties as assigned.

My first boss, Frank Iossi, the man who brought me to Mayo Clinic, was himself a former journalist and had also had a career working with the health systems agency (HSA) back when Minnesota had one. He had also served in the Navy during Vietnam. Frank was old-school, a disciplined man who believed in the hierarchical order of things and was completely dedicated to the Mayo values and traditions. That said, he did hire me to help modernize Mayo's approach to media relations.

In Tucson, I had overseen a group that had started using one of the first personal computers, KayPros, for word processing as soon as they were commercially available. By the time I left, we had a local area network, used email profusely, sent copy by email to our in-house typesetter, and generally had operations very automated. That doesn't sound like much now, but in the 1980s, we were riding the wave, if not actually ahead of the curve. After I'd been hired by Mayo Clinic, but before I moved to Rochester, I was musing about my new office and it hit me that there was no computer in it—at least, not that I could remember. I called Frank and said, "Is there a computer in my office?"

Frank said, "Oh, you want one of those?" I then realized that none of the managers had a computer in his or her office, nor did Frank. Some of the administrative assistants did, and a few of the specialists, mostly for desktop publishing. When I got to my office I discovered an old IBM 286. It squealed when I switched on the power and emitted a high-pitched tone as it slowly did its work. Sometime later, a tech came by to set me up with OfficeVision, one of the early email programs. This would not be the first time I would be dumbstruck by the contrast between the cutting-edge medical aspects of Mayo and the relatively unsophisticated aspects of its administrative approach (which, I can assure you, is no longer the case).

To Frank's credit, a few months after all this, he and I sat down with the computer group, made plans, and, in due course, the office was completely wired, everyone had a desktop computer, and we were soon burying each other in emails.

Frank trained me in what Mayo Clinic expected in its future leaders, making it clear, without ever actually saying it, that he saw me as one and, for that, I am eternally grateful to him. He told me, and I soon saw for myself, that there was no better training in Mayo Clinic operations than handling the weekly press call. I always felt Frank loved his news bureau. He chose the people with care and he called them, privately, "thoroughbreds." This metaphor struck me as odd, until I'd handled a few months of press call and experienced the intense, fast-paced, very public and highly accountable job of interfacing with the outside world on behalf of one of the world's greatest institutions. The news bureau staff developed into experts in all manner of crisis communications, issues management, media relations, and brand building. Days, weeks, months would speed by and, on Monday mornings, we would gather and review our status sheets and often end up laughing until we cried about some of the crazy things we had to deal with the previous week.

One day during the first President Bush's term in office, I received a call from a *Wall Street Journal* reporter asking to speak with our expert on sinusitis. Although we received dozens of calls a day about all manner of subjects, I was just a bit wary of a *WSJ* reporter calling the Mayo Clinic about something relatively mundane (in most cases). As any of us would do in the news bureau, and, in fact, is quite common practice among any media relations professional, I asked him what the story was about. Instantly, the reporter turned hostile. "Listen, I don't have time for this shit. Just tell me who I should talk to about sinusitis."

Well. My dander was up, and so, I calmly repeated my question. The reporter lost it. "Goddammit, do you know who I am? I'm W____. B_____. I'm a fucking Pulitzer Prize–winning journalist and I am not going to be stopped by some PR flunkie. Who's your CEO?"

Well. I was happy to give him the number for Dr. Waller's administrative assistant. She and Dr. Waller had been through this sort of thing dozens of times before. I called them to give a heads-up. Turned out Dr. Waller was away, so another board member, Dr. Cameron Strong, one of the nicest people you will ever meet, talked to Mr. Pulitzer Prize–winner. Dr. Strong then called me and said he'd answered some basic questions, and all was well.

A day or two later, the story came out. Mr. B____. had written a story investigating the treatment the president was being given by his White House physician for sinusitis. I was pleased to see we did not make the story. I was also happy we had been on our guard, since the piece was vaguely critical of President Bush's physician and we had a policy of not commenting on the care of patients that were not our own and who had not given us permission to speak. Now, the Health Insurance Portability and Accountability Act (HIPPA) would have made it illegal for anyone to comment on this case without the proper permissions, but this was before that law passed. Dr. Strong had obviously stuck to generalities you could find in any reference book, so Mr. B didn't get what he was looking for—a critique.

This anecdote points out a few important points about media relations at Mayo. First, Dr. Strong immediately responded. Not with "I'm too busy," or "You handle it," or any other dodge. Second, I was supported, even though *The Wall Street Journal* is an important outlet for any organization. Third, the story sticks in my mind because no journalist before or since, no matter how famous, was ever as rude to me as Mr. W____. B____.

As our news bureau gelled, we developed simple practice guidelines for ourselves. One of them was the following statement about our priorities:

1. As per the Mayo Clinic primary value, the needs of the patient come first. If the patient doesn't want to have any information released or does not want to participate in a story, we are done. We will not cajole or pressure. In a few high-profile cases, we did suggest that a simple statement that fills the information vacuum is usually better than complete radio silence. The decision was always the patient's.

2. Our second priority was to the caregivers. They are at Mayo Clinic fifty, sixty, even more hours per week saving lives. If they can't do a story, okay, we will find another option if there is one.

3. We are advocates, not reporters. We are here to protect and enhance the Mayo Clinic. We were never asked to lie. We told the truth, even if it was painful. Yes, we would investigate and draft carefully worded statements, but there are many examples of Mayo Clinic being forthright about mistakes or "bad news." Some of these were difficult indeed but, in the end, preserved Mayo's unparalleled reputation for integrity.

4. If the other three conditions are met, we are here to help the media.

We cultivated relationships with media, of course, just as any medical center does. In 2002, Chris Gade—by then, head of external relations—and the team put together a conference on medicine and the media that was attended by many prominent journalists, with Ted Koppel of ABC's *Nightline* as conference chair.

We were discriminating about who we would talk to, all part of preserving Mayo Clinic's brand attribute of integrity. Integrity in the Mayo Clinic set of brand values does not merely mean that Mayo Clinic follows the laws and regulations. It even goes beyond patient confidentiality. For consumers, Mayo Clinic's integrity represents the idea that their needs will come first, ahead of any commercial considerations, ahead of individual pride or ego, and that they will be taken care of as individuals and families. This aspect of Mayo's brand has been a key aspect of the organization's brand promise for more than 150 years and it was the news bureau's job to help keep it that way.

Most inquiries were legitimate, although we would often have to draw the line between information we could share and information the patient did not want disclosed. Before HIPPA, the American Hospital Association guidelines for condition reports were somewhat helpful. When it comes to a celebrity or other notorious patients, though, the guidelines don't help much when a camera crew from Arkansas shows up unannounced because they want to talk to someone about the governor's medical issues. He was the successor to Governor Clinton and was at Mayo Clinic for a liver transplant, something we never disclosed from the news bureau but, as it happened, the Arkansas news team staked out a spot on a public sidewalk near our campus and, by some coincidence, ran into a physician who knew of the governor's case and agreed to do an interview. Any of us in media relations know the kinds of problems this can cause—not the least of which is an irate patient who had asked for confidentiality. A statement was released, the governor received his organ, and the physician was reminded of the Mayo Clinic rule: no one talks to the media without first going through the news bureau.

CURB YOUR EGO

One of the great pleasures of working for a culture like Mayo Clinic's is that the staff are almost 100 percent voluntarily compliant with the proven processes and procedures. When the occasional physician deviated, as did the physician in the story above, the leadership of the institution—in this case, Mayo Clinic in Rochester—would go ballistic, albeit in a very polite, Minnesota-nice kind of way. After the dust settled on whatever tempest was created, the next question I'd be asked would be, "Has this person had media training?" Almost all mistakes such as this one were first seen as a learning opportunity. Although the CEO may be upset, the remedy was education and counsel, not reprimand or censure. Repeat offenders, of course, were then causing themselves their own heartache.

One such recalcitrant researcher we worked with refused to get with the program. My first encounter with Dr. K occurred when he happened to be away from the clinic. We received an invitation for him to appear on a talk show in Chicago—I don't remember which one, but it certainly wasn't *Oprah*. The subject had to do with organ transplantation, his particular research area. His studies could be controversial and, if memory serves, this particular question had to do with organ transplantation for prisoners—as in, whether or not taxpayers should be footing the bill for such care for criminals. We in the news bureau thought it best not to involve Mayo Clinic in such a debate, since it is really a matter of law and public policy and ethics, not a strictly medical issue, and we declined the interview. When Dr. K returned, he learned of this and, in his fury, wrote a long letter to the CEO and other top leaders, copying me, more or less defaming my staff, me, and the entire policy of the news bureau mediating among the staff and the reporters. I remember the line, in paraphrase, where he said, "No one will decide which media I talk to, when, on what subject, except me."

Since I was still fairly new, this letter scared me. I called Bob Smoldt and asked him if I had anything to be concerned about. His answer spoke volumes about the culture of Mayo and his particular style of leadership. He said, "John, the letter reflects far more poorly on Dr. K than on you or your staff. You don't need to worry about it."

In a culture like this, professionals can do their job, use their skills, make decisions, and not be continually watching their backs for the next knife to be thrown. Understand, Mayo Clinic is a consensus culture and, when necessary, decisions about media relations would involve many people weighing in on a critical issue. The news bureau staff did not just wing it all day long—they consulted with many others at all times. As I was told more than once, though, physician leadership didn't mean that physicians were experts in all fields. Brilliant though they may be, they relied on the professional expertise of the financiers, the human resources staff, the news bureau, the IT group—and made sure they did indeed hire experts. One of my colleagues, Kent Seltman, said it best one morning in my office early in our careers: "The Mayo Clinic culture allows me to do my best work, and motivates me to want to do my best work at all times."

As sometimes happened at Mayo Clinic, an individual such as Dr. K found himself in the wrong culture, since Mayo Clinic abjured self-promotion and individualistic shenanigans and, instead, rewarded humility, teamwork, and being able to get along with others. Someone joked—I don't know who, though it was often repeated tongue in cheek—that Mayo Clinic was the best socialist organization in the United States. We weren't socialist by any means. The team, though, was the heart of the culture.

The *coup de grace* for Dr. K occurred when I received another call that *60 Minutes* wanted to do a story on the issue of whether the families of organ donors should be compensated for their loved one's organs as a method of helping to ameliorate the chronic shortage of organs. Dr. K was an expert on the subject of transplantation and had done much research on various aspects of the subject. He had invited *60 Minutes* to come to Mayo Clinic to do a story. I didn't know if the issue of compensation was his suggestion or not. All I knew was that *60 Minutes* was coming, and that Mike Wallace would be the journalist.

When I was a kid, Mike Wallace used to do a program about the lives of famous people called *Biography*. I loved history and loved the show. He narrated each episode, and so I grew up hearing that grave, masterful voice of his. As I became seasoned in the media business, and *60 Minutes* gained its legendary influence, I learned that there was no call to be dreaded more than the one from *60 Minutes* and no journalist more to be feared than Mike Wallace. And Dr. K had invited him.

I should mention that we could have said, "No, we don't want to participate in the story," even though they'd been invited by Dr. K. I discussed this with the Clinic leadership. We all agreed that we had nothing to fear or hide on this subject and, of course, Mayo Clinic avidly supported the need for organ donations and, in fact, when one considered all three Mayo Clinic locations as one institution, Mayo Clinic had the largest transplantation program in the country. So on with the show.

Segments like this one for *60 Minutes* are usually partnerships between the media relations person—in this case, me—and the segment producer—in this case, a young man who worked with Mike. The producer and I planned out who Mike should interview, and we walked the Mayo Clinic and Saint Marys Hospital campuses scouting suitable shooting locations. This would take a few days, and then I could expect a call from him as to when they'd be back to do the segment.

One person Mike Wallace was going to interview was the physician in charge of Mayo Clinic's transplant program at the time, Dr. Syl Sterioff. Besides being a brilliant surgeon, Syl was extremely personable, articulate, and passionate about the need for organ donors. He was opposed to the concept of paying for organs on ethical grounds. Imagine the impact if a family knew that they could donate an organ and be compensated. You might say that donations could be restricted to those who were deceased. Yet we do have living donors and we live in a world where, in some areas, desperately poor families will sell a child rather than see their family starve. One can easily see the unintended consequences of such a policy.

Admittedly, it's a complicated subject. Dr. Sterioff was the expert, and he knew the issue backward and forward. Still, during the hiatus until the *60 Minutes* crew returned with Mike, I paged Dr. Sterioff to suggest he might want to have a refresher on media training to prepare.

MESSAGING

During my career, I have often heard people reference media training and message development as if it were something nefarious. When Al Gore robotically referred to the safety of the Social Security funds as being in a "lockbox" during the 2000 presidential campaign, the whole notion of developing messages and testing them with focus groups came under suspicion and ridicule. Perhaps many people didn't realize that these activities had been used by companies and individuals all over the world for decades, including political candidates, advertising agencies, even the armed forces, and, by the way, pretty much anyone facing a job interview. Who hasn't been told to think through what they will say in response to a tricky question about a gap in their resume? You can wing it or you can think it through and be prepared. Most importantly, don't lie. As with any tool, the efficacy and ethicality of messaging depends on how it is used.

I have worked with CEOs who wing it, who believe they are intelligent enough and fast-thinking enough not to need preparation. They're busy people, they're on top, so they have great faith in their own abilities. In my experience, this approach is ultimately dangerous and leads to major faux pas, sooner or later.

I've never been a CEO, but I have had this happen to me more than once. At a large meeting of my department when I was the chief public affairs officer, I presented a slide program about the future of our department. I moved to the next PowerPoint and everyone started laughing—my secretary had inadvertently typed "Pubic Affairs." At the podium, I wasn't thinking about her; I was laughing along with the group and made a couple of jokes. Only later did I learn that my secretary had been mortified, and she felt I was making fun of her. Many apologies ensued.

One of our physician CEOs came in late to address a meeting of all the top administrators at an outside conference room. He ran in, whipped off his coat, and proceeded to deliver his keynote address with nary a note or prompt. I suspect he felt he'd done a good enough job, and then hurried off to his next meeting. This was fairly early in his tenure, a successful tenure, I dare say, yet that morning, many of the administrators formed an opinion of him that lasted for the rest of his career: that he disrespected the administrative staff, and couldn't be bothered with giving his listeners five minutes of his time to speak to them, let alone answer questions. He had done himself unnecessary harm.

Words have consequences. Once spoken, they cannot be retrieved. These days, they exist on the Web, forever. I often think of Abraham Lincoln, riding the train to Gettysburg, repeatedly revising those few hundred words that the audience almost ignored, they passed by so quickly. Yet, in that moment, Lincoln redefined the meaning of the Civil War and the United States it perpetuated. He was there to dedicate a gravesite, something he might have done without much preparation, but he didn't wing it, although he may have been our most literarily gifted president.

At Mayo Clinic, the anomaly of the previous story aside, our leadership (even the CEO I spoke of for issues he deemed worthy) worked hard to convey the right message. Message development and media training were a standard part of our operations. Nothing deceitful or obfuscatory occurred—in fact, the working principle was to tell the truth, from our point of view. I deeply resent the notion of a spin doctor or flak. At Mayo Clinic, the task was to express ourselves so as to preserve the bond of trust between Mayo Clinic and the patient, a bond we held sacred. Our most important job in the department of public affairs, whether in marketing, media, internal communications, government relations, or any other public activity, was to preserve that trust. No one at Mayo Clinic ever asked us to lie or distort the truth. No one ever said to me, "You're the flak. You handle it." We were partnered with leadership and the entire staff to preserve and protect the integrity of Mayo Clinic.

This all sounds very high-minded. However, what makes Mayo Clinic the great institution it is, is the fact that this is the truth. I lived it. Even in the direst circumstances, Mayo Clinic staff go to any necessary length to tell the truth and preserve that bond.

So I paged Syl Sterioff to see if he would do some preparation. Perhaps I caught him at a bad time. When I used the priority paging system at Mayo, I always wondered what I was intersecting with on the other end. Did the physician step out of the exam room to take the call, just when he had given a patient some bad news? Had the doctor lost a patient that day? Once, I had a surgeon answer a page while he was in the operating room. He was cool with it. I was kind of amazed at his *savoir faire*. At any rate, for whatever reasons, Syl—usually the most gracious of men—did not take kindly to my suggestion.

"John, do I really have to do this? I don't have half a day to give to this stuff. I've already had media training. I know the issues. And besides, it costs a fortune."

We often used an outside consultant for media training, in partnership with one of the news bureau staff, since it is sometimes easier for an outside person to critique a colleague's performance. The cost was actually quite reasonable, although the policy was to charge it to the participant's budget.

"Syl, I understand, but this is Mike Wallace we're talking about. How about if I pay for it out of my budget? And we can make the session very focused, two hours, just to help you get your thoughts organized."

"John, I know my thoughts." He paused. "Okay, I can do it next week. Call Carol to set it up. Just set it up and I'll be there." Click.

We had our consultant, Bob Aronson, in the room along with me, and two of my news bureau staff, Chris and Shelly. Bob had been helping Mayo leaders with media for many years. He had just the right touch with physicians, authoritative without being condescending or aggressive. He reminded the trainee over and over again—talk to the patient out there. This is all about the patient. Not you, certainly not the reporter. It's about the patient. When a physician gave a long, technical answer to a question, he'd replay the interview and, at the end, ask the doctor, "If I'm a patient, what do I get out of what you just said?"

Usually, the doctor would laugh, acknowledging, "Not much."

Chris, Shelly, and I were there to not only make suggestions on messages but also to pose as reporters, asking Syl the toughest questions we could devise. Shelly relished this role and always had the best time asking the hardest questions. Dr. Sterioff was back to being his professional, collegial self and participated with all due respect and engagement.

A few weeks later, the *60 Minutes* crew arrived. A small crew, really: the producer, a camera man, a sound man, maybe one or two others at times, and Mike Wallace. He had an air of dignity and also a bit of a sense of not being approachable. A couple of years before, I worked with Lesley Stahl on a *60 Minutes* piece and she couldn't have been friendlier or more approachable. Mike kept his distance. Often, he'd check out the setup, then wait in the hotel room (which was literally across the street) while the shot was being set up. The producer would call him, he'd do his bit, and then he'd go back to his room. He was never unpleasant. Just remote.

It happened fairly regularly at Mayo Clinic that we'd meet famous people. Not all of them were as legendary as Mike Wallace, particularly for someone in the media business. My most vivid memory of him is when he interviewed Dr. Sterioff. They set up a shot, with our permission, in a dialysis unit. Syl and Mike sat on stools, and all around them were patients in bed receiving dialysis. As they do for TV interviews, Mike and Syl were very close together, their knees only inches apart. Tape rolled, and Mike Wallace bore in for the interview. Whereas before, he had seemed rather lethargic and disinterested, suddenly he perked up, seemed ten years younger, and, with bright eyes and that commanding voice, tore into Syl Sterioff for more than thirty minutes—maybe almost an hour. I worked with many great journalists over the years. He was the best interviewer I've ever seen. He knew the subject, knew what he wanted to get from Syl, and did his absolute best to get Syl to crack and admit that compensating families for organs could be a good thing. At one point, Mike waved his arm around the room and said something to the effect of "Shouldn't we do everything we can to save these people who are waiting for an organ? Their lives depend on it. Isn't that your job, to help them at whatever cost?" It was very dramatic, with a touch of compassion, and someone else might have been driven to at least give an inch, maybe say that it might work if this and that were done. Syl didn't budge. He stuck to his beliefs for the entire time, and then, finally, we wrapped.

As he walked out of the room, Syl whispered something to me like, "Damn. That guy is tough."

I barely had time to say, "You did great," before he was down the hall.

For months afterward, nothing happened. The organ transplant story was what is called "evergreen," meaning it could be aired anytime to fill a slot in the program, provided something bigger or more urgent didn't pop up. Frustratingly, the segment kept getting bumped. Each week at our news bureau meeting, we'd review the status of our stories. The organ donation segment became a weekly joke. At first, I'd say the spot would air next week, then in two weeks, then I'd say it was pending, and finally I just put on the sheet "Not dead." The group would beat me to it and say, "Still not dead yet," and we'd all laugh.

Then, out of the blue, the producer called to say the spot would air that Sunday. As was our policy, we sent out a notice to a large distribution list to let people know. Even though I'd been present at every step of the filming I couldn't predict how they'd put the show together. It was as new to me as it was to anyone else. Although I'd been anxious about some of the statements Dr. K made, which were included, I felt a great sense of relief after it had broadcast. Besides Dr. K's controversial sound bites, everyone else had come off just fine.

A few minutes after the show ended, I got a call at home. It was Syl Sterioff. He thanked me for pushing him to do the training. He said he realized how much of a difference it had made, and that he felt good about the way he had come across on the segment. That's the kind of person he is.

WE'RE IN IT TOGETHER

Mayo Clinic had strict policies for engagement with the public, including the media, originally written into a booklet called *Representing Mayo*. This handbook was given to every staff person and covered everything from what to do if a reporter from *The New York Times* calls you directly (call the News Bureau) to how to handle an FBI agent knocking at your door (call the legal department). One of the aspects of Mayo culture I always found fascinating was how voluntarily compliant most of the staff were. I attribute this largely to the manner in which Mayo Clinic governed itself—that is, collectively through committees, which in turn gave the staff assurance that their voices were being heard. I would add to that the open doors of leadership, the many two-way communications vehicles in place, and the widespread understanding that we were working for a great place. We had a good thing going and no one wanted to be the one to mess it up.

The news bureau had a more detailed and specific manual for handling media relations, crisis communications, and issues management. When I started, we revised the manual and, during my tenure, the document evolved with the time and Mayo's needs.

Originally, the policy stated that Mayo would never discuss a patient not under Mayo's care. You, no doubt, have seen physicians on TV regularly discussing the medical issues of a person in the news, even though that patient is being treated by someone else. That's what Mr. Pulitzer Prize winner wanted Mayo Clinic to do for him, either directly or indirectly—critique the care being given by the White House physician. Dr. Strong handled it by giving him the kind of generic information one could easily find in a textbook or, now, ironically, on MayoClinic.com. How would Dr. Strong know whatever was going on with President Bush at that moment, and why his physician was treating him in a certain way?

Over time, the news bureau section evolved into the external relations division as we became far more proactive about our media presence and added the Web and social media and a video news feed to the mix. Often, we pushed the edges of Mayo's conservatism so that we could remain competitive in the crowded media world. For instance, in reference to statements about other people's patients, the rule was finally relaxed a bit, and we were able to have our physicians speak generically about a particular illness or syndrome. We were very careful not to make any statements about the patient or speculate about outcomes, whether something was correct or not, and there were still many stories we passed on because of the inherent danger of Mayo Clinic appearing to weigh in on someone's medical care. The new freedom served us well and I'm not aware of the change damaging Mayo or any other institution or caregiver— or patient.

Another policy that set Mayo Clinic apart was their refusal to announce a study that was being fielded. We only wanted to discuss published results. Again, it is quite customary for institutions or individuals to seek publicity for a study they are conducting, even though the results may not be known for years, or may be inconclusive, or even useless. One evening, I was watching Keith Olbermann on MSNBC when he was still doing *Countdown*. A physician came on as a guest and announced he was heading up a study that would cure breast cancer. A stunned Olbermann asked him if that's what he meant, that he was going to cure the illness. The doctor repeated his claims. I was appalled that anyone would say something so wildly speculative on national television. Interestingly, I never heard mention of this study or that physician again, even though he worked at a very prestigious academic medical center.

For years, we had great difficulties getting researchers to give us advance notice about a study being published. They were so accustomed to Mayo Clinic frowning on self-promotion they simply went about their business and, if they had the lead article in the *Journal of the American Medical Association* (*JAMA*) or *the New England Journal of Medicine* (*NEJM*) or *Lancet*, they'd say nothing and let the world hear about it when the magazine was published.

The news bureau staff approached this problem in a number of ways. We created a presentation that demonstrated the value of publicity regarding studies, not just for the authors but for Mayo Clinic and, most importantly, the patient. The presentation included research that showed citations for a given article rose substantially as a result of media coverage. We also demonstrated through data that more patients availed themselves of advantageous treatments and protocols as a result of the coverage, including increased volume for a given disease treatment center at Mayo Clinic. We also fielded a year-long study about how our patients felt about having been in a news item. Every patient but one said it had been a positive experience and they would do it again in a heartbeat. The mildly negative patient said she wasn't really upset about being in the news; she just didn't realize how much attention she would get, and so probably wouldn't want to go through that again. But she also made sure to tell us she still loved Mayo Clinic.

Like other medical centers, we had our staff cover certain beats, such as cardiology or neurology. The person with that account served as the liaison between public affairs and the specialty department. For many of these departments, it was their first experience of having a dedicated communicator and marketer and, therefore, a consistent, long-term relationship with public affairs. Over time, in most cases, a close bond developed among the medical staff and their representative, since the account person could help them get publicity, marketing, consumer research, and internal communications. Meanwhile, the account person learned more and more about the specialty and so the physicians became increasingly trustful of her. She would become part of the team.

Naturally, there was the occasional mismatch. A few times, I received a request from a department head to replace his account person. Usually, the given department wanted more, faster, and sometimes higher-quality service, and felt the current public affairs specialist wasn't up to the task. Often, the concern was a lack of aggressiveness, or sometimes poor follow-through and missing deadlines. It does require a particular temperament to succeed at managing, for instance, the wants, needs, and aspirations of a department of more than two hundred highly skilled, intelligent, and demanding cardiologists. A person needs a lot of self-confidence and backbone mixed with a good deal of tact and a fierce sense of urgency. Equally important is a good grasp of how the department's goals melded with the overall institutional brand and strategy, which were not always perfectly aligned and, at times, would require the public affairs specialist to deny the request or find another path. Most of the time, staff people would grow into and relish these roles, demanding as they were. Embedded in the medical practice, they would have a strong sense of purpose and felt they were making a real contribution to the mission and success of Mayo Clinic. A few discovered this was not their best fit, would burn out, and gladly returned to the role of writer or production specialist of some kind. The most difficult cases were those in which the perceptions of the specialist ("I'm doing everything I can for them.") and the department head ("She's just not the right person. We're not getting what we need.") were wildly askew. Then we would go through rounds of meetings, coaching, laying out expectations on both sides. Sometimes this worked, and sometimes there was nothing to do but make a change.

The "beat" system, as it is known (from newspaper reporters' beats), worked well for us, so long as the specialist assigned to the department learned to manage expectations on the client side and the many resources available at Mayo on the production side. Inevitably, matters would get out of hand when the public affairs specialist devolved into an order-taker. She would burn out, unable to fulfill all demands on her own, yet was still driven by the Mayo culture to exceed expectations and excel in all things.

For brand management, the beat system proved essential. As specialists became more deeply embedded in their respective departments, fewer and fewer random acts of brand malfeasance surfaced. Over the years, the self-regulating nature of Mayo Clinic's culture made acrimonious brand decisions the exception rather than the rule. Eventually the brand committee disbanded, replaced by a duo of the brand administrator (the public affairs chair) and a high-ranking physician. For the vast majority of issues, the operational level Brand Team sufficed for adjudication and enforcement.

Throughout my tenure at Mayo, media relations comprised the mainstay of Mayo Clinic brand building, outside the medical arena. Many studies have shown people put more stock in news media than in advertising, despite the prevailing distrust of media in general. Naturally, media relations grew to encompass cable news, blogs, Twitter, YouTube, and all the other avenues engendered by the digital communications explosion. Mayo grasped the importance of these media relatively quickly compared to other medical centers, even though the inherent Mayo skepticism necessitated a careful approach. In the long run, this put Mayo at the forefront of modern media in the health-care category.

At conferences, I was often asked how we had convinced the Mayo Clinic leadership (especially the CEO) to embrace social media despite the obvious pitfalls of crazy comments, misinformation, and even—perhaps especially—legitimate complaints. Notwithstanding the numerous measures we employed to ensure such complaints were handled professionally, I am proud to say the initiative did not require a great deal of convincing. On one level, the benefits of social media to an institution more or less built on word-of-mouth marketing were fairly obvious. To my mind, what really prevailed were two other aspects of Mayo culture:

1. A long, deeply embedded tolerance of academic freedom, encompassing not just scholarship but freedom of thought and expression.

2. An even more deeply held faith in the quality of Mayo Clinic's services, products, and staff.

Bottom line, the risks were seen as relatively small and manageable compared to the likely benefits.

To be sure, much debate ensued as Mayo's social media presence grew increasingly significant and—I have no doubt—continues regarding the degree of access and transparency digital communication provides. The occasional digital outrage usually prompted calls from some quarters for tighter controls or even, rarely, "turning it off." These opinions never garnered much traction. The needs of the patient come first, and in the twenty-first-century digital communications are undeniably necessary to any business model and increasingly vital to patient care and well-being.

CHAPTER 7

IN SEARCH OF SYNERGY

ONE BIG HAPPY

As the department grew, the job of integrating and coordinating across the increasing number of divisions within public affairs became more complicated, and also more important. In 1996, I was promoted to division chair of communications, which grew to include:

- ○ Institutional communications
- ○ External relations (the transformed news bureau)
- ○ Marketing communications
- ○ Patient and visitor communications
- ○ Support for Mayo Clinic Health System
- ○ Support for Mayo Clinic Medical Ventures
- ○ MayoClinic.org

One of Mayo Clinic's secret sauces is synergy. In synergistic systems, the whole is greater than the sum of its parts. As the Mayo brothers often said, two heads are better than one. In an ideal system, all members, all parts, are working in harmony to achieve the same goal. The Mayo Clinic culture abounded with teamwork analogies. One of the favorites was a symphony orchestra. Each member may pursue individual excellence, yet each member also needed to subsume their individuality for the greater good.

Another favorite metaphor at Mayo Clinic, and indeed all over the corporate world, is family. Health-care organizations love to call themselves a family. Of all the health-care systems that I am aware of, Mayo Clinic came closest to earning that distinction in the positive way it is intended. As has been said repeatedly throughout this book, the spirit of teamwork, the *esprit de corps*, at Mayo Clinic was exceptionally strong.

Just the same, the family analogy can cut both ways. I am reminded of an anecdote from one of our messaging focus groups. As with many health-care providers, Mayo Clinic was fond of saying that we treat patients like a member of the family. One time, we tested a message to that effect with a group of consumers. The response was telling. "Please treat us better than that," they said.

They weren't kidding. Families can be loving and nurturing, or they can be dysfunctional and stultifying. Sometimes on the same day. Of course, it's a spectrum. We all know, though, that every organization has its positive familial aspects and its negative familial aspects as well. It is delusional to pretend otherwise.

At Mayo Clinic, conflicts such as jealousy, poor communication, and disrespect arose and were generally dealt with in the long run. Often, the situation, whatever it might be, had to worsen before it was resolved. This was due to a culture of self-regulation and peer review. The staff, as a body politic, did not accept bad behavior. The offending individual would often find herself isolated and unable to accomplish much. Usually, the person would "get the message" and leave of her own accord.

Understand I am not referring to overt malfeasance or unethical behavior. I am happy to say such matters were dealt with swiftly and firmly. I am speaking more to the friction that inevitably arises as a consequence of competing ambitions and divergent visions of the desired future of the organization. Mayo places an enormous value on harmony within the organization—on getting along.

These types of problems call for strong leadership and skillful management. Mayo Clinic leadership works diligently to lay out the vision and strategic plan for the institution. These plans are developed in consensual fashion and thoroughly communicated. Medical and administrative departments devise strategies and tactics to effectuate the vision. At its best, the outcomes are synergistic and improve the patient experience at every level. All of this can happen because of the foundation of collegiality, teamwork, and trust that exists among the staff.

INTEGRATION GATHERS STEAM

During my time at Mayo, the drive to achieve ever greater synergies intensified. Many factors coalesced to engender a sense of urgency about the need to raise Mayo's interdisciplinary approach to new levels. Some called it the "perfect storm"—declining reimbursement, increased competition, consumerism, an aging population, digital communications, evolving technologies for long-distance care, all played a part. Equally important, perhaps more so, were the explosive growth of Mayo Clinic and the increasing diversity of its activities. The centrifugal force of each component entity hoping to fly off on its own path threatened the centripetal strength of bodies staying in harmonious orbit around the core values and goals. Integration was seen as the best mechanism to balance these forces.

Originally, integration across the medical provider side of the enterprise—mainly at the three Mayo Clinics—took priority, and it soon became apparent that medical integration would be most effectively accomplished if accompanied by administrative integration. After all, medicine and administration had always operated hand in glove at Mayo. Now that the enterprise had grown beyond the borders of Rochester, Minnesota, the ties that bound the three Clinics were frayed, though not yet broken. For economies of scale, resource management, indeed, the best needs of the caregivers and the patients, integration on a global scale became a critical necessity.

By the early twenty-first century, Mayo Clinic leaders recognized that fundamental integration would improve the patient experience. This meant quite a lot of change for everyone. For example, the three Clinics had each implemented separate medical records systems decades earlier. If a patient seen at Arizona subsequently went to Rochester, the record had to be sent to the Rochester office manually. With the advent of digital technology, the record could be made available electronically. Even so, the records were separate, not the integrated record that is one of the hallmarks of Mayo's approach to care. Given that the three clinics had different computer systems, integrating the record across the three sites was trickier than it seems. Over time, major initiatives were implemented to create one system out of three, with interoperability across the enterprise. Although the number of patients treated at more than one Clinic was relatively small, the number was increasing and, over time, the Mayo Clinic Health System and other entities became more intimately connected to the Clinics, and so an integrated information system served many purposes.

So physicians and other providers had to learn new ways of doing things. Change is hard under any circumstances. When you mix in the lingering animosities about a Rochester takeover or a physician's sense of eroding autonomy, you have an enormous change-management problem. Nevertheless, the initiatives took hold and clinical and administrative areas became more integrated than ever.

INTEGRATING PUBLIC AFFAIRS

In public affairs, we integrated many of the diverse functions that managed Mayo Clinic's "outward facing" and brand-building activities. In 1996, five years after I was hired as director of the news bureau, I was named division chair for communications, reporting directly to Bob Smoldt. The division included internal communications, external relations, patient and visitor communications, and support for Mayo Health System and Mayo Medical Ventures. The offices in Scottsdale and Jacksonville were not yet included. The division was strictly a Rochester endeavor.

Even so, there was much to be done bringing these sections together. I'm often asked, "How did you do it? What was the imperative?" Much of the mystery comes from the questioner's experience with unsuccessful attempts at bringing common purpose, cooperation, and information sharing across these little fiefdoms. Never underestimate the desire of a manager, no matter how small their territory, to drive a stake into the ground and hoist the banner of their sovereignty. Never underestimate the ferocity with which that manager will defend that territory against all forces of change.

These impulses existed in my group, just as they do everywhere. They were tempered by Mayo Clinic's avowed culture of teamwork and humility. One could push the individual power envelope only so far before one's reputation would suffer irreparable damage. Mayo's committee structure and consensus culture, though, gave resistance many paths to voice concerns, raise objections, and search for compromise. Ergo, change could be slowed, although, in my experience, sensible change won out in the end, with a few exceptions—and, even then, necessary changes might be deflected in one year and rise up again in the next, until the social fabric of Mayo had worked its magic and the previously debunked idea would now have the patina of a change whose time had come.

In public affairs, the key area for integration was between internal and external communications. More than once, the news bureau had sent out a news release only to find that employees had yet to hear about whatever the release contained. A mantra evolved that employees shouldn't find out what was happening at their workplace by reading about it in the newspaper or seeing it on television.

Since the original Mayo Clinic was in Rochester, Minnesota, this was harder than it sounds. When I arrived in 1991, Rochester's population was only about seventy thousand. When you consider that roughly thirty thousand people worked at the Clinic and hundreds more in the attendant hotels and restaurants, it becomes evident that just about everyone knew someone or was related to someone who worked at Mayo.

Rochester then was served by an NBC affiliate, and a local afternoon newspaper, the *Post-Bulletin*, known locally as "the PB." (Now there is also an ABC affiliate and a Fox News affiliate.) The PB saw it as their mission to cover Mayo Clinic extensively, including, at times, the need to "expose" the inner workings of the Clinic. For us in the news bureau, the dilemma was that our focus was national and international. Many times, we sought maximum publicity for a story and found the PB would resent the fact that we'd pitched the release to *The New York Times* or *The Wall Street Journal* instead of them. From a business perspective, it made perfect sense, unless you arrive at the conclusion we eventually reached—that is, that, in many ways, the PB was an adjunct to our internal communications.

Consider a story from the 1990s when Mayo Clinic needed to revise how employees paid for health insurance. As it is for any American company, employee health insurance and medical care is very expensive. As costs rose, Mayo Clinic made the difficult decision to have employees pay a modest premium for coverage. Up to that point, Mayo had covered the costs 100 percent. Being self-insured, this meant a huge cost for Mayo.

Employees were told that a change was coming, and then a period of time elapsed before the details were decided and then announced. This was not accidental. Rumors fly fast, and the purpose of our communication was to keep employees informed about each step of the process.

One morning, I received a call from the PB. Employees had called the paper with rumors that enormous premiums would be imposed upon them and other draconian changes were coming to the health coverage. All the information given to the PB was incorrect, I knew, but on the very morning they called, Mayo was having the first of an extensive series of employee town halls, at which the complete details of the new plans were being revealed. So my dilemma was: Do I give the PB the correct information, decline comment, or devise some other statement? I decided to confer with the CEO of the Rochester Clinic.

Knowing Dr. H as I did, I entered Philips Hall, Mayo's largest auditorium, with a bit of trepidation and asked him to step out of the meeting for a minute. Fortunately, someone from human resources was speaking and he was available. In the hallway outside the auditorium, I asked Dr. H his thoughts about the PB call. Dr. H hated the PB. He saw them as a constant thorn in his side. As soon as I told him about the inquiry, he exploded.

"I don't want you to tell them a goddamn thing!" he said.

Rarely had I encountered this sort of overt anger at Mayo. Somewhat shocked, I kept quiet for a minute while he seethed. Then I tried reason. "We can't say nothing. They'll print the misinformation and that will be very bad for us."

Dr. H thought for a minute. "Do what you want," he said, and went back into the meeting.

In truth, the solution was fairly simple. I called the reporter back and told the truth. The information he had was wrong, we were rolling out the plan that very day, and once we'd had a chance to inform our employees, we'd give them the story in detail.

So the tempest in a teapot was abated. Over time, we learned to include the local media in our planning, even though, for most stories, they were not our target audience. For internal issues at Mayo, they were, of course, critical. Consistency between our internal and external messages was paramount. Later, when I was made division chair of communications, we introduced the standard operating procedure of creating detailed communications plans for both internal and external communications, ensuring that both audiences were accommodated in our thinking and our tactics. Hard as it may seem to believe, this had not been done before. For internal matters, the local media had been seen as an afterthought.

As digital communication evolved, we developed various lists for disseminating information quickly throughout the organization. Instances of employees learning about developments inside the Clinic by reading the PB were almost eliminated.

Another unanticipated glitch in communications arose among the three geographically disparate Clinics. Opened in 1986 and 1987, respectively, the Jacksonville and Scottsdale clinics antedated the widespread application of digital communications. They operated, more or less, in three communications bubbles. News about each would be shared with the other two, usually in the monthly employee magazine or at the periodic staff meetings. Real-time communication among the three in matters of public affairs was almost nonexistent.

For the first few years of the new sites' existence, this had not presented a major problem. Over time, though, situations arose when a story in *The Florida Times-Union*, say, or *The Arizona Republic* would spread to the other clinics and would spark consternation among the staff that they were not being informed of actions by the organization. In the worst case, some would feel there was something of a cover-up or, at least, information definitely withheld. If the Jacksonville campus had decided to build a hospital, shouldn't everyone be told? In those days, the Clinics each had separate provisions for budgeting and capital allocation. Ultimately, the budget decisions were vetted by what was then the top governing body, the executive council, and, in major instances, the board of trustees—Mayo's body of internal and external directors. Lacking an institutional forum, enterprise-wide information dissemination did not frequently occur and, often, when it did, it did not function as quickly as the grapevine.

During the time I was division chair of communications, 1996 to 2001, this persisted. In 2001, I was named department chair for public affairs for the entire foundation when my boss Bob Smoldt became chief administrative officer. At that time, I was then asked to work on reengineering the Mayo Clinic Scottsdale communication and marketing group and, later, do the same for the Mayo Clinic Jacksonville team. The eventual outcome was, among many things, a common portal for news about the enterprise and email distribution lists that covered all of the business entities of Mayo Clinic.

This probably seems obvious to the reader. At the time, it was revolutionary. Resistance to the idea was fierce. Each entity wanted to "control" its own messaging. Entity CEO's felt some of their authority eroding, seeing evidence of another Foundation (Rochester) takeover. Within my own group, the practitioners at the sites had to relinquish some of their individual control and modify procedures they felt worked well as they were. When it came time to merge the organization, news sites on the intranet sites for each of the Clinics, battle lines were drawn. Interestingly, one of the key issues was the color of the banner at the top of the site. Each site had adopted a local flavor for their graphics palette: desert earth tones for Arizona, tropical greens and blues for Florida. Besides the indigenous flavor, the colors served to differentiate them from Rochester and the foundation, which both used the classic Mayo blue. Meetings were held, leadership weighed in, weeks passed by, and, eventually, the decision was made to use blue.

The situation reminded me of a time early in my career, in Tucson, when St. Mary's and St. Joseph's hospitals merged under a corporate banner, Carondelet Health System. As the newly appointed head of communications for the corporation, I decided we should merge the two weekly newsletters into one. This was in the early 1980s, well before the Web. My staff took the bull by the horns and we rolled out a weekly newsletter for both campuses. Not long after, I was in my office at St. Joseph's when my secretary let me know Sister Beatrice wanted to see me (not her real name). I walked over to her office, sat down, and, after a very few pleasantries, heard this: "How dare you? How dare you rob this hospital of its newsletter? You have ripped the soul out of this institution. You should be ashamed of yourself."

St. Joseph's and St. Mary's were Catholic hospitals. The CEO was a nun who lived with Sister Beatrice. And I was raised Catholic. Here, I had made my first big move as a corporate executive and I was being condemned to perdition for all eternity.

In truth, I listened politely and said something along the lines of "I'll take it under advisement." Part of me was somewhat bemused. I doubted that I had ripped the soul out of St. Joseph's. Just the same, I learned something. I had ordered the change in the newsletter and implemented it by fiat. I had not consulted with one person at either hospital. Going forward, we revamped our approach and came up with a new format that had input from both hospitals and was well-received. For the rest of my career, I never forgot to get the opinions and buy-ins of the constituents that I was allegedly there to serve.

As with all change management, the best remedies were persistent communication and a simple unwavering mission. By this time at Mayo, in the early 2000s, the push for integration was gathering steam and the CEO and CAO of the foundation were behind the effort. Without their support, my task would have been impossible.

Our efforts bore fruit, demonstrated by the very high marks Mayo received in the subsequent employee opinion surveys. When asked if they felt informed about the direction of the organization and about the content of Mayo Clinic's strategic plan, an overwhelming majority of employees said they were.

INTEGRATING ACROSS BUSINESS UNITS

In 2001, when I became department chair, I inherited the following functions:

- MayoClinic.org
- Internal communications
- External communications
- Government relations
- Marketing
- Mayo Health System marketing and communication
- Development communications
- Mayo Clinic Scottsdale public affairs
- Mayo Clinic Jacksonville public affairs

These were all in various stages of integration. In some cases, the areas reported to me and, in other areas, they did not. Lines of authority were unclear, budgets were still controlled separately, and much friction persisted at the level of individual activities. Any merger creates winners and losers—it is impossible to avoid. I have found that most efforts at amelioration of those pains are ineffective and merely prolong agonies and the mourning period. Sops such as inflated titles and comanagement arrangements or "vice this" and "assistant that" simply cause confusion and, often, even more conflict than was originally present. Organizations must be structured in ways that are clear and simple.

Easier said than done, of course, and, in my career, I became well-known (some would say infamous) for frequent reorganization. I confess that there was some truth in this. My reasons were basic. The organization evolved at a rapid pace and we had to keep up by matching our resources to the current needs of Mayo Clinic and its patients. Concomitantly, as the structures evolved we found ourselves continuously improving our methods for working together.

I say "we," to acknowledge that public affairs had an administrative team that was excellent. Like any executive, I could do nothing on my own. My direct reports, known collectively as the public affairs leadership team (PALT) matured into a committed, courageous, and effective team upon whom I depended and upon whom I could rely without fear.

To effectuate the necessary level of integration, constant communication is essential. Also critical are common projects that transcend organizational boundaries. Nothing builds a team or exposes the fault lines in a potential team more quickly than having the members work together toward a common goal. PALT met quarterly face-to-face, usually in Rochester to cut down on travel costs. We would have brief retreats on campus with one overnight and hash out plans and actions in concert. In turn, I would visit the other sites at least quarterly, usually more often. This gave me a chance to meet with leaders of the sites and spend time working beside the staff at those locations.

As previously mentioned, I was asked to reengineer the Scottsdale group in 2001 and then, later, the Jacksonville group. To accomplish this, I commuted from Rochester to Scottsdale and then Rochester to Jacksonville every other week, for two and a half years and a year and a half, respectively. When you commute that much, the flight attendants and gate attendants know you by name. Frequent flying such as that is brutal, but the investment was necessary since, at that time, I was interim director of those groups in addition to being department chair for foundation public affairs. A critical intangible benefit was that I became a known entity at each campus rather than being seen as a "Rochester interloper." Even after my commuting stint ended and I returned to my quarterly visits, people were not surprised to see me on their campuses. I was more or less accepted as a member of their teams. I don't know how it can be done any other way than to be physically present.

Blending communications was low-hanging fruit. More challenging was brand management across the sites. Assessing the scope of Mayo Clinic's activities and their effect on consumers, my group and I concluded that Mayo Clinic would benefit greatly from an integrated brand presence. I suppose a globally integrated brand presence is the Holy Grail for any brand manager. Some companies do it brilliantly—Apple, Disney. Others, not so much. In health care, we had a wide-open field on which there were very few players, and we were starting with a big lead.

At national conferences, I have often been asked by my colleagues from other institutions how Mayo did it. They are aware of our level of integration and brand integrity, and they likewise fight the good fight against unnecessary territorial barriers and powerful egos. Every organization has different cultures and challenges. Even so, the reader might find it useful to hear about our experiences.

Initially, our concern was elevated because of some alarming (to us) brand data that we had unearthed. Without revealing anything proprietary, I can say that the data showed some erosion in certain attributes that we valued. While the degree of change was small, a few studies pointed to a possible trend. Importantly, the data showed us that our situation was not caused by any activities of our competitors. They had not "taken" any of our brand position. In essence, we were doing it to ourselves.

We in public affairs regarded this as the canary in the coal mine. The core issue was the many ways through diverse business entities that Mayo was approaching the public. While there were many anecdotes around the enterprise hinting at some of the concerns, this was the first time we had hard data. Mayo Clinic is a learning organization. Physician led, research driven, evidence based. The best way to influence decision making in such an environment is to present a rational data-driven case. Accordingly, my colleagues and I assembled an extensive presentation to be given at the then-annual 'Three Clinics Retreat" in Scottsdale.

The presentation included quantitative and qualitative data. We also gave our analysis of causes and remedies. Essentially, the recommendation was that, to perform effectively in the current marketplace, Mayo Clinic needed to strengthen the integration of its brand presence. In previous chapters, I have discussed the burgeoning Mayo Clinic enterprise as it extended its reach across the country and the world. By the time of this presentation, Mayo Clinic entities were impacting millions of people a year with materials, media, and events that were not generated by the clinical practice. Additionally, there was little central oversight of messaging. Most importantly to our minds were the lost opportunities to present a powerful brand message across multiple platforms if all the entities and functions were working synergistically. If development wanted to raise money for a proton beam center, didn't it make sense for the media relations team to promote stories about a proton beam? Or to put information about proton beam on the Mayo website? Or social media? As I've often stated, those ideas were nothing new in the "outside world" but, because of the peculiarities of health-care organization and governance, they were seen as practically revolutionary.

The leadership at the retreat accepted the fundamental issues. Predictably, the remedies were harder to swallow. The familiar themes of autonomy and inherent suspicion of centralized authority reared up again. Nonetheless, we left the meeting believing we'd been given the go-ahead to implement some changes. At Mayo, this means more planning, more committee visits, more data, in what often seems a repetitive and even circular process that, despite the time involved, eventually produces a positive outcome.

One initiative that later showed the benefits of cross-platform integration was called destination medical center (DMC). Mayo Clinic planned a truly significant investment in capital projects at the Rochester campus over a five-year period. To enhance the overall patient and visitor experience, Mayo proposed that the city of Rochester and the state of Minnesota endorse a plan that would facilitate investment in the Rochester community for infrastructure upgrades, new businesses, lodging, restaurants, and other amenities.

Naturally, the state legislature faced many conflicting priorities for funding. The attitude from the capitol, St. Paul, usually centered on the belief that Mayo Clinic did very well financially and didn't need any "handouts," even though Mayo wasn't actually asking for handouts. This prejudice was deeply rooted and opponents who wanted their budget priorities approved didn't hesitate to use that particular club. During one particularly testy time, our CEO had heard one too many times about the wealth of Rochester and said publicly that there were "many states other than Minnesota that would love to have a Mayo Clinic." He was bashed a bit for daring to speak the truth, which could be perceived as a threat, although recall that Mayo has two other campuses primed for growth. My view was it was about time someone had called this out.

Mayo met with civic leaders, business people, and legislators. We also used news media and our internal communications to keep people updated. We created websites to explain the proposals and illustrate the benefits. Over time, public sentiment swung in Mayo's favor and the legislation passed.

The requisite functions for this initiative—government relations, community relations, external relations, internal communications— were within my administrative purview, so integrating messaging was more easily facilitated. The process became much more difficult in the realm of true shared services, which, in Mayo terms, meant working across department and business entity barriers.

To be sure, Mayo had gradually implemented a shared services organization. In typical Mayo fashion, the initial meetings were advisory in nature. Over time, pilot projects were instituted. Eventually, the difficult task of reassigning staff and merging budgets began.

One of my methods for achieving a major goal was to write a brief white paper on the subject. Being a writer by trade, I am most comfortable working out a problem or set of problems on paper. Fortunately, this was a common approach at Mayo, so I felt at home.

In one key respect, though, my tendencies did not align well with Mayo Clinic. At Mayo, I became known as a visionary—some might say dreamer. I was never satisfied with the status quo—not for me, not for my staff, not for Mayo Clinic. I completely internalized Peter Drucker's admonition "adapt or die." I might have added a corollary to this, had I known then what I know now: "adapt *and* die." As the author John Updike once wrote, "Every growth is a betrayal."

Let me pause here to mention that this "visionary" tag was not my invention. During my long career, I received innumerable assessments of my character and performance, whether it was from Myers-Briggs surveys and the like or vast numbers of personal performance reviews. The visionary label came up consistently. Like any blessing, it can also be a curse.

I wrote a white paper proposing a major reorganization of shared services functions that I thought belonged in public affairs. My motivation was in response to the brand analysis we had presented at the retreat in Scottsdale. The forum for sharing this white paper was the Mayo Clinic administrative team (MCAT), led by then chief administrative officer Shirley Weis, who had succeeded Bob Smoldt. This group consisted of the various department chairs for all administrative areas, such as finance, human resources, IT, and the three Clinics. Shirley had read my paper and was generally supportive.

She knew, though, that at Mayo, she could not implement something like my proposal by unilateral fiat. The entire administrative organization would have to endorse the plans. As we talked through the proposal, it was clear that the ideas provoked resistance on the part of many team members. An underlying subtext was the issue of a person (me) trying to agglomerate staff and funding (power). Given that I am an idealist and a visionary, I knew this could be a possible perspective, but I thought the obvious benefits would speak for themselves, being Mayo's success on the global stage. I also believed that, after so many years, the people around the table would know that was not my intent. To me, my motives were pure. Unfortunately, others had their doubts. The discussion was, as they say, robust. At the meeting after the meeting, I had to be told that I had been somewhat pilloried. I hadn't seen it that way at all. For me, it was a healthy discussion. No one had flat-out refused the ideas. Moreover, I never expected the path to be without potholes and pitfalls. That just went with the gestalt of change.

RESISTANCE

With Shirley's guidance, I continued to tackle different areas that had been identified as contributing to the slight fragmentation of the brand presence. One of the most difficult was with the development department, which I have learned is a situation many in my position have struggled with at other medical centers. For the first century of its existence, Mayo Clinic did not have a formal fundraising operation. With the establishment of Mayo Medical School in the 1970s, the institution decided to begin fund-raising to pay for the school, so as not to drain resources from the clinical operation to support it. By the twenty-first century, development had grown into a significant adjunct to Mayo Clinic's economy, raising upward of $300 million a year for medical research and education. Considering the growing reimbursement shortfall, this funding was a critical component of maintaining the viability of Mayo's research and education mission.

Like so many other of Mayo's "diversifications," development had maintained a rather separate existence, fostering a culture and, one might say, an attitude about its own exceptionalism. This attitude of specialness is something I have encountered in many departments in my career. It seems every collection of professionals has an unspoken hierarchy and a simultaneous need to set themselves apart from others. Specialists are superior to generalists, cardiologists are superior to pediatricians, surgeons outrank everybody (just ask them). Among administrators, there are the "line" functions, such as nursing and other caregivers, and the "staff" functions such as finance, human resources, and public affairs. At times, it seemed as if the medical and "line" staff saw departments like human resources and public affairs as sanctuaries for people who couldn't hack the "real" stuff like calculus or organic chemistry. Once, I watched a very prominent surgeon present a series of slides about various functions at Mayo and their cost and how they related to the cost per Medicare patient. The idea was to lower the costs for Medicare patients to better align with reimbursement. The surgeon came to the administrative staff functions and said, without hesitation, that he had no idea what "these people did" but it sure as hell cost a lot and "I don't know why the hell we need all this."

During the first few weeks of my time at Mayo, I was sent out on the obligatory tour of all the major functions and meetings with their leaders. At one memorable appointment, I knocked on the door of one of the executives in charge of some of the "real" stuff, who looked up from his desk and said, "Who are you?" I told him I was the new director of the news bureau and we had an appointment.

"What for?"

"It's an orientation. I tell you something about what I do, and you orient me about what you and your department do."

"I don't care about what you do."

Thus ended my orientation to a department that shall remain nameless.

Although development was often perceived by the medical staff as residing in that unpleasant category of "staff function Siberia" (along with human resources, public affairs, and a few other groups), they had a special twist that gave them something of an edge: they raised a great deal of money. Like some other departments, they could fall prey to seeing themselves as institutional saviors. Sometimes they seemed to forget that it was the actual medical work that earned the money on whose behalf they made the asks, yet no one could deny their success in performing a highly specialized task that very few wanted to do and was actually rather undervalued and often misunderstood. Over the years, they had hired their own support infrastructure, including communications and graphics. They had their own communications staff, produced their own marketing materials (although the word "marketing" was anathema to them), and even developed campaigns, messaging, logos, and graphic identities separate from the rest of the enterprise. Eventually, development was reaching millions of people each year with separate messaging and appearance—that is, separate branding. Often, this approach conflicted with the messaging and priorities of other areas. Because of the cultural issues, polite attempts at coordination through collegiality and negotiation had not worked.

When I started, in 1991, this arrangement was considered untouchable. Now, more than twenty years later, we were looking at goring a very sacred cow. At one point, my colleagues in public affairs leadership and I met with the then-chair of the development department and his leadership team to talk through the issues. We had one of those horribly awkward and painful corporate meetings that are obligatory but almost useless. We were supposed to work out a solution together when the situation was that the one group (mine) was trying to push through a change that many perceived necessary, that is bringing the development communications staff closer to the brand management and overall brand strategy component of Mayo, while the other group was absolutely determined to resist the change at all costs. Repeatedly, the department chair asked why this particular aspect of integration was necessary. Was there a business case? Or was this another integration for integration's sake (a common sticking point at the time). Since the development department raised hundreds of millions of dollars each year, their perspective was understandable when viewed from the narrow viewpoint of one department. My arguments were that development would be even more successful if all the resources at Mayo Clinic, not just the few under their direct control, were integrated behind the scenes to help enable their cause, and, second, that Mayo Clinic as a brand, as an institution, would better serve its constituents and thereby be more successful globally if all its strategies, messaging, materials, and priorities were coordinated synergistically. In truth, the second half of this argument was compelling to many of us. Unfortunately, this all fell on deaf ears, with the development chair growing visibly angrier by the moment. When we decided to give it up, he punctuated the meeting by putting his face into my face and criticizing my choice of suit, shirt, and tie, since they were all striped, which worked well to my mind, but he thought was absolutely a sartorial *faux pas*. On that note, the kumbaya phase of our labors together was terminated.

Some months later, development had a new chair and the initiative to merge the development communications staff into the larger public affairs group gained new momentum. The CEO and chief administrative officer made it clear to the new chair that this was the direction Mayo wanted to pursue. To her credit, unlike her predecessor, she had a more global vision of the Mayo enterprise and, being new to the position, she did not take these initiatives as a personal affront. Although she had to endorse a direction many of her staff disliked, she did it with magnanimity.

It's important to understand some of the mechanics about how integrations such as this worked. The communications staff remained housed in the development offices. The new leader of the development communications division reported to the chair for public affairs but also sat with the leadership team of Development. Both departments were represented at high-level meetings with the CEO and CAO regarding relevant development matters. The development chair worked with me on the budget for development communications and in evaluating the division chair's performance. Everything possible was done to maintain team cohesion in Development.

Besides the larger, more abstract reasons for making the change, the reader should understand the very definite operational reasons behind it, which were even more sensitive and perhaps more compelling. As part of the process of integrating this group into the larger program, I met individually with the development staff charged with producing their materials. As so often has been the case when nonmarketing noncommunications professionals manage these functions, I found unhappy staff, disarray, waste, and lost opportunities—in fact, all the ills enumerated in previous chapters: the job shop mentality, the lack of strategic direction, an absence of effective operating procedures, and the overt and covert abuse of the "writing staff." The department as a whole did not know what they didn't have, since the situation had persisted for decades. Once we righted the ship, made some staff changes, and produced some professional materials, some of the development staff gradually appreciated the new order of things. Old habits die hard and deep wounds are slow to heal. Anyone involved in mergers or similar transitions should not underestimate the emotional turmoil produced, particularly the passive-aggressive animosity that is directed at leadership. The management team needs to be geared for some turmoil and some tears. Not everyone, however competent in her field, has the temperament to steer a group through these rough waters. Compounding the problem is that it is almost always necessary to change the leadership of the group, since it is almost impossible for a leader from the past, with his or her alliances, attitudes, and history, who was largely responsible for the situation as it currently stands, to adapt the different behaviors and vision necessary to make the new ideas a reality. I have found that the wait-and-see, let's-give-it-a-try-and-hope-for-the-best approach simply prolongs the inevitable. Besides, usually, the team members know the fix they are in is due, largely, to bad management and rightly will question the wisdom of keeping the manager responsible.

PURSUING A GLOBAL BRAND

This first tier of integration of public affairs and branding activities consisted largely of coordinating groups that were possessed of a common communications or marketing function at Mayo. In a sense, they were no-brainers, notwithstanding the amount of time, effort, and turmoil that had to be overcome to achieve a larger teamwork. Eventually, though, my reading and interactions with chief marketing officers and other leaders from outside health care compelled me to think that a global, multifaceted enterprise like Mayo Clinic could attain a level of brand, product, and service integration rivaled only by such companies as Disney and Apple. The vision incorporated the principles of branding and marketing but also, at its most fulfilled, a kind of integrated business planning that Mayo was already pursuing, although in a fitful and somewhat unconscious manner.

I always found Mayo Clinic to be something of a marvelous organism. The term "learning organization" is thrown around rather loosely these days. Of all the places I've worked, Mayo Clinic was the only one that truly deserved that label. In a sense, this was almost inevitable. Physicians and nurses and other caregivers are, by nature and by professional requirements, perpetual learners. The

Mayo brothers themselves modeled this behavior their entire lives and bred it into the culture of the organization. Mayo Clinic seemed to me to demonstrate these behaviors *en masse*, as a body politic— an enormous collection of people working together in a community, whether or not they were directed to do so.

So much good occurred at Mayo during its first century and a half as a result of this relatively undirected volitional teamwork that the notion that Mayo should codify such activity with policies and procedures was slow to take hold. As Mayo grew and grew during the last thirty or so years, it became apparent that the enterprise had simply become too big and too geographically diverse to expect the same kind of spontaneous integrations to occur. Accordingly, more specific policies and, dare I say, *rules* had to be put into place. One could not simply depend upon the Mayo organization to take in new staff and breed good Mayo citizens by osmosis as had occurred for so long. Even so, Mayo had a way of finding its true north, time and again, because of the essential goodwill and pride the staff brought to the intelligent pursuit of a common mission.

From my vantage point, Mayo Clinic was on the verge of a new level of greatness, becoming a global brand operation that would make it unbeatable in the marketplace. No other institution in health care had a stronger brand foundation. Much of the essential integrative infrastructure was either completed or underway. The principle of data-driven brand management had been inculcated into the organization. Missing was a complete horizontal approach to integrated business planning and brand management across Mayo's various business platforms.

A number of factors influenced my decision to pursue this wider integration. First and foremost, I believed it would provide better information to consumers and therefore, ultimately, better decision making on their part. Mayo Clinic had so much to offer businesses, families, donors, and other constituents; a fully integrated multiplat-form approach would demonstrate the powerful synergies available to them. When Mayo completed the global integrated infrastructure and decision-making apparatus that was underway, it would enable an unheralded kind of customer-relationship management and life-time partnership with patients and families.

I was convinced that the relationship of the patient to the American hospital needed an upgrade because I believed it was broken. Episodes of care were mostly transactional, expensive, and sporadic. Little attention—or money—was given to wellness, prevention, or mental health. Everyone in health care knows this. The trouble is they are trapped in an insane American "system" that often rewards behavior contrary to their best instincts.

Mayo Clinic was already different, but to my mind not different enough to maintain its preeminence. Many initiatives were underway, and I saw the potential to pull them together and focus talents and energies in support of a new vision. This vision would encompass using every means of digital communications available to enable patients' interactions with their providers and empower them to self-manage their health. Monitoring and other transactional episodes of care could be done at home or in connected community clinics and hospitals. Information, testing, and follow-up care could be connected to Mayo Clinic through those community centers at a lower cost. Mayo would provide its unparalleled specialty and subspecialty care at the times and places it was most needed and most cost-effective.

Again, much of this was already happening in a fragmented fashion, particularly regionally in Florida, Arizona, and Minnesota. To me, the most exciting possibility for this kind of interconnect-edness and expansion would be for these efforts to be globally integrated and branded. Similarly, activities such as the reference lab, health information, the Mayo Clinic Web presence, and product development could be cross-pollinated and cross-sold for the benefit of business and patients.

I wrote white papers, met with colleagues, and presented at various meetings. The effort generated a great deal of attention—not all of it positive. At a series of retreats, my fellow administrators and I reviewed these ideas. Many saw the intellectual merit in them, at least as a long-term goal or dream. Reality, though, has a way of making dreams seem untenable. In other words, culture eats strategy for lunch and dreams for dessert.

Ultimately, we held a massive retreat facilitated by an outside group for a few days. All the stakeholders were there. It was quite a production, with numerous subgroups working out solutions to various problems, including achieving the synergies I had proposed.

One anecdote in particular will sum up the experience, at least from my perspective. I was in a work group—I don't remember which one—and the conversation drifted a bit, in a way I found amorphous and inconclusive. One of my tendencies, I have learned, is that, in such a situation, I cannot bear the frustration of endless meandering without a destination. So, almost involuntarily, I found myself, first, talking a lot and then, eventually, at the white board drawing an organizational chart that depicted the future as I saw it. The group had asked me to do it, so I did. One of my other traits, I have learned, is to believe passionately in what I am doing, and so I am sure that the group saw in me a person possessed, perhaps not only by a vision but by ambition.

What I didn't know and found out later was that they also thought I was passionately creating an empire for myself and they didn't like it very much. The merits of the ideas paled in comparison to the institutional dread of someone trying to agglomerate power. Coupled with the resistance of any of my fellow administrators to the idea of giving up a piece of their individual departments to fuel this global effort, which they probably believed was an ego trip on my part, and you have an institutional nonstarter.

To be fair, some shifting did occur. Elements of a media production group that had been led separately were put into public affairs.

Communications was rearranged to combine external and internal relations into a single group (which probably should have happened years before). A full-fledged medical director for public affairs was named, an essential component for ongoing influence. Other tweaks were made, but nothing on the grand scale I had imagined.

During this period, a colleague who had been at Mayo even longer than I had said to me, "John, Mayo Clinic is a place where progress is made in baby steps. We do one thing, then the next, building on what went before. You like to make giant leaps. That's hard for us."

Such a comment could be seen as discouraging. I saw it as sincere and somewhat helpful. After the dust had settled from this sojourn into institutional no-man's-land and I saw that my vision would not be fully realized, I took heart in the notion that I had set certain wheels in motion. Although the relatively large centralization I had proposed did not materialize, I believe that the institutional consciousness had been raised and the organization had taken not only tangible, though incremental, steps in that direction but a major leap in culturally recognizing the possibilities thereof and in how Mayo Clinic might compose itself in the years ahead.

MAYO CLINIC AND THE MALL OF AMERICA

During the last few years of my career, I had one of those experiences that shapes you for the rest of your life. When I started at Mayo Clinic in 1991 I was invited to a meeting with some of the people developing Mall of America (MOA), located in Bloomington, Minnesota, and, to this day, the largest indoor mall in the United States. At that time, the MOA group proposed that Mayo lease space at the mall to house something akin to a medical museum combined with a Mayo Clinic exhibit. Given Mayo's reluctance to overtly promote itself (especially back then) or be involved with blatantly commercial activity, this idea went nowhere. Besides the cultural barrier, there was the cost and, truthfully, the unknown—that is, what would the mall be like and will it be successful?

That last question is almost comical now, given that the MOA is hugely successful, having become a destination for shoppers around the world and an icon of Minnesota. As the years went on and both Mayo Clinic and MOA occupied premier positions in their respective categories, it began to seem to some within Mayo that some kind of association with the mall might be beneficial. For a while, the idea of a retail store was bandied about, to be populated by products from the Medical Ventures group. They ultimately declined, not finding the venue financially viable.

The idea was rekindled when MOA announced plans for a major expansion of the mall, to include a town square concept with recreational facilities, a cinema, and, they hoped, a health-care component. The traditional mall experience was losing its luster. MOA had already changed the nature of mall shopping by including an amusement park on the premises. The current thinking was to turn a mall into more of a community center with shops and services and a more human feeling to the environment.

Mayo Clinic and MOA discussed what could be done in this type of space. Unlike the tenor of earlier times, Mayo had finally embraced the concept of wellness and prevention. Plans had been approved for a comprehensive wellness center on the Rochester campus. The new strategic plan adopted wellness as a core principle. Now a presence at the Mall of America offered an opportunity for Mayo Clinic to touch many more people in meaningful ways with wellness, prevention, health information, and a connection to the Clinic.

At first, the possibilities seemed limitless. We had the opportunity to invent something totally new and, on the surface at least, leadership appeared ready to take that leap. The clean slate appealed to me and I volunteered to participate in the creation of this new center. I was made secretary of the committee charged with developing the plan, along with a physician leader.

Thus began the least satisfying, most difficult, and ultimately biggest failure of my career. Despite my sense of the auspicious onset, signs of trouble emerged almost at once. Members of the committee could not agree on the charge—that is, the material purpose of our committee. Despite weeks of discussion and research, various members interpreted the mission in different ways. At the heart of the debate was the question of Mayo Clinic's traditions and direction. Many thought Mayo should "stick to the knitting" and establish a patient-care operation at the mall, preferably centering more on a subspecialty that would have high demand, such as sports medicine. Others thought it should be a primary care facility along the lines of MinuteClinic. A third faction, of which I was a proponent, saw the attraction of creating something entirely new in health care, a facility that offered wellness, prevention, and alternative care in a people-friendly setting combined with some primary and secondary medical services, with an ability for people to be referred to Mayo Clinic in Rochester when appropriate.

Many months were spent following dead ends with business models and consumer studies. Frustrations mounted as members felt their time was being wasted, since little was getting done. Internal conflicts intensified. Eventually, some members left the group to be replaced by others who either had divergent views or were completely in the dark. After a year, a new physician leader chaired the committee when the original chair left Mayo for a new position at a system elsewhere. I remained on the committee but moved out of the secretary slot. A very capable new administrator was named as secretary and work commenced anew.

Under new leadership, a plan came together, eventually. A stint working with IDEO resulted in quite an ambitious plan for a facility along the lines I previously described that I supported. This was shot down by leadership as too expensive and too risky. Thus died the idea of doing something bold and innovative. Leadership asked us to go back to the drawing board.

At this moment, had I possessed a better perspective, I would have resigned from the project. My read of the organization had been faulty. I had been told to think big, be bold, help lead Mayo in a new direction. People said such things. Trouble was, they didn't really mean them. If memory serves, I did offer to leave the project but was told to stay on, although then the new committee secretary was appointed, and I stepped back somewhat.

As I look back, I see that I exhibited a few traits that are probably endemic to my personality that manifested in responses to the situation that weren't always helpful. Usually calm, levelheaded, and tolerant, I became louder, more insistent, more polarizing. I saw myself as a lone advocate for radical change. I believed in the cause and wanted to be courageous. Around this time, I made a presentation to a gathering of my administrative peers about the project. For the first and only time in my career, I publicly crashed and burned. The problem was my overconfident enthusiasm, which some saw as arrogance. Also, the presentation was short on specifics, since we had few, and long on vision and abstractions. Given the operational nature of the audience, this was fatal. Taken all together, these issues gave people the notion that I wasn't taking the project seriously, that I was cavalierly glossing over details and issues. In the following days, I received some very negative feedback. I had done the project no favors and, thereafter, resolved not to be its face, at least as much as I was able. There was another aspect to the reaction that wasn't my fault. I was chair of public affairs and marketing. Many wondered openly why "the communications guy" had been given this assignment. My presentation cemented their fears.

While I personally roiled with internal conflict, the project proceeded apace with compromise upon compromise until, finally, a store was erected fronting on the Mall of America rotunda, a prime location. The fact that it was a "store" symbolizes everything that was wrong with it. Though it had a retail component, it also had some high-tech gadgets for information and a few erratic opportunities for alternative therapies and occasional consultations. No one knew what to make of it. Even as it was being constructed, I knew in my heart it would fail. Even when it was a shell, I could tell that the whole concept didn't gel and that the public would not get what it had really wanted from a Mayo presence at Mall Of America.

During the opening days, various Mayo leaders came through Minneapolis on their travels to and from the Clinic and stopped by the store. Almost inevitably, in those first weeks, our high-tech gadgets broke down just as Mayo visitors tried to use them. My colleagues were just as perplexed as the public, and they made their feelings known relentlessly. So then came months of tweaking, rebooting, retweaking, and re-rebooting. Nothing worked. We made our last push with a dramatically revised plan that might have turned the tide, a different center in a different location more focused on the traditional patient services of patient care and referrals to Mayo but, by then, it was too late. Leadership and the staff in general had lost faith in the project and it was shut down.

WHAT I LEARNED

In the years since the store folded, Mayo Clinic established a Sports Medicine Clinic in a redeveloped section of downtown Minneapolis. The center opened after I retired from the Clinic, so I don't know much about it except that I hear it is doing well. The Mall of America project, I believe, helped Mayo leaders adjust to the concept of having a presence in the Twin Cities. Some of the same people who worked on the Mall of America project were involved in the Sports Medicine Clinic. Although I have not spoken with them, I would surmise they learned from our experiences.

It is often said in the corporate world that failure is an important educator. Some business gurus encourage leaders to allow their employees to fail occasionally, for without taking big risks, one cannot make big gains. This nostrum may be true for individuals like Steve Jobs or certain companies with a strong entrepreneurial spirit. In my experience, it is not true in health care.

So one must be careful about risks. As I evaluate the circumstances of the project's demise, I see now that we failed to bring leadership along. For many weeks, we labored in obscurity. This was partly due to the length of time we took to pull a plan together. It was also due to a simple lack of upward communication on the part of the chair and myself. This led to the grapevine carrying the message. If you aren't in control of your message, you are standing on thin ice indeed.

This lack of understanding was also enabled by top leadership's inability to articulate what they wanted us to do. They told us to tell them. When we told them, they didn't like it. When we changed it, they didn't like it. To us, it seemed they'd only know it when they saw it. We were guessing and guessed wrong. Part of this problem was mixed messages. On the one hand, we were told to create something wholly new. On the other hand, we were told the presence had to make a profit, basically immediately. These two items are almost always *prima facie* incompatible in the early going of a "wholly new" venture. Over time, it became clear that the latter criterion was the most important, and we had not realized that until it was too late. Had we focused on that alone, what we created would have been vastly different.

In a more abstract sense, we misread and overshot the organization. The culture was not ready for a radical brand extension. In retrospect, this seems obvious. At the time, many voices were expressing a belief that Mayo would benefit from a visionary outpost in the Twin Cities. As it turned out, they didn't mean what they said. They weren't interested in spending millions of dollars to initiate something revolutionary and nurture it and carry it for a few years until it took shape. They had no confidence it would ever be viable financially. One cannot blame them. We were not able to show definitive numbers because our proposal was fraught with all the problems I've mentioned. Without a cohesive sense of purpose, services, and target consumers, you are swimming in the dark.

As I have pointed out *ad infinitum*, at Mayo Clinic, you cannot move forward on any project, traditional or radical, without deeply committed physician involvement. We never had that for the Mall of America project. A few physicians rose to the occasion but, for the most part, Mall of America was a nonstarter with them, since it required staffing a facility ninety miles from home that had an ambiguous purpose, a setting in a shopping mall, of all places, and would ultimately detract from the revenue generated by the physician's home department. Such issues can be overcome with the right kind of support and buy-in: practices can be reimbursed, money can be applied from other budgets, etcetera. Remember, Mayo Clinic physicians are salaried, so we are not talking about affecting an individual physician's salary. Nonetheless, these barriers were close to insurmountable, given all the other problems with the project.

As so often happens with visionary ideas, we suffered from trying to do too much. Unclear as to our primary focus, we tried to do a little bit of everything. Then, when we faced the realities of institutional uncertainty and limited funding, we ended up building a facility with a little bit of some services, and none of others that, in the end, were probably more important to consumers, all of it in a mishmash that had no rhyme or reason.

The Mall of America project was conceived as an experiment. Sometimes experiments teach through success. More often, they teach through failure. Mayo Clinic learned from the experience, as did I and my colleagues. In the end, one must be prepared for the consequences of such endeavors.

CHAPTER 8

HEALING A BROKEN DEPARTMENT

OUT OF BALANCE

Over the years, I was often assigned the task of healing a broken department. The words "healing" and "broken" have not been chosen cavalierly. Time and again, I have found that departments—teams—that need "reengineering" comprise good people with useful skills that have been broken—dispirited and ill-used— by unfortunate circumstances, usually by bad management.

The most common circumstance resulting in the dysfunction of a team is when they are out of sync with the organization. As one CEO said to me, "I have all these people over there doing all this stuff but I have no idea what they're doing or accomplishing. All I know is it costs a lot of money." The team in question knows that something is terribly wrong. The poor fit is evident in every interaction with leadership, every edited or rejected piece of copy, every slashed budget. Their individual reactions to such a situation vary. Some will be angry, others depressed; all will fear for their jobs.

Invariably, the team believes they are performing the functions for which they were hired or would gladly do if they were allowed. They resent their inferior, powerless position in the organization. They feel they are being disrespected. They do not understand how things could have gotten as bad as they have become.

The incumbent manager in these situations may fight for that missing respect in ways that are not helpful. They make outright demands to be respected without changing anything about how the team performs. Or they kowtow excessively and make their subordinates do whatever is asked of them in an attempt to court goodwill. The manager, at first, struggles just as mightily as the subordinates, sometimes even more so. After all, they are responsible for the output of the team and the well-being of its members. Few are so insensitive as not to be affected by the disaffection of their colleagues. By the time I am involved, however, the frustrated manager is usually furious or, more commonly, so beaten down that they have checked out, becoming caretakers of a job shop, subject to the conflicting whims of numerous superiors and losing all respect in the eyes of the subordinates they are supposed to lead.

In one extreme case, the CEO of an organization that I worked with was so fed up with his marketing team that he banished them to an off-campus location. The office walls were concrete block, the cubicles in the center of the space had partitions six-feet high, and the entire area was littered with cardboard boxes full of the brochures and mailings the CEO disdained. The previously committed manager of the group gradually withdrew from any pretense of engagement, arranging to take postgraduate classes during work time and, according to the team, letting the group basically fend for themselves. Since the team was so far off-campus as to be virtually invisible, few people had any sense of the group's behavior. Every group I have been asked to repair has been invisible, metaphorically speaking, except the leadership team knew they weren't getting the services they needed, although they did not know the reasons why.

MANAGEMENT PROBLEMS

In my opinion, the desire for change, for the department in question to be rehabilitated, almost always rose from a change in leadership at the very top or, at least, a serious change in thinking on the part of a very senior leader. When a new CEO takes the helm of an organization, he or she will necessarily assess the assets at his or her disposal. The CEO usually has been put into position to effect change. The status quo is not an option. She will evaluate what tools are available to her to have the greatest chance of success.

In health care, marketing is not usually the first order of business. Naturally, the medical aspects take precedence—that and the overall strategic direction of the enterprise. Sooner or later, though, the CEO realizes that one cannot bring meaningful change about without effective communication with the medical staff and employees, and that a professional internal communications program is an essential component of her strategy. I say component because many have theorized, and I agree, that leadership behavior is the most important aspect of internal communications. Some say it is as much as 65 to 75 percent of the overall success factor. This is often summarized by the well-known adage "If you talk the talk, you have to walk the walk." If leadership is not walking the talk, the staff will figure it out in a heartbeat. Trust will erode. Change will be difficult, if not impossible, to achieve.

Many others have written extensively about how managers and leaders can be seen to be walking the talk. From the communication and marketing perspective, there are a few points to make.

Leaders need to demonstrate authenticity, the sense of integrity that comes from saying what you believe and believing what you say. In the age of video and digital communication, this is more critical than ever. It is impossible to hide behind a formal portrait, a staged grip-and-grin, or a written statement. Sadly, perhaps unbelievably, many health-care leaders retreat into these secure comfort zones, even as the world around them proves every day the foolhardiness of such an approach. Leaders hate to feel exposed or vulnerable. Social media, town halls, and a twenty-four-hour-a-day news cycle increase the sense of risk. This is why critical thinking, careful expression, and professional guidance have become so endemic to the culture of business. All of this, though, must emanate from a leader's internal consistency, or the persona will evaporate.

For me, the greatest exemplar of that philosophy was Dr. Robert Waller, the first CEO of Mayo that I worked for. Dr. Waller spoke, wrote, and carried himself with a Lincolnesque dignity and humility. When I became chair of institutional communications, I asked Dr. Waller what he wanted me to do for him. As he always did, he thought for a minute before he spoke.

"John, I don't know enough about your field to tell you how to lead communications. After a number of years in this job, though, I can tell you that everything I do is communications. In a meeting, if I call on Dr. Jones first and fail to ask Dr. Smith for his thoughts, everyone in the room will wonder why. If I am talking to Dr. Anderson in the hallway, the people who see us are sure something is up. I'm not sure how you manage that, but I know it's true and I know it's important."

Perhaps any leader at a high level of the organization learns this truism eventually. What is noteworthy about the best leaders, such as Dr. Waller, is that they don't just realize the truth of the adage intellectually but have the capacity, empathy, and courage to absorb and internalize its meaning and use it to the organization's advantage. This may seem simple or obvious when written in black and white but, over and over again, I have seen leaders observe or experience the reality of how their behavior affects an enterprise or a team and reject the feedback out of hand, or worse, see it as a personal affront, often saying, in so many words, "I am who I am and I cannot or will not change my personality." This is nothing short of arrogance and, in the end, is destructive to the team and the leader.

Scholars say the second most important factor in successful internal communication is the reward system, roughly 15 percent. Through the reward system, leadership literally either puts its money where its mouth is, or it does not. As with behavior, the workforce will soon decipher which behaviors are rewarded and which are not. We all know the corporate archetypes of the empty suit, the human deadwood, and the furtive incompetent. As these types of employees are carried, protected, or just ignored, the resentment of the vast majority of the staff who work hard, exhibit excellence, and otherwise give a large portion of their lives to the corporate "family" turns into a toxicity that can dissolve even the strongest bonds of teamwork and allegiance to the company's mission. Years ago, a young person on one of my teams, let's call him Doug, came into my office specifically to ask about the phenomenon of an empty suit. He was referring to a particular senior executive whom everyone considered unreliable, phony, and overly political. Doug asked me how such a situation could persist. Doug was in his early twenties, very sincere, and hard working, and this was his first corporate position. What could I say? "There are people like him in every company," I said to Doug. "It seems to be an unavoidable human phenomenon. After all, a large company is pretty much a microcosm of society in general. If you expect everything here to meet an ideal of complete fairness and just rewards, you will always be disappointed."

I meant this with no cynicism, just, to me, a statement of the obvious. Nonetheless, I absolutely believe, as I told Doug, that every effort should be made to achieve that ideal of a level playing field, fair play, and just rewards. It is not easy. Health-care corporations impose systems to ensure equality in compensation, hiring, firing, and other aspects of human resources. This is necessary and appropriate. Unfortunately, these policies also protect the underperformer, compensate the average worker at a level similar to a star, and often make it that much more difficult to reward the outstanding individual.

Still, one must find a way. I worked with a woman, we'll call her Jane, who endured the hardships of an especially arduous assignment for many months. Not only was the work itself difficult, but she had to work with complete jerks from outside the company. We've all had to cope with those "partnerships," when the group on the other side cannot get themselves together, or make ridiculous demands, or just behave badly, day after day. At Mayo, partnerships can be rife with hazards, since the Clinic has such high and restrictive standards regarding product endorsements and use of the brand. Our experience was that we were often the outliers compared to the business world at large. We were fine with that. Partners, though, sometimes rebelled. Despite all this and more, Jane succeeded in her mission.

I wanted to reward her, preferably with money. At Mayo Clinic, though, monetary bonuses just weren't done (with some very rare exceptions). I wanted my boss, the aforementioned Bob Smoldt, to make an exception and allow human resources to cut Jane a check. He would not, since he believed in applying the compensation fairly and by the rules. Bob always upheld the Mayo Clinic values, personally and professionally. After I proposed the bonus and he declined, he thought for a moment and then said, "Say, I tell you what I will do. I'll write her a letter. Give me some of the specifics of what she did, and I'll send something to her."

I left somewhat disappointed, Bob's words of "a letter" repeating themselves in my mind. I imagined Jane reacting to her reward as if a doctor had just given her a lollipop after getting a shot, or her parents had given her socks and a fruit basket for Christmas. A few weeks later, though, I visited Jane in her office and found her beaming. "Look at this," she said. On her desk was the letter from Bob, framed, thanking her for her outstanding work with a very difficult project and also for her overall dedication to Mayo Clinic (Jane was a very long-term employee). She was clearly over the moon, and I could see the letter meant more to her than any short-lived monetary supplement.

Bob's actions were consistent with overall Mayo Clinic policies and values. Leaders fail when their actions contradict their words and the expressed values of the company. Many hospitals and medical centers like to refer to themselves as a family. In fact, at every health-care organization I have worked for, the top people used that metaphor, time and time again. Yet when the chips are down, those same hospitals will hire a management consultant to slash hospital budgets and move to remove scores of staff. The contradiction is inescapable.

I raise these issues from the perspective of internal messaging and communications. Innumerable sources are available regarding effective leadership. From my vantage point, leaders need to abandon the fantasy that an article about values written in corporate-speak and published in the weekly newsletter has any meaning to staff who can see that the actions and rewards of the leadership team contradict every word of the article.

STRAIGHT TALK

At Mayo, there were many examples of the value of having those three aspects of organizational communications—leadership behavior, rewards, and formal media—synchronized. Some years ago, Mayo leadership decided that the time had come to ask employees to pay a small portion of the cost of their health-care benefit. Heretofore, Mayo had paid 100 percent of the medical costs for employees. That decision was made shortly after I came to Mayo Clinic. To give you an idea of the relationship Mayo had with its staff, I remember attending one of my first Mayo employee "town hall" meetings where this change was announced. An employee stood up and asked, with no trace of irony or anger, "Does this mean that Mayo isn't going to take care of us anymore?"

Despite the employee contribution, over subsequent years, the costs had become untenable. The time had come, not merely for an employee premium, but a complete overhaul of the benefit program with different options rather than the single all-inclusive plan Mayo had been funding. With a great deal of collaboration and fore-thought, the leadership team and our internal communications team collaborated on the best way to manage the potentially very divisive decision. Mayo employees are exceptionally loyal. Survey after survey shows that, as a group, they are well above national norms for loyalty, pride, dedication, and trust. No one in leadership wanted to damage those essential bonds, one of the benefits of which was the typical Mayo staff person's willingness to go above and beyond for the patients, families, and each other; in other words, a strato-spherically high degree of discretionary effort that everyone knew was a key component of Mayo's brand and success.

Accordingly, a program was rolled out across the organization called "Straight Talk." In essence, the program was quite simple. We told the truth, in specific detail. Leaders spoke at meetings with employees at all locations during all hospital shifts. Armed with detailed PowerPoint charts, speakers described the costs, the trends, and the prognosis for the generous Mayo Clinic health-care benefit. Then they stood for candid question-and-answer sessions. As I said, this was not revolutionary. I must say, though, that such a program of candid information sharing can only be successful if the organiza-tion has laid a foundation of trust, and only if that trust is rewarded with honesty and authenticity.

The remarkable thing about "Straight Talk" was that the infor-mation shared did not specify the changes that would be made. Rather than wait months for all the decisions about plan types, coverage, and premiums, while the rumor mill worked itself into a frenzy, the choice was made to let employees in on the planning. The rumors didn't stop, but they were contained. Since "Straight Talk" clearly outlined the working principles leadership would be guided by, the conversation, even the grapevine, had parameters. Again, a leader saying, "Your benefit will continue to be best in class and will be affordable" doesn't work without a reservoir of trust between leaders and staff, which Mayo Clinic had in abundance.

When the program was rolled out several months later, the response was quite positive. Any complaints were muted and reasonable. It seemed that, even with the guidelines laid out, some employees feared brutal measures might be taken, so the reality, once the changes were announced, struck the vast majority of people as no big deal and were met with a collective sigh of relief.

WALKING THE TALK

Another example highlights the critical synergy necessary to communicate successfully with purpose. After the Great Recession of 2008, Mayo Clinic, like every other company, faced some hard choices. Most universities and nonprofit organizations saw their endowments decrease substantially. Mayo fared better than many, but still took a big hit. As economic troubles hit the United States and other countries, travel slowed, which meant some decrease in visits to centers like Mayo. Many organizations, including medical systems as close to home as some in Minneapolis and St. Paul, were laying people off. Naturally, questions arose as to whether Mayo Clinic would have to follow suit.

A simple principle was adopted by the leadership team and promulgated throughout the enterprise. Every necessary measure would be taken to reduce expenses without laying anyone off. Asking someone to leave his job would be a last, desperate resort. This might mean reassignments, job sharing, even pay reductions. Everything possible would be done to keep people employed. We would all ride out the recession together.

Months of work followed, with every level of management involved in implementing the program. Leaders held meetings, formal communications were distributed, and the actions taken conformed to the stated goal. In the end, fewer than twenty people left Mayo, out of a workforce of more than sixty thousand.

A STRATEGIC PARTNERSHIP

In both of the situations I have described, the writing and production of formal media were important. By themselves, they would not have been sufficient. The close partnership of leadership with the institutional communications team was essential.

During my time at Mayo, I observed a continuous improvement in that relationship. From a small group of people bred in traditional written journalism churning out feel-good puff pieces and jargon-laden corporate missives, the team had evolved into a dynamic engine of multimedia services intimately involved in helping Mayo Clinic achieve its mission.

As stated earlier, this was the outcome of years of work with leaders and the members of my various teams. Over time, I developed a process that enabled me to bring these disparate groups to a new level of engagement and effectiveness. I did nothing by myself. Without senior leadership support, I was dead in the water. Without talented, committed staff, I was worse than useless. My job was to bring these two groups together and then disappear (to a point).

When I first tackled the task of remaking a group, my assignment always came at the behest of senior leadership, usually a leader in a new role. The impetus was internally driven—not so much marketing as using effective communications to help chart a new strategic direction, keep staff informed, and raise morale. Study after study has shown that, more than anything else, employees want to know what's coming next and what the rationale is for those actions. And they want to hear it from their direct supervisor first. Formal communications assist this process, fill in the gaps, and reinforce the message throughout the enterprise.

I always asked to read and understand the strategic plan of the organization. A few times, I was invited to participate in its creation. Regardless, the staff I was to lead had to have a deep understanding of the plan if they were to fulfill the basic prerequisite of any staff function—to partner with leadership in the achievement of the organization's mission and vision as described in the strategic plan.

Back in the 1990s, when I became division chair of communications for Mayo Clinic in Rochester, I was asked by the CEO at that time, Dr. Robert Hattery, to reengineer the function. As a new CEO, he had a firm grasp of how important internal communication could be to him and the Clinic. At a board meeting, together with a senior consultant from Towers Perrin, I presented a host of findings and recommendations regarding the current state of the division. The concept of strategic partnership with leadership was the central takeaway for just about everyone on the board. A few days later, Dr. Hattery asked to see me. "Okay, La Forgia," he said. "I get it. A strategic partnership with leadership. Okay. I'm in. So what do you want me to do?"

What a great question! There you have it. The crux of the biscuit, as Frank Zappa would say. It's all well and good to bandy a shibboleth about. Tell me what you want me to do!

Over the years, I've had occasion to refine my answers to that simple, important question. Each side has responsibilities—the organization's leaders and the public affairs staff. On the part of leaders:

1. *Tell us the truth.* If we are to be valuable assets to you, then we need to know the truth about whatever issues are confronting the organization. This involves mutual trust, of course, the platform upon which confidence in our services can be built. We cannot simply be the "propaganda machine" or "writers for hire." To truly add value, we have to know what we are talking about and *why*.

2. *Engage us early.* Preferably in the planning stages of the project or issue response. There comes a point in every project or issue that arises when a leader should know that some kind of communication or marketing (usually both) will be needed. All too often, the tendency is to wait until every "i" is dotted and every "t" is crossed before even thinking about the need to communicate outside the conference room. By then, the rumor mill is in high gear. Marketing data haven't been considered or requested that could inform decision making. Sometimes products are named, project acronyms created, a host of decisions are made that would have benefitted from expert counsel from communications and marketing. All of which affect the brand. Engaging us early eliminates rework and missteps down the road.

3. *Require communication plans.* At Mayo, as at most organizations, major decisions and issues management occur at the senior leadership team, management or operations team, or the board. It became standard operating procedure at Mayo that these bodies, when making major decisions, would require the responsible parties to contact public affairs for a communications or marketing plan. Almost every decision, issue, or crisis will have an internal and an external component. Often, marketing data will be needed. Everything affects the brand. Requiring a robust communication plan ensures a professional, effective, and timely communication component to any undertaking.

4. *Let us do what we do.* I've made the point repeatedly that the tendency to use the functions of public affairs as order-takers or afterthoughts is counterproductive. So, by extension, is the outdated perspective of seeing the personnel in these groups as somehow less capable, less astute, less valuable than personnel from "harder" functions such as

finance or IT. Is this because, often, the field is heavily populated with women? Is it due to the fact that "everybody
communicates"? Marketing is "easy" or "fun"? Regardless, nowadays, these attitudes are just plain wrong. Often,
I wanted to tell my superiors to get out of the way and let
us do our jobs. What makes physicians think they should
draw logos, design brochures, or write copy? I've never
seen a good product arise from those napkin scrawls. Then,
when the item fails, they come to me and say, "Maybe we
should hire a real (i.e., external) firm to do this for us." I'd be
thinking: *You mean the firm from which we hired our latest
marketer—designer—writer?*

5. *Involve us operationally.* One of the clearest signs that
   public affairs had arrived at Mayo Clinic was when various
   members of the group were included in regular meetings of
   the important committees, from the board of governors to
   the clinical practice committee to regular meetings of the
   many administrative and clinical departments. By staying
   in touch in that manner, keeping their finger on the pulse,
   they learned the ins and outs of the organization firsthand, making them better able to add value when needed
   and be involved in important matters at their inception. It
   had the added benefit of making the public affairs person
   feel needed and respected, which is an incredible boost to
   morale, commitment, and productivity.

OUR OBLIGATIONS

Conversely, if one expects leadership to adhere to these principles, the public affairs group has the obligation to perform to those
standards. First and foremost, the team must possess and be able to
apply a particular set of skills. If one claims to be able to serve as
a strategic partner with leadership, it is necessary to have the skill

set to back up that assertion. When I have worked with groups to elevate their performance, I would explain that individuals in our positions needed to provide three kinds of services: consultation, project management, and execution. Consultation naturally is the ability to provide expert advice, to draw upon knowledge, and to experience and apply them to new situations strategically and effectively. Project management is that aspect of the skill set in which the specialist acts as an account executive, gathering resources from the broader public affairs department, the wider institution, or from outside firms; in short, whatever is necessary to achieve a given goal. Execution is the ability to write a script, shoot a photograph, publish a Web page, produce a video, and the like.

I found that most health-care communications and marketing staff were heavy on execution, somewhat lighter on project management, and often very sparse indeed on consultation skills. This is the other side of the "order-taker, job shop" syndrome. We are taught as a society that the physical output of a worker is the valuable commodity. Even though, in the postindustrial world, this is no longer true; in health care, the "manufacturing" perspective still holds sway. Physicians are measured and rewarded by throughput, relative value units, and the like: that is, widgets. Specialists who "do things" to patients—surgeons, invasive cardiologists, gastroenterologists—are paid more than those physicians who spend most of their time thinking—diagnosticians, pediatricians, psychiatrists, and so on. I found many hospital CEOs see their facilities, more or less, as factories at the service of physicians. They may understand that the success of a practice is hugely dependent upon intangible factors such as patient satisfaction, but they mostly measure their success in terms of numbers of surgeries, beds filled, and financial bottom lines. For the communications professional, this extends to their performance. How many news releases were sent out? How many brochures? How many ads? Did they drive up the numbers?

The previous paragraph is not meant to imply that those issues are not important. Of course, they are vital. My intent is to delineate the world in which the public affairs team operates. Just as the public affairs team needs to understand how the patient and family see the world, they need to also understand how their employers view things. Many in my field will complain that their superiors just don't "get it." Thing is, administrators say the same thing about them. Obviously, a meeting of the minds is needed.

This manufacturing mentality is pervasive and insidious. Once, I was working with a long-time employee, let's call her June, who was a superior writer. She had spent her career composing copy for newsletters and brochures. As we remodeled the department, I asked her to work with her client, the human resources department, on being more consultative and less buried in the execution of materials, which was basically impossible for her to do by herself. She confessed that this was a new role for her and she had some apprehension about it, but she'd give it a try. I should mention that I had also given the staff permission to lessen their individual burdens of writing by hiring freelancers to augment their capacity. (A word on this: Many managers in my position fear that giving such permission opens the floodgates for staff to use extensive outside help, thereby spending exorbitant sums and perhaps, at worst, avoiding doing much work themselves. In my experience, the vast majority of people will remain reluctant to use outside help. The natural tendency is to do the job oneself. Additionally, the rare individual who is abusing the privilege is easily spotted and dealt with through budget management and other means.)

A few weeks later, I visited with June in her office to see how she was getting on. She was excited to share a project she was working on and a decision she had made. "I thought about our conversation," June said, "and I felt like it really helped. Human resources asked me to develop a communications plan for a rollout, and they also need a series of letters to go to employees ASAP about some benefits changes. So I hired a freelancer to write the communications plan and I'm writing the letters. Everybody's happy."

Well, not everybody, I thought. My heart sank, since she was obviously trying hard and was somewhat pleased with herself, but she had completely missed the point. As supportively as I could, I explained that I would have expected the exact opposite arrangement, that June, as the strategic advisor, would develop plans in concert with human resources leadership and would hire freelancers to help with execution when necessary. Happily, in the subsequent months, after some practice, June became quite adept at advising human resources in a strategic manner.

Eventually, to perhaps make the notions clearer, I would draw a triangle and divide it into three bars, with "execution" at its base, "project management" in the middle, and "strategy" at the apex. Most staff would spend a large percentage of their time performing execution and project management tasks, less on strategy. Conversely, a position like mine would be heavy on strategy and lighter on the other two areas. We tied our career ladder for promotions to these concepts as well. To achieve a higher position, a person had to demonstrate increasing abilities in project management and strategic consultation. I found that some individuals were perfectly happy to stay in the execution realm. Others desired the higher calling but had no talent for it. Others rose rapidly.

LEARN THE ROPES

One of the toughest aspects of this kind of transition during the makeover of a department was helping people develop skills as internal consultants. Not everyone enjoys the role of going face-to-face with a powerful person in the institution in the name of steering them away from a bad idea and toward a good one. The writer mentality, in general, tends to be somewhat introverted, and many of the people I worked with saw writing as their core skill.

Our remedies were to mentor, to review, and to educate. We used the book *Flawless Consulting* as a springboard for conversations about being a strategic partner. Each person had a copy of the book and we reviewed it chapter by chapter, not in a schoolroom sense, but simply as a conversation as part of a staff meeting. By way of review, often, a colleague would come to my office frustrated by their unsuccessful attempt to consult. We'd go through the conversation they'd had, sometimes line by line. "What did she say?" I'd ask. "What did you say then? How did she take that?" Insights would emerge as to points that could have been made or different reactions given. Mentoring is a no-brainer, although often overlooked or given short shrift. We learned to assign new or junior people a capable mentor skilled in strategy and consulting. This worked wonders for a person's training and also their sense of belonging.

One of the most neglected aspects of truly functioning in a superior manner as a consultant, partner, and strategic advisor is for the communications and marketing professionals to *know the business*. How does the medical center stay afloat financially? What are the referral patterns? What are the brand perceptions? What do the leaders care most about? What does the reimbursement profile look like? How do insurance contracts, government regulations, demographics, and other factors affect the hospital? Health care is exceedingly complex, with many constituencies, each needing attention and nurturing if the medical center is to flourish. It is essential that the marketing and communications staff understand these relationships if they are to acquire the coveted seat at the table.

Many times, I have encountered individuals working in positions in hospitals who have no idea of the answers to any of the questions posed above. Often, they have never seen a surgery, never spent time on a night shift, don't know how physicians get paid, don't understand how Medicare works. Even at the department, division or section level, I would ask team members basic questions and receive blank stares for answers.

Once, I began meeting with a new group and the discussion turned to a particular project consuming a fair amount of staff time. A medical department services brochure was to be mailed to thousands of people. "What's the budget for this?" I asked the assembled group. No one knew. "Is there a communications plan for this area?"

"Not that we know of" was the reply.

"This brochure is about primary care. Did you know that I was just told yesterday not to promote primary care at this time?" No one had heard that preference, even though it had been discussed at the leadership team months ago. Then I asked, "Have you seen the budget for this department?"

"No," they said. "The previous manager would prepare it by himself. We never see it." This was more common than you may believe. I encountered it time and again. How can one have a "seat at the table" if that is one's level of knowledge about the work and the company and patients on whose behalf the work is being performed? It's a self-fulfilling prophecy for marginalization and lack of respect.

Health care is an art, a science, and a business, whether for profit or not for profit. Every aspect is important and complex. Health-care systems are replete with highly trained individuals in all aspects of health care. It is incumbent upon the communications and marketing professional to learn the concepts, the lingo, the facts, and to keep abreast of the ever-changing forces that affect this extremely dynamic and enormous sector of society. I would urge my staff to pursue advanced degrees, whether masters of business administration (MBAs), masters of public health (MPHs), or whatever education would further prepare them for their chosen career path in health care, especially if they had any ambitions to pursue positions beyond the "execution" phase. In fact, after years of discussion, Mayo Clinic finally made the decision to require an advanced degree not just for department chairs (equivalent at most organizations to a vice president) but for division chairs (which at Mayo are the components of departments and, in turn, are composed of various sections that are often called departments at other institutions). By the time I retired, each of the division chairs in public affairs had acquired a relevant master's degree.

I cannot stress the point enough. Nothing will build trust faster than if the public affairs person exhibits knowledge and insight not only in their own discipline but in that of physicians and business executives. Conversely, nothing will alienate that same person or group more quickly than an obvious lack of understanding of the health-care center and its environment as seen by leadership.

SKILLS AND STRUCTURE

Ultimately, of course, the functions must deliver. Meeting deadlines and budgets are the two most fundamental obligations. If that's all you do, though, you're not really delivering on what you've promised. As discussed previously, meaningful content supported by data is critical. I have also found that a consistent presentation format that can be quickly read and understood saves much time and misunderstanding. After all, in health care, you are most definitely not preaching to the choir, rather, you are communicating with a group of people who do not know your jargon, your assumptions, or your outlook. In public affairs, we developed a template for our communications and marketing plans. We learned to keep them short, to tie them to organizational strategic objectives, and to do a lot of premeeting with clients and others to ensure buy-in and support.

Another key aspect of delivery that often causes trouble when neglected is keeping the client informed. Nothing is worse for a department than getting a reputation as a "black hole" where ideas, requests, and projects go to disappear and never be heard from again. It takes years to rebuild the trust of clients who have experienced the delays, broken promises, and cost overruns of a broken department. In this day of texts and emails, there really is no excuse for not keeping the client informed on a regular basis.

In the process of healing a broken group, I would naturally introduce whatever aspects of the foregoing were missing or inadequate. My preference was to meet with the staff collectively and individually. Rather than approach the team as a collection of underperforming individuals, I preferred to see them as trapped in a web of neglect, misuse, and bad management. Before meeting individually with staff, I would ask each of them to answer six simple questions on a single sheet of paper (not long treatises):

○ What are you currently doing that you consider a strategic contribution?

○ What are you currently doing that you consider a waste of time and resources?

○ What part of your job do you love?

○ What part of your job do you hate?

○ What would you like to be doing?

○ What advice or observations do you have for me?

Simple as this seems, this exercise caused some commotion and also opened some channels of communication. Many people would stop by and ask me what I meant by "strategic." I assured everyone there were no wrong answers and no penalties for honesty. Once the meetings occurred and I demonstrated the sincerity of my assertions, the exercise began the process of showing the team members that they were valued, would be listened to, and would have a say in how the department functioned going forward. In other words, it gave them hope.

For me, the most important and the most difficult aspect of any reengineering project was the emotional toll it took on the staff. Usually, their boss had been fired or moved to a different position. Whether they welcomed or resented that change, it made them afraid for their jobs. Major change was not just imminent, but it had actually occurred, and now they wondered who would be next. This situation's difficulty was amplified by the fact that I could not discuss the reasons for the previous supervisor's departure, due to employee confidentiality. That didn't stop staff from telling me what they thought the reasons were. The staff know what's what. They could see for themselves what the difficulties were. I've always noted that you really can't keep secrets from the staff—one way or another, the truths come out.

The other side of the difficulty was that I could not make any guarantees about who would keep their jobs and who would not. That would be sheer lunacy, given that I hardly knew them. Certainly, some of them had reputations that preceded my being placed in charge. My philosophy, though, was that each of them had a shot at showing me their value. In fact, that is more or less what I would say in our first meeting. For obvious reasons, this would be essential. One cannot build trust if the staff believe you are sitting in front of them with a pocketful of pink slips. So my message was simple. "Yes, we are in a period of change. For me, at this juncture, you are the team. We will work together to reshape this team and improve our performance. I don't have a pocketful of pink slips. Each of you has an opportunity to show me your good work. I can't guarantee the outcome, but it's as much up to you as it is up to me."

Closely related to job security was status, responsibilities, and salaries. Again, it was common, almost without exception, that I would find an organizational structure that made no sense. Staff knew that there were problems in the hierarchy, not because organizational charts are important *per se*, but because they lived every day with the consequences of unclear lines of authority, confusing paths of approval, unclear delineations of responsibility, and inequity in job titles, compensation, and status. At times, it seemed as if managers just made random decisions about such matters or reacted to situations as they arose, with each solution to a problem aggravating the staff and only contributing to the overall sense of anarchy. People need some kind of rationality behind decision making. Perhaps the universe is random, and perhaps human beings are fundamentally irrational but, in the closed system known as work, individuals need to know that there are rules to the game they are supposed to play and that those rules will be consistent, communicated, and fairly enforced.

Years ago, when I was moving from Tucson to Delaware, the president of the Carondelet system I was leaving after ten years, Sister St. Joan Willert, gave me some advice. "When you take your new position, don't go in there with guns blazing and make big changes right away," she said. "Give yourself six months to get the lay of the land, see what's what. It'll save you from making mistakes you wouldn't even know were mistakes."

I never forgot that bit of wisdom, although six months, in this day and age, is a long time. Even so, the essential idea of knowing the dynamics, especially the political dynamics, before making decisions is the difference between success and failure. In my meetings with staff about the issues delineated above, I would find a great deal of political machinations behind many of the decisions previously made. These would be sources of great discontent. Again, there are no secrets. People know who the favorites are, who got the bigger salary for the same position, who got promoted because they deserve it, and who got promoted even though they didn't deserve it.

The remedy is a system. Much as I personally favor an approach to management that is flexible and tailored to the individual, a system of organization solves many problems and makes personnel decisions fairer and more transparent. At Mayo, we developed a career ladder of public affairs Specialist I, II, and III. The salaries were commensurate with progress and the criteria for each were clearly spelled out. I've done similar models at other organizations, always in consultation with human resources. I also always included the staff in the planning.

Job titles are a similar source of concern when they are inequitable and seem to be handed out willy-nilly to appease a particular person. Again, nothing is more aggravating to a team than for one person to receive a random reward for no apparent reason.

As you can see, a great deal of the task of healing a broken department is to provide an environment of structure and predictability to decision making. Paradoxically, perhaps, within that structure, one needs to provide employees with freedom to act, latitude to adapt to situations as they arise, and the independence to solve problems for the institution on their own. In other words, get out of the way and let them do their jobs. This might be the biggest challenge of all. By the time I stepped in, the staff had been beaten down, particularly for showing the kind of initiative I was now advocating. Time after time, I heard the story of the employee who met with a senior executive, made a decision that the executive didn't like, even though it was the *right* decision, only to have said executive call the director and demand that he or she get what she wanted, however foolish or unnecessarily expensive or against policy, and so the director would back down and tell the employee to "just do it." Don't ask questions, don't think for yourself, just obey orders. One hardly need describe the level of disrespect this shows to the suddenly lowly staff person. Multiply this a hundred times and you have a cynical staff almost incapable of doing superior work for the same executives who are in their suites wondering why they can't get truly professional marketing and communications.

MANAGING UP—AND DOWN

Talk is part of the remedy for healing the staff, as is guidance in consulting. One can make assurances of support. Nothing matters, though, until that first situation when the executive calls the director, now me, to complain about a staff person not "doing what they're told." The degree to which I stood up for an employee was completely proportionate to the amount of trust the group would have in me and, by extension, the degree of success we would have as a team. The first few times it happens, the staff are almost shocked, because it seems so unusual to them. Trust me, they tell the stories to each other. Confidence and trust begin to supplant mistrust and fear. Eventually, a staff person comes in the office and says, "Thank you. That's never happened before."

One cannot go around an organization thwarting some of the desires of senior executives without (a) advance preparation and (b) making waves. Advance preparation, for me, meant spending a great deal of time making presentations, writing reports, but, most importantly, meeting with the leadership as a group and individually to achieve some common understanding and buy-in. I would always stress that we were empowering the staff to be the kind of strategic partners they said they wanted. The compact was that they had to deliver. If they did not, I would deal with it. The compact did not call for always blindly doing the bidding of the executive. This kind of arrangement would take some getting used to for everyone. Some accepted the idea of collaboration and the partnership would flourish. For a few who, I must say, were generally the more authoritarian types, it was a struggle. Eventually, most would find when their support person was finally delivering the kind of service they had always wanted, the relationship was no longer command and control, but a conversation, a partnership, with give and take on both sides. Human nature being what it is, there is always someone who cannot accept true collaboration, and I will admit this is a perpetual tussle. In my experience, it is unavoidable and something to be endured in the name of making a living, in the same realm as dealing with the perpetually nasty administrative assistant, or aggressively arrogant colleague down the hall. To that, I advise *illegitimi non carborundum.*

Regarding making waves: without CEO support, the waves created will become a tsunami that will drown even the most politically astute executive. It is the CEO who will eventually hear about the upstart marketing staff, the CEO who will need to appease his disgruntled executive, the CEO who will be the leader in charge of seeing the marketing and branding plan through. After all, the CEO is, or should be, the ultimate keeper of the brand and the champion of any strategic direction. Without the support of the CEO, the chief marketing officer cannot bring the marketing plan to fruition, and the marketing and communications staff will not hold any sway with their clients.

Assuring the current staff that they are the team must be framed carefully, for the unfortunate fact is that not everyone will make it through the transition. I would make it clear that everyone had a fair chance but that, in my experience, there would be people who either would not or could not adapt to the new world order. Some people don't really want to be self-starters or independent agents or strategic consultants. They want to be given an assignment, given the parameters, write the script or the article, and go home and forget about it. Indeed, in a larger department, there is a definite role for good soldiers, teammates content to execute on time and on budget without carrying the risks or the stress of a larger role. I have found a few of these folks will self-select out of the group to fill positions that are a better fit. In a smaller department, these roles are hard to sustain, since the team member must wear many hats, in fulfilling each of the three sections of the triangle, as it were.

By far, the most difficult situation is the person—or people—who cannot raise the bar on their performance. Sometimes they are employees with a bit of history with the organization who suddenly find their world turned upside down. They may struggle mightily for a while or they might simply withdraw from the get-go. Either way, they don't succeed. Almost always, some will recognize their situation and find new jobs on their own. Other times, the manager either helps them with placement elsewhere in the company or they need to be asked to leave.

No one that I know enjoys firing people. The unavoidable truth is that poor performers sow discord and drag the whole team down with them, including the manager. Early in my career, I would wait too long to deal with such problems, except in obvious cases of malfeasance. The struggling good-hearted employee would break my heart. Over the years, I had to harden myself to the emotional aspects and recognize that, for the good of the team, the person had to go. In truth, most often, the individual would eventually find a situation to which they were better suited. I'm not trying to sugarcoat this; firing is traumatic for all involved. Some individuals deal with it better than others. If you're responsible for dozens or even hundreds of people, you have to think of the greater good. Generally, the remaining members will know that the person was underperforming, even as they whisper among themselves to conjecture who the next victim will be.

With vacancies, the opportunity arises for enhancing and broadening the skill set of the team. In our reorganization retreats, the staff and I would lay out the skills and capabilities that either needed to be augmented or acquired for the team to thrive. In seeking qualified candidates, we would search nationally. Perhaps more importantly, we would search outside of health care as well as within it. We wanted to find excellent practitioners of marketing and communications, not experts in health care, necessarily. In general, the sophistication of other industries in marketing and communications was far ahead of health care, especially in advertising, data analysis, marketing strategy, and digital media. Once at Mayo Clinic, the new hire learned health care soon enough. We wanted the years of experience they could not have acquired from having worked at a medical center. By the same token, although we certainly had our fair share of journalists, writers, and media people, we searched outside of those areas as well. Eventually, we had people from finance, advertising agencies, government, the sciences—even a veterinarian, who was an excellent science writer.

As has been pointed out repeatedly, Mayo Clinic stresses the team concept, almost, occasionally, to a fault. In public affairs, we made a big effort to ensure that a new hire would work well in our department as well as in the Clinic as a whole. A key component of that, for us, was the application of behavioral interviewing. Mayo Clinic had adopted a behavioral interviewing system for the entire enterprise. Departments had some latitude to adapt the catalog of questions to meet their particular needs. Besides creating a list of relevant questions, we would start by doing a preliminary screening of candidates, first by sifting resumes and then by phone interviews, to create a short list of good prospects. We would invite those individuals to Jacksonville, Rochester, or Scottsdale for a panel interview. The panel would consist of five to eight people, comprising the person's potential colleagues, administrative assistant, supervisor, and, often, the supervisor's boss. I found that this worked beautifully to unearth the person with the best skills and best fit, and also gave the existing staff a stake in the outcome, all of which enhanced *esprit de corps.* Early on, I participated in every panel. After the panel interview, another round of interviews would be scheduled for the top two or, sometimes, top three candidates. These interviews would include people from within and outside the department, especially potential clients and physician partners. As the department grew, it became impossible for me to be part of every panel, but I did insist on meeting every person to whom a job offer was being considered, so that I had an opportunity to vet that candidate personally. Only a few times did I vote down a chosen candidate. The process took a considerable amount of time and resources. Occasionally, we would review the process to find ways perhaps of saving some steps. In the end, we always decided that the positive results in terms of strong teamwork, employee engagement, and, most importantly, hiring the right person was worth it.

Once having made a deal, so to speak, with leadership, and then creating a plan based on the institution's vision and goals, then having put the right staff in place with the right skills, we had to be accountable, and that compelled measurement and reporting. Health-care leaders are not generally in touch with the goings-on in the marketplace until something big arises: a competitor opening a facility or getting a front-page article in the local paper. At those times, a senior leader is likely to place a phone call or send an email to the marketing director with a comment along the lines of, "How come they get that kind of coverage and we don't?" Even at Mayo Clinic, I would get those kinds of calls. Ironically, I then would present the data that showed we *were* getting that kind of coverage, to an even greater extent than the competitor in question. It seems to be a trait of human nature that we pay more attention to the good fortunes of others and hardly notice the good fortune that we ourselves acquire.

Of course, data had more important purposes than simply quieting tempests in teapots. Leaders want to know if their investment in the revitalized function is paying off. My approach was to create a report that could be shared with groups on a regular basis. Our methodology was to focus on parameters of output, outgrowths, and outcomes. Commonly, output is a simple productivity measure and is the dimension most commonly used in health-care organizations. How many ads were run? How many news releases were distributed? How many hits were recorded on the hospital's website? These numbers matter, but the trouble is they have nothing to do with the effectiveness of any of the activity. They just show the group is producing a requisite number of widgets.

Outgrowth consists of the consequences of an activity. For example, the institution may invest significant funds in an advertising campaign. Many hospitals do, in fact, spend large sums on imaging campaigns. The output factor, of course, is the number of ads created and the spend for the ad buy. Presumably, this all shows the staff have been productive. Outgrowth could be measured by various brand parameters, such as growth in awareness and favorability. Other outgrowth questions to be measured could be: Has the market become more aware of the hospital? Are people more inclined to think favorably of the facility? Do more people have a better understanding of the range of services available there?

Although outgrowths lay an important foundation for marketing, the ultimate measure is outcomes. Outcome measurements provide answers to my favorite marketing and communications question: So what? We ran ads and more people know who we are and what we do. They even like us. So what? Has that increased referrals? Is there any evidence that our activity has changed consumer behavior? Have we increased revenue, however marginally? Have we recovered our costs and then some?

These are the tough questions that have to be answered. In my experience, they're the only answers that will justify the existence of a marketing program. Internal communications, media relations, and government relations will always have a place out of sheer necessity. One simply must communicate with staff, deal with the press, and work with government. The marketing proposition is always dicier. The ads may be well done, may even win awards but if they don't drive consumer choice and add to the business, what's the point? There is more to marketing than advertising. Social media, other kinds of engagement programs, physician relations, all matter a great deal. At the end of the day, though, they should be keeping existing markets secure and helping the brand extend and capture new customers and new markets.

Most leadership teams in health care don't have much tolerance for long reports on subjects pertaining to marketing and communications. At the board level, we learned to share pertinent data on a quarterly basis and include a more extensive report in the reading packets distributed before the meeting. What worked best with clients was to report on a specific project and show outcomes. These were more immediate and compelling, were simpler to absorb, and so had more impact.

When all is said and done, a plan—or a function—is only as good as its relevance to the current situation and the organization's needs. We regularly changed the department's structure, strategies, and tactics to adapt to the changing needs of the Clinic and the marketplace. This is not as easy as it sounds. Staff become comfortable with a certain structure and approach. When these change, disruption always follows. It's important to keep the staff informed about the "thinking at the top" so they can understand the rationale for changes in direction when they arise. By the same token, one can't allow the department to be whipped from one priority to another, day by day, because of transient political whims. There needs to be some consistency. At Mayo, we'd always say the mission and vision change almost never. The approach to fulfilling the mission and vision, however, require periodic adaptation.

An adage suggests that the job of a leader is to make herself unnecessary, that is, lead herself out of a job, something like raising a child to be independent of his or her parents. In the remaking of various departments, I definitely would experience that my direct involvement with the operations of the group would diminish over time. Eventually, we'd hire a new permanent leader to replace me and, once I mentored that person, the group would be on its own. Done properly, the healing of a broken department leaves a lasting legacy of a high-functioning team with a positive culture that consistently contributes to the organization's success. Such an outcome is fulfilling for everyone involved.

CHAPTER 9

IN CONCLUSION

THE PRACTICE OF marketing and communications for health care is a tricky business. The practitioner is trafficking in the health and wellness of human beings. Presenting accurate and useful information that can help people get healthy and stay healthy can be a worthwhile and satisfying pursuit. On the other end of the moral spectrum, selling medical procedures to increase a person's or an institution's profits at the expense of ethical considerations is unacceptable, even criminal.

Administrators, physicians, and marketing professionals occupy many points on that moral spectrum. To be sure, most inhabit the realm of trying to be of service to people, although, at every juncture, they are pulled toward the need to increase their margins to support their missions. The inherent tensions this creates puts the marketing and communications professional in a precarious position. Sell too hard, appear too commercial, and one risks offending client and consumer alike, and debasing the medical profession in the process. Fail to improve the bottom line, and one is perceived as not doing the job successfully.

My hope for this book is that it will enhance a person's ability to navigate the dangers of these rocks and hard places. Open communication among all participants in the enterprise is essential, as is continuous adaptation. At Mayo, every proposed brand extension was met with an inherent skepticism. The drive to preserve and protect the invaluable Mayo Clinic brand was the life force of the culture. Yet most leaders knew the truth of Peter Drucker's adage "adapt or die." This warning is especially apt for the slow-to-change and factionally warring American health-care "system."

In the past few years, Mayo Clinic leaders, along with other health-care experts, became fond of saying that American health care faced a "perfect storm." The forces driving this storm included:

- An aging population
- Rising consumerism
- Declining reimbursement
- Escalating costs
- Increased regulations
- Millions of underinsured or uninsured
- Employer cost constraints
- Global medical tourism
- Increased competition

The list could go on. It is hard to imagine any sector of the economy coping simultaneously with so many critical, potentially disruptive, challenges, let alone a sector that is approaching 18 percent of the entire country's economy—and growing. In such an environment, change is inevitable; indeed, it is already upon us. Recent health-care reforms such as the Affordable Care Act represent the tip of an iceberg. For health-care leaders, the question is "Will we make the necessary changes or will the changes be made *for* us?"

Mayo Clinic and other medical centers have commenced a host of initiatives, hoping to take the lead in improving the situation. Concierge medicine. Remote Web consults. Telemedicine.

Accountable Care Organizations. Remote monitoring. Smartphone apps. Wellness centers. MinuteClinics. Internal cost-cutting. System consolidation and integration. Despite these random efforts, the pace of systemic change is slow. Many initiatives suffer little or no reimbursement. Insurance companies continually press for bigger discounts. Physicians feel their autonomy eroding, their status diminishing, their income threatened.

A major difficulty is the seeming impossibility of bringing together all of the warring factions that have a piece of the $3 trillion pie. Attempts have been made at having physician groups, insurers, hospitals, and the government collaborate, either voluntarily or by fiat, so far, with limited success. Few souls are courageous enough or altruistic enough to willingly divest themselves of some of their income or power. Yet that is what is required.

And what of the patient in all this? Sadly, mostly forgotten, marginalized, and powerless. At Mayo Clinic, we asked a cross-section of Americans how they felt about the American health-care system. Generally, people express a positive attitude toward their individual physicians. When considering their experience with the system as a whole, however, people said they feel the system is failing them. Cost is a major worry. Besides that fundamental concern, two other key issues emerged: patients feel the system is hopelessly fragmented and they feel personally abandoned by the system.

Typical stories relate a patient's journey from one generalist, specialist, and testing location to another, usually with appointments days or even weeks apart, with seemingly little coordination among the caregivers and, often, only spare explanations as to the reasons for the various stops on the journey. A patient will tell Dr. Adams that Dr. Madison has said such and so, and Dr. Adams will reply, "Oh, is that what he told you?" implying that the two had not communicated at all. When my own mother was in the hospital dying of cancer, one physician at the hospital ordered a second bone marrow biopsy, which I questioned. When my mother's primary care doctor came to do her rounds, I asked her about it.

"Why does he want to do that?" she asked, as if I would know. No coordination. No communication. Her whole episode of care was like that. Although one may dismiss my story as anecdotal, I can attest to hearing many similar tales in focus groups and through surveys over the course of decades.

The sense of abandonment is subtler, but equally pernicious. Most people have only a tenuous grasp of the intricacies of modern medicine and its delivery. Diagnosed with a chronic illness, patients experience transactional care—that is, a prescription, a pamphlet, and some sort of care plan, but feel lost as to how to rearrange their diet, activities, and, in short, their entire lives to accommodate their condition. Likewise, an acute illness such as a cancer diagnosis often leaves patients and families to find their own way through the morass of immediate and future consequences for the patient and everyone else affected.

This is not to blame the caregivers. Many go above and beyond to help patients—offering personal cell phone numbers, email addresses, home care options, and support groups. The system, contrarily, is not set up to reward or compensate such behaviors. Health-care reform tends to focus on expenses as an absolute panacea. Cut this, eliminate that, costs will go down, and everyone will be happy. Trouble is such an approach solves nothing, since it ignores root causes and merely treats a symptomatic manifestation of a deeper problem and, in the end, serves to put more of the burden on the patient for coordinating their care and paying for it.

The elephant in the room is that true systemic health-care reform would require a massive redistribution of resources and, therefore, individual and corporate wealth. Imagine a system that compensated prevention, primary services, pediatrics, home care, mental health services, and other services that help prevent serious illnesses and are currently at the low end of the revenue hierarchy.

Where would the money come from for such a system? From the surgeons, specialists, insurance companies, and medical centers that receive huge revenues for treating the problems the aforementioned services could prevent.

The elephant has a companion in the room—lifestyle. One Mayo Clinic ear, nose, and throat surgeon, renowned worldwide for his specialty of rebuilding, as best he can, the heads and necks of patients ravaged by cancer, told me his practice would diminish by 70 percent if people didn't smoke. The issues of substance abuse, obesity, gun violence, poverty, racism, and other social ills have all been extensively documented as placing an enormous preventable burden on the American health-care system. This is where the lost, the victimized, the downtrodden of our society often end up—the emergency room, the operating room, and then a hospital bed, then home again for the cycle to repeat itself.

I believe a higher calling for marketing and communications in health care can help address these issues. People need information—honest, straightforward, plainly explained information—about the highly complex fields of medicine and health-care delivery. As much recent history has demonstrated, this is harder to do than it sounds. During the debate over the Affordable Care Act, aka Obamacare, many of us in health care would watch in utter disbelief as people swallowed the lie that end-of-life counseling constituted the establishment of "death panels" or, even more bewildering, when individuals who received Medicare, a completely government-controlled, government-financed health-care program, would be seen on TV saying, "I don't want Obamacare because I don't want the government involved in my healthcare." One's head threatened to explode.

Of course, these examples represent politics at its basest, the more so because the matters at hand concern people's very lives. So the duty falls on the experts in health care to get their act together and communicate. The essence of the necessary communication, and perhaps the major theme of this book, is to understand the situation from the point of view of the needs of the patient. Health-care marketers are uniquely positioned to "pull the outside in"—that is, to figuratively break down the hospital walls and bring the patient's perspective into the mind-set of decision makers. Conversely, marketers are also equipped, through hospital staff and the center's numerous modes of communication, to report back to the patients and the larger world about the needs of patients and their families. Just as the "Big Three" in Detroit thought they were in the car-selling business rather than the personal transportation business, health-care leaders easily fall into the trap of believing they are in the health-care facility business, providing a factory, as it were, in which physicians can perform operations and procedures, rather than seeing they are in the business of providing health and well-being to the communities they serve.

The difficulties are compounded by the current system, which does not reward alternative behaviors and, in fact, obliquely penalizes them. The alleged trend of consumerism in health care has not changed this dynamic. Mention consumerism to the average physician and they will tell you about the nettlesome patient who visits their office carrying a sheaf of Internet printouts and proceeds to ask irrelevant questions or demand to be provided a discredited drug or treatment. Moreover, as studies have shown, consumers rarely make a personal decision as to where they will receive hospital care, nor do most people reference the innumerable and sometimes contradictory quality reports available. Rather, most people simply go where their doctor tells them to go.

Marketers and communications professionals in health care can play an important part in bringing about a deeper understanding of health care in the United States and changing attitudes about how it could be improved. However much I believe this to be true, it is only a small part of the solution. What is needed is an entirely different approach to consumerism, one that addresses the patient's authentic concerns. The information is there, the tools are available. What is lacking, and is desperately needed, is the will and the courage from our leaders in health care, the government, and from the general public to adopt the revolutionary measures necessary to meaningfully change the American approach to health care and meet the needs of patients as the patients themselves perceive them.

ACKNOWLEDGMENTS

As will become evident to the reader, my thinking about the interplay of brand, marketing, communications, and organizational culture has been shaped primarily by my career at Mayo Clinic. It was at Mayo Clinic that I learned how an organization becomes truly great, and how it sustains that greatness for more than 150 years. It was there that I met the colleagues and mentors that I could learn from, admire and respect. For almost twenty-three years, it was there that I found a professional home. Nevertheless, the ideas contained within are purely my own.

Although so many people have helped me in my career that I hesitate to name names, there are a few individuals I would like to thank personally.

It was my privilege to work with four physician CEOs at Mayo Clinic: Robert Waller, Michael Wood, Denis Cortese, and John Noseworthy. Each in his own way shaped the Mayo Clinic and led the enterprise to greater heights. They served as mentors for me throughout my career, sometimes without even being aware of that designation.

For many years my physician partner for marketing and brand management was Patricia Simmons, MD. She was a courageous and astute champion for Mayo Clinic, its brand, and for best practices in marketing and communications. She could not have been more helpful or supportive as my professional partner and I am very grateful to her for all she did.

The man who hired me into Mayo Clinic was Frank Iossi. I doubt he could have known at the time what a gift he was giving me. My next boss, Robert (Bob) Smoldt, was the kind of leader I think all leaders should aspire to be—intelligent, generous, humane, and selfless. As chief administrative officer, Bob's influence was enormous although often undetected, so capable was he at leading through others.

Bob's successor as chief administrative officer was Shirley Weis, with whom I shared many struggles and triumphs. As a change agent she helped me be the change agent of my aspirations. Although she was in every way my supervisor, I saw our relationship more as a partnership and I am forever grateful for the opportunities and support she gave me.

No one accomplishes anything alone, and that goes double for me. I was blessed to have an incredible staff at Mayo Clinic: division chairs, section heads, administrators, and administrative assistants who made me proud and without whom nothing described in this book would ever have occurred. Of particular note was my group of direct reports, known collectively as the public affairs leadership team. They worked with me for many years, some for as long as I was at Mayo. They were Adam Brase, Lisa Clarke, Amy Davis, Chris Gade, Kathleen Harrington, Misty Hathaway, Nancy Jacobs, Bruce Kelly, Kent Seltman, Marti Sichko and Michael Yardley.

Most importantly, my wife, Pamela, read the manuscript, gave me honest feedback, and kept me moving forward with this book, especially during those brief times when motivation flagged or circumstances—such as moving to another country—made writing less than convenient. My life changed for the better the day I met her and each day is better than the day before.

I hope you enjoy the book and find it useful.

ABOUT THE AUTHOR

In his thirty-nine-year career, John La Forgia has been an integral part of the transformative changes in marketing, branding, and communications that have helped shape the health care industry. He spent twenty-two of those years at Mayo Clinic, and twelve as Chief Marketing Officer.